Trans-Himalayan Traders

TRANS-HIMALAYAN TRADERS

*Economy, Society, and Culture
in Northwest Nepal*

James F. Fisher

UNIVERSITY OF CALIFORNIA PRESS
Berkeley   Los Angeles   London

University of California Press
Berkeley and Los Angeles, California

University of California Press, Ltd.
London, England

Library of Congress Cataloging in Publication Data

Fisher, James F.
  Trans-Himalayan traders.

  Bibliography.
  Includes index.
  1. Magars—Commerce. 2. Magars—Economic conditions. 3. Com-
merce, Primitive—Nepal—Dolpo. 4. Dolpo (Nepal)—Economic conditions.
5. Dolpo (Nepal)—Ethnic relations.
I. Title.
DS493.9.M3F57 1985   306'.09549'6   85–5834
ISBN 0–520–05375–3

Printed in the United States of America

1 2 3 4 5 6 7 8 9

For my parents,
Frank L. Fisher
and
Helena Salmon Fisher,
in gratitude

Contents

Acknowledgments

This book, based on field research conducted in a village deep in the mountains of northwest Nepal, is a revised, expanded, and generally overhauled version of an earlier formulation that was presented as a Ph.D. dissertation to the University of Chicago in 1972. Although the modern intellectual roots of this study extend from Mauss and Malinowski through Barth, its more immediate muses are the faculty of the Department of Anthropology of the University of Chicago. I have followed theoretical tacks increasingly divergent from those of my mentors over the last ten years or so, but I remain profoundly grateful for the general aura of intellectual ferment, stimulation, and creativity exuded by the Anthropology Department at Chicago during my time as a student there. I am particularly grateful to Professors McKim Marriott, whose unbending rigor has made me deal more honestly with the South Asian context than would otherwise have been the case, and Manning Nash, whose general anthropological approach and theoretical orientation have provided the stimulus and sustaining energy for this effort. In addition, I am thankful for penetrating insights and criticisms from Professor (now Sir) Raymond Firth, whose pioneering work in problems of economic anthropology and social change are an obvious and invaluable influence, and to Shepherd Forman for a careful and critical reading of sections of the work which contributed to its transition from chaos toward coherence.

I am indebted also to Professor Christoph von Fürer-Haimendorf of the School of Oriental and African Studies in London for much helpful advice, counsel, and generous hospitality during our delightful six-month stay there en route to Nepal, as well as for the suggestion of Tarangpur village as a research site. I am grateful to William Douglass, Stephen Tobias, Joe Reinhardt, and David Jordan, each of whom helped clarify and consolidate my argument. I thank Mike Frame for giving me the benefit of his unparalleled knowledge of Nepalese agriculture. At the University of California Press, Martin Orans and two anonymous reviewers provided excellent, detailed, and constructive critiques. Victoria Scott performed meticulous copyediting. Richard and Vivian Waite hand-carried the edited version from California to Kathmandu and back. I am greatly in debt to all of these people.

During our year in Tarangpur, my wife and I were for all practical purposes sealed off by the high passes that enclosed us from the rest of the world, with which we could communicate only sporadically by mail. The runners of the Postal Service of His Majesty's Government of Nepal perform an onerous, essential task efficiently and reliably, but under the best of conditions it took at least a month for letters to reach us from Kathmandu, so we had to rely heavily on other people for more favors than would be necessary under less logistically austere circumstances. I am grateful to Dipak Mathema and Susan Southwick of the U.S. Educational Foundation for efforts to get the mail through which went far beyond the call of duty; to Tom and Marilyn Vernon and Richard and Marleane Mitchell for morale-boosting care packages; to Dr. Larry Wilson for medical advice and supplies; to Peter and Martha Fritts for their welcome contribution of warm clothing; to Sir Edmund Hillary for his emergency donation of a tent after our own failed to arrive until we had already been in Nepal for a year; and to Barry and Lila Bishop for massive infusions of peanut butter from their camp in Jumla when our own supplies were exhausted.

Our expedition would never have gotten off the ground without the permission of His Majesty's Government of Nepal and the friendly and helpful assistance of its officers. I am especially grateful to two pioneering Nepalese social scientists, Mr. Dor Bahadur Bista and Dr. Harka Bahadur Gurung, for their support, advice, and encouragement. Of course the research would have been out of the question without the participation and cooperation of the people of Tarangpur, who put up with my presence, persistence, and infernal questions with restraint. To two of its leading citizens, Mr. Takla Tsering Budha and Mr. Chandra Man Rokaya, whose lives have followed very different paths but who each in his own way personifies the highest qualities of his people, I owe a special debt for aid in helping me understand the Tarangpur world. Mr. Rokaya has also devoted considerable time to discussion of various questions by mail, and his cooperation has been invaluable. The late Sirdar Changchu Sherpa, the third permanent member of our expedition, managed all the nuts and bolts details, from arranging for porters and looking out for their loads to buying and cooking food, as well as innumerable other small but vital tasks. No detail escaped his careful attention, and he performed his tasks with enormous enthusiasm, initiative, and unfailing good humor. We would never have survived without him. In Kathmandu, after our return from the field, Mr. (now The Honorable) Keshar Bahadur Bista helped uncover and analyze archival data, and Mr. Govinda Bahadur Shrestha assisted in intensive linguistic work with a village informant. My thanks are due to them both.

Closer to home, I am greatly indebted to my colleague at Carleton, Dan Sullivan, for helping me present information more clearly in the graphs and tables. I thank Karen LaViolette for much artistic, editorial, and typing assistance; to Betty Kendall and Nikki Lamberty goes credit for typing the bulk of the manuscript. Carleton College has been typically generous and supportive in providing funds for typing, a term's leave for writing (provided by the Bush Foundation), and a subvention toward publication.

The whole enterprise, from beginning to end, would have been impossible without the encouragement and support of my wife, Catherine, whose continuous contributions to my physical and mental health, as well as to the research itself, sustained me throughout the entire endeavor.

Finally, I acknowledge financial support in the form of research grants: a Fulbright-Hays Graduate Research Fellowship (GFH 7–82) and an International Development Fellowship awarded by the East-West Center in Honolulu. An earlier draft was written at the University of Chicago with support from the Research Center in Economic Development and Cultural Change and a Ford Foundation Indian Civilization Fellowship.

Kathmandu, Nepal James F. Fisher
January 1985

Note on Orthography

The orthographic complications which normally vex nonlinguistic scholarship involving an exotic language are in this instance compounded by the phenomenon of trilingualism. In the interests of general intelligibility and readability, I have consistently attempted to use English equivalents of local terms wherever possible, sometimes adding the original Nepali, Tibetan, or Kaike in parentheses. Where an indigenous term is used, I have italicized it and added diacritical marks at its first appearance, but place names have not been italicized, and I do not use diacritical marks on familiar place names (e.g., Kathmandu, Jumla).

In the case of Kaike, an unwritten and undescribed Tibeto-Burman dialect, I have transcribed words phonetically (see Fisher 1973), since a phonemic analysis has not yet been done. Because Nepali written in the Devanagri script is a broad phonetic transcription, I have transliterated most Nepali terms directly into Roman letters, generally following Turner (1931). Tibetan is an altogether different matter, since a direct transliteration from the Tibetan script is incomprehensible to anyone not literate in the language. In Tarangpur only lamas can read Tibetan; few—if any—actually write it (except to copy texts), and what is written is of course classical Tibetan, not the local dialect. In view of these considerations, and because this study is an exercise in social anthropology with little relevance to the constricted concerns of Tibetology, I have transcribed Tibetan terms phonetically also. Although I have generally tried to avoid cluttering the text with distracting diacritical details, where they are used, (¯) denotes long vowels, (ṇ) indicates nasalization, and (.) marks retroflex consonants. To distinguish between categories of social organization and occupations, I capitalize the former but not the latter—for example, Lama lineages and devout lamas; Blacksmith caste and skilled blacksmith.

1

Introduction

It is easy to see that in the long run, not only objects of material culture, but also customs, songs, art motives and general cultural influences travel along the Kula route. It is a vast, inter-tribal net of relationships.

—Bronislaw Malinowski
Argonauts of the Western Pacific

THE RESEARCH PROBLEMS

At its best, anthropology is the studied and stimulating attempt to mine the richness of John Donne's insight that no man is an island—that we are, as Geertz (1973:5) has put it, animals suspended, ineluctably together, in webs of significance that we ourselves have spun. Yet it has taken anthropologists a long time to extend the epigram to the analysis of the societies we live in and observe. Society is not isolable any more than an individual human being is. Webs—cultural or otherwise—are always supported or in some other way connected to the natural world, and cultural webs always merge with other, similar webs at their geographic and conceptual borders. While Radcliffe-Brown (1952) and Marriott (1955) have each raised questions about the definition and analytical viability of traditional anthropological units,[1] it was left for Barth (1969:9) to observe that:

Practically all anthropological reasoning rests on the premise that cultural variation is discontinuous: that there are aggregates of people who essentially share a common culture, and interconnected differences that distinguish each such discrete culture from all others. . . . The differences between cultures, and their historic boundaries and connections, have been given much attention: the constitution of

1

ethnic groups, and the nature of the boundaries between them, have not been correspondingly investigated. Social anthropologists have largely avoided these problems by using a highly abstracted concept of "society" to represent the encompassing social system within which smaller, concrete groups and units may be analyzed. But this leaves untouched the empirical characteristics and boundaries of ethnic groups, and the important theoretical issues which an investigation of them raises.

The village in the mountains of northwest Nepal which I call by the pseudonym Tarangpur is probably as geographically isolated a community as an anthropologist is likely to encounter today. Yet the ways in which Tarangpur is not economically and culturally self-sufficient are far more interesting than the ways in which it is. This fact led me away from a finely drawn description and definition of Tarangpur society, the delineation of its internal structure, and detailed analysis of its symbolic order, although these are all of course interesting and legitimate topics. My concerns are of larger scale and wider scope. Straddling the larger South and Central Asian Worlds, Tarangpur exemplifies the interstices of the multiethnic society of Nepal, and I therefore attempt to describe and explain Tarangpur's convoluted and changing integration within those worlds.

Tarangpur is a cultural, linguistic, and economic hinge between the Buddhist, Tibetan cultural area to the north, and the Hindu, Nepali regions to the south and west. As such, its people are marginal to both these traditions, and they do not bear any very great affinity even with Magars elsewhere in Nepal—for example, the Magars south of Tichurong described by Hitchcock (1966). While I am concerned with the mechanisms that maintain ethnic boundaries between these mediating mountain peasants and other groups with which they regularly interact, I am not interested here in the similarities and differences between different populations in western Nepal which call themselves Magars.

The word *Magar*—like Gurung, Rai, and Limbu—refers to a "tribe" or "caste," depending on the point of view of the social scientist who is translating the Nepali word *jāt* (Hindi, *jāti*). I do not find either translation satisfactory. The Magars of Tarangpur and its surrounding villages are not tribal in the corporate, territorial, or political sense usually implied by that term; nor, given their concentration in a limited part of Nepal and the lack of traditional relations with Brahmins and other high-caste Hindus, are they a caste in the conventional Indian sense. If a sociological label is required, "peasant," in Redfield's (1953) use of that term, or "ethnic group" (Marriott 1965) is as appropriate as any, but I am skeptical about the utility of several kinds of anthropological labels for a people who are marginal in so many ways. In these mountain communities, Magar is simply a convenient status summation which can be readily and incontestably claimed by anyone (except untouchables) who wants it. I call the inhabitants of Tarangpur Magars as a shorthand device to place them in ethnographic context, not to describe a specific structural or cultural type.

Tucked away in an obscure fold of the Himalayas a two-week walk from the nearest motorized transportation, Tarangpurians are acutely aware of the world beyond their valley and have evolved various strategies for dealing with their remoteness. In each case they exchange their way out of isolation. These multifarious transactions can be interpreted through the processes by which they are maintained and adapted to the environment, as a way of organizing interpersonal behavior, and as an index of social and cultural change. In adopting a transactional perspective I lean heavily on the ideas of Fredrik Barth, whose *Models of Social Organization,* according to Kapferer (1976), marks a "paradigm" shift in British social anthropology, although he has been less influential in America. However that may be, I do not believe in or argue for transactional analysis as any kind of specially privileged or uniquely insightful theory. It is simply an intellectual framework that helps to elucidate the problems in which I am interested and to organize the data I present (which is all that what usually passes for "theory" in anthropology ever does).

Fundamental to Barth's concept of transaction is the notion that in any social relationship we are involved in a flow and counterflow of prestations, which is one way of describing the movement of goods and services. The flow of goods and services is determined by our own and our counterpart's ideas of appropriateness and value. These ideas determine not only what we exchange but which statuses may be combined in a set in a given exchange; only those involving commensurate prestations are relevant counterparts in a social relationship. Such ideas also affect the course of interaction in a relationship: the flow of prestations is not random over time, since each party's behavior is modified by the presence and behavior of the other in a progressional sequence (Barth 1966).

By viewing interaction in terms of transactions, says Barth, we can interpret behavior by means of a strategic model. That is, a sequence of reciprocal prestations represents successive moves in a game. Each actor keeps a ledger of value gained and lost, and each successive action affects that ledger, changes the strategic situation, and thus "canalizes" subsequent choices. Barth's game theory analogy is unfortunate because it casts his model in zero-sum terms, whereas the fundamental notion of transactions is reciprocity. The ledger is a personal one, and under certain conditions (e.g., between players from ecologically differentiated, symbiotic zones), the "game" can have more than one winner. Nevertheless, Barth's model does have the advantage he claims for it of depicting a succession of events over time—in other words, it is a model of process.

One measure of the analytical importance of such a concept of transaction is that it provides a way to assess the strength of values. It is meaningless, Barth maintains, to say that something has value unless people in real life seek it in preference to something else of less value. This can only be the case when they act strategically with respect to it—that is, make it the object of transactions between themselves and others.

I believe the transactional model has the additional advantage of providing an analytic framework for the study of change, since it allows for specifications of the continuity that links two situations in a sequence of change. Different analyses of change can then be generated depending on the nature of the continuity described. This study makes explicit certain assumptions about the nature of the continuity that exists between Tarangpur today (i.e., at the time of the research, 1968–1970) and Tarangpur forty years before the ethnographic present—specifically, the striking shifts in the transactional patterns, as measured in changing allocations of time and resources.

I attempt to deal with two distinct but interrelated kinds of transactions in which Tarangpurians engage. One is the transactions in trade—the exchange of material goods (counted and measured as best I could for the present, and estimated for the past) between and across distant but contiguous symbiotic ecological zones. I argue that these economic transactions are the bedrock in which the second set of transactions—those consisting of interactions between adjacent ethnic groups of different cultures—takes place.

Data for the latter (unlike the former) frequently had to be gathered indirectly because cultural interactions could not be so frequently or directly observed. To obtain data on the economic set of transactions (and to understand the village cultural setting generally) required more or less continuous residence in the village for the entire fieldwork period. To fully observe the transactions in ethnicity would have required constant travel with the traders. This would have been not only logistically incompatible with the requirements of obtaining the economic data set but also politically impossible, since the necessary permits to visit the sensitive northern border area could not be obtained. Hence both the data and the conclusions on ethnic interaction are frequently inferred from what Tarangpurians said and did while in Tarangpur. Examples of this kind of material are found in the discussion of culture and impression management in chapter 4.

Data on the two kinds of transactions (economic and ethnic) do not represent unconnected domains but two empirical sides of the same conceptual coin. To discuss the latter while ignoring the former, as is sometimes done in ethnicity studies, is an error I have tried to avoid. A central theme of the book is that economic transactions changing over time have profoundly affected the interactional transactions, which have in turn generated changes in the ethnic identity and orientation of Tarangpurians. Baldly stated, economic change has been the cutting edge of cultural change. Assessing the material in terms of transactions and attempting to place the concept of choice on a par with that of structure (Firth 1954) is one tentative, halting, but determined step away from the paradigm fatigue of structuralism, in both its Radcliffe-Brownian and Levi-Straussian varieties.

A final, obvious fact may be too easily lost in the abstractions: namely, that the problems addressed here—even the question of choice—are, like all anthropological problems, primarily the problems of the anthropologist and not of the people whose collective lives are the basis for the solutions (people who, like us, just muddle along and struggle through their lives day after day as best they can). As one Tarangpurian said to me, replying to questions which were to him, of course, childishly simple: "We go to the fields, plow, and weed; we put heavy baskets on our backs and go trading—that's it! This is all there is to discuss about our life here."

Attempting to come to grips with the symbiotic links between regions and the bonds between village and nation is not an entirely novel endeavor. But it does warn of a shift away from intensive analysis of the internal dimensions and organization of Tarangpur and toward the manner of its integration into larger networks. Such an intensive internal analysis could be done—even transactionally, in the manner of Marriott (1976)—but that would be another book. The anthropological investigation of choice and decision-making is still in its infancy, but such approaches all too often focus on unnecessarily narrow concerns—whether to use a new kind of seed or whether to plant one crop rather than another, for instance. What I attempt here, in contrast, is to understand why people choose one culture rather than another. The analysis that attempts such an understanding is incomplete, as all such cultural understandings intrinsically are. As in any anthropological enterprise, there are loose ends; in the spirit of Valery, I have not really finished the project, but only abandoned it.

Most of the book grapples with these analytical issues by placing them in the specific ethnographic context of Tarangpur. After the methodological interlude that concludes this chapter, chapter 2 outlines some of the basic geographic and historical facts that have shaped life in Tarangpur. The central point is that the evidence from all sides describes a land and people who are, above all, marginal—politically, geographically, logistically, linguistically, even mythically. Their cultural identity is up for grabs and must be chosen from competing models.

Chapter 3 sets out the fundamental ecological dimensions of the agricultural cycle on which the rest of the economy (and, I maintain, the rest of the culture) rests. The discussion—much of it a quantified and, I fear, tedious analysis of such items as field size, crop yields, and consumption patterns—establishes that a net grain surplus is generated. I take pains to be clear on this question partly because precision is, ceteris paribus, a virtue, and also because if people are making choices in their lives, it has to be shown that there are choices to make. If the alternatives imposed by the environment are so harsh and restricted that sheer survival permits no other course, the basic economic and cultural decisions are preordained; transactions and choice would not exist.

Chapter 4 describes how the grain surplus has satisfied the demand for salt and become the basis for a long-established grain-salt-rice trading system. I describe how this cycle of transactions has led Tarangpurians out of their valley and into cultural confrontations to the north and south. Chapter 5 details a second, coexisting circuit—which has now largely replaced the first—of animals, wool, and manufactured commodities, and compares the cultural implications of following each cycle. Chapter 6 deals with forms of local wealth, generated mostly from the trading cycles (which rest in turn on the agricultural base) and how this wealth is stored, used, and circulated. Chapter 7 returns to the transactions theme and assesses the impact of the different spheres of exchange for the internal social, political, and symbolic life of Tarangpur. Chapter 8 is a summary that concludes with a discussion of ethnicity and interaction in this unusually complicated cultural shatter-zone.

THE PROBLEMS OF RESEARCH

It would be unwise to assess the data that follow without a methodological pause, since the resolution of the theoretical research problems is illuminated by considering the practical problems of research. Anthropological fieldwork is the type of undertaking in which the theoretical scaffolding as well as the tools of the trade must be displayed along with the finished product.

The field research was conducted in Tarangpur village, Dolpo District, Dhaulagiri Zone,[2] between October 1968 and November 1969.[3] Because of Tarangpur's isolation from transportation services, we were never able to take a vacation—a trip to Kathmandu and back, for example, would have required a month in travel time alone. Added to whatever additional time would be spent in "rest and relaxation," this constituted a total far beyond what we felt we could afford and still get the work done. The full year was therefore spent in the village and its vicinage, except for a survey trek to Jumla, a small bazaar town a week's walk to the west which seemed to us, after several months in Tarangpur, more like Times Square than anything else.

Despite fairly extensive treks in Nepal in the early 1960s, in the Mt. Everest area and to the west and south of Pokhara, I had never been anywhere near Tarangpur and did not even have any clear notion of how to get there. There were small airstrips at Jumla, a week's walk to the west, and at Dhorpatan, a week's walk to the south, but no scheduled service to either. We attempted at every point to keep the size of our expedition at a minimum, so that we would be, if not inconspicuous, at least not egregiously obtrusive. We were too small and impecunious a group to charter a plane, so we took the regularly scheduled Royal Nepal Airlines Corporation DC-3 to Pokhara.

Not knowing whether any food would be available where we were going, we brought with us from Kathmandu what we hoped (optimistically, as it turned out) would be a year's worth of rice and *dal,* flour, peanut butter, sugar, tea, and a can of peaches to open for Christmas dinner. Our Sherpa assistant, Changchu, busily organized the packing of all these items and their distribution— along with our clothing, books, film, typewriter, paper, and other supplies—into what eventually amounted to thirteen porter loads of 35 kilograms each. By the standards of other expeditions, even scholarly ones, this seemed an alarmingly small amount of provisions to keep us going for a year. (The American Mt. Everest Expedition of 1963, for instance, needed more than 900 porters to carry supplies for three months.) Although we were not entirely sure of our ultimate destination—or that its inhabitants would even allow us to live there—we knew that wherever we settled would be so isolated that we could not afford the time (not to mention the energy) for a trip out to collect more supplies.

But there were some advantages, too, in being a small and mobile operation. We were not only less obvious as we passed through the countryside and into the fieldwork area but we were able to muster the few porters we needed. Changchu found thirteen able-bodied men, about half Tibetan refugees and half low-caste *Damāis* (Tailor caste) in Pokhara. Packed into conical wicker baskets, the loads were hefted onto the back and stabilized by a rope under the basket tied to a leather strap pulled across the top of the forehead, so that the neck muscles provided most of the support.

We proceeded north of Pokhara over a ridge to the Modi Khola (Modi River) and up the Kali Gandaki River to the zonal capital of Bāglung, took the Myagdi Khola fork at Beni, then went over the pass to Dhorpatan. At Dhorpatan our Damais decided that they would prefer not to cross in their bare feet the snow-covered passes about which we had been hearing ominous stories along the way, and so they quit. We also paid off the Tibetans, and I belatedly regretted my earlier agreement to pay them at half-rate for their empty-handed return to Pokhara. Fortunately, Changchu was able to rustle up eight Tibetan ponies and their owners to take us, for an exorbitant sum, the rest of the way.

From Pokhara to Dhorpatan was a one-week trek, and from Dhorpatan to our destination was another week, but the two legs of the journey were quite different. During the first week we were never far from villages and the supplies and food we could buy from them. But during the second week we were traveling through high, alpine, largely uninhabited country, with only two adjacent villages in our path—Pelma and Yama. We slept in our tent, while the horses were hobbled to graze during the night. The two passes (Jangla Bhanjyāng) near the end of our journey, both close to 15,000 feet high, were already quite deep in snow, and we quickly learned to conserve our strength by letting the horses break trail for us. From the top of the last pass it was a long, grinding, knee-jarring descent to the Bheri River Valley. We headed for the first signs of habitation we saw and dragged ourselves into the village just as darkness fell, only to discover that we were in Gomba, not Tarangpur, which we belatedly saw beyond a stream and around the hillside, another hour's walk away. All of us— horses included—were so exhausted that we decided to sleep where we were and proceed the next morning to Tarangpur.

We were startled to discover that a police border checkpost had been installed at Tarangpur just a few months before our arrival. This was an external presence I had not anticipated, would never have requested, and did not relish, but it did provide unexpected opportunities to observe the interaction of national and local levels of government. A measure of the remoteness of the area was the fact that even after we had lived in the village for several months, one neighbor thought that we and the Nepali constables were from the same country—for many of the villagers, all people from outside the valley are indistinguishable. Toward the end of our stay, a friend excitedly ran to our house to tell us that five Americans had just arrived from over the pass; I rushed up to their campsite to discover five Japanese dentists on a vacation trek.

In any case, the checkpost commander was helpful in our search for accommodations. Between his efforts and our own, we finally found a newly rebuilt house right in the middle of the village. In addition to its convenient location, it was the only house in the village with the attractive feature of a ceiling high enough so that I (at 5 feet, 10 inches) could stand erect under it. Believing that ghosts cannot enter a house if they have to bend over, Tarangpurians had always built their houses with low ceilings. But as no ghosts had appeared for some time, our landlord daringly built a higher ceiling, to our considerable relief. The owner suggested a monthly rental of about $5; we offered $4 and the deal was closed. Our landlady and her two sons continued to live in another part of the house which had not yet been refurbished.

Our quarters consisted of a single large room, which we subdivided by hanging our tent fly down the middle. Tarangpurians sit, eat, and sleep on the hard dirt floor, so we hired low-caste *Kāmis* (Blacksmith/Carpenter caste) from a nearby village to make us a bed, an enormous desk, and a small table and two chairs for our "kitchen." On one side of the tent fly were our bed, desk, clothes, and medicines, and on the other were the cooking fire that Changchu designed from stones and empty kerosene tins, table and chairs, food, and—within a few days—our four chickens, which occasionally provided us with eggs. Opening onto our single room were four windows, each about the size of my fist; it was so dark inside that we usually needed a flashlight to search for things even during the middle of the day. A smoke hole in the ceiling over the fire added a little more light, but not much.

The first task I set myself was simply to map the village, but the houses are so closely clustered and piled on top of one another, with so many little paths separating them, that I found it impossible to make an accurate map until the Panchayat (the local governing body) secretary finally agreed to walk around with me and name the houses. I also wanted to take a complete census of the village, with such details as age, clan membership, place of birth, and preliminary genealogical connections. But I immediately discovered—as I was to find constantly throughout the fieldwork period—that people were reluctant to answer questions. Even if they were willing to answer a question, they would almost always insist—for perfectly good reasons, from their point of view—on initially asking why I wanted to ask the question in the first place. I answered by saying that I was a student (in the "21st grade"), that I had come to learn about their customs and history, and that if they didn't tell me what was going on I would fail in school. They sympathized with my plight, but not to the extent of becoming enthusiastic informants.

Although we had excellent relations with the villagers, who came to appreciate not only our medicines and material goods but also our honesty in dealing with them, most never lost their suspicions of what might come of my knowing too much. Gathering data was frequently like pulling teeth. People in some cultures are very anxious for outsiders to know about them; indeed, I marvel at the good fortune of a colleague who worked in Sri Lanka and found that he sometimes had to ask his informants to stop giving him so much detailed information that he couldn't record it all. My situation seemed more reminiscent of Evans-Pritchard's account of working with the Nuer (1940) or Malinowski's (1922) comments on the Amphlett traders,[4] although I would not be so harsh.

There seemed to be three major reasons for the Tarangpurians' reticence. First, because outsiders—including other Nepalese—are virtually unknown in the valley, there was an entirely reasonable suspicion and fear that whatever they said could be used against them. I was interested, among other things, in economic questions—amounts of land owned, taxes paid, and the like—and since the villagers shared the universal fear of higher taxes (a cultural universal, no doubt), they saw no advantage in handing out information that might fall into unfriendly hands, even if we ourselves were benign.

Second, a number of Tibetan refugees had passed through Tarangpur in the early 1960s following the political instability in

Tibet in 1959. Indeed, some still lived in Tarangpur or returned to spend the winter months there, and the stories they told of difficulties with the Chinese had made the Tarangpurians very apprehensive about foreign intervention in their valley. As it turned out, we did many of the things the Chinese did when they first arrived in Tibet—handed out medicine, gave candy to children, and were generally polite and interested in local affairs. Many people just assumed that we were the advance guard of an American invasion force, which would arrive after a discreet period to take over the valley. When we arrived, one of their first queries concerned the state of Chinese–American relations. When I said that I personally did not harbor any ill will toward the Chinese, this only confirmed their worst fears. When I later understood their concern, I told them that America and China were bitterest enemies (this was before Kissinger's secret trip to Peking and the subsequent rapprochement), and my reputation and trustworthiness improved markedly.

Third, Tarangpurians believe that natural and human objects are endowed with certain kinds of powers (*shakti*), which must be carefully guarded against dissipation. My request for soil samples met with a refusal that was irate as well as adamant, since taking a sample away would place the power of the soil in jeopardy—a not inconsequential consideration in an agricultural community. Later, even my short-term research assistant, Chandra Man Rokaya—who had been born and raised in Tarangpur and still had family and property there, but who was at the time earning his B.A. in agriculture at a college in India—returned for a short vacation and aroused the collective wrath of his fellow villagers when he too wanted to take some soil samples for testing. I encountered the same difficulty when I tried to inventory the Tibetan books (handwritten or printed from woodblocks) kept in most houses. My efforts to copy just the titles met with great resistance, because it was felt that copying the title would drain away the power of the book.

Still another problem I encountered—which I have not seen discussed in the literature of fieldwork—is the problem of the pathological liar. I discovered that two or three people in the village consistently gave me answers that had nothing whatsoever to do with anything that might be called truth. They gave information which seemed reasonable, or at least plausible, but which after cross-checking turned out to be fabricated out of whole cloth. Other informants then admitted candidly that one could not believe anything these people said, but it took me a painfully long time to become aware of that fact.

Under these conditions, the intensive fieldwork techniques I was using—insistence on obtaining information directly from individuals without using special informants—were yielding frustratingly little information. Later, I discovered that working with a young man who was a respected village leader, Takla Tsering Budha, opened doors that I could never have opened myself. Once it become clear that it was acceptable for me to find out certain kinds of information, the data began to flow much more easily. Thus I owe much of my information to the assistance of Takla, whom I paid for his help. I avoided paying other villagers, preferring to interact with them as a friend who could sometimes be helpful—for instance, by treating medical problems or by loaning money without interest. As our landlady's son told us early in the fieldwork, if we gave him ten cents for every relative he named, he would give us an unprecedentedly detailed and extensive genealogy.

I tried—on most occasions successfully—to type up my notes every evening, so that gaps and inconsistencies could be noted immediately instead of after my return to Chicago. At night during the winter, it was frequently below freezing inside the house, so I sometimes found it too cold to type (on such occasions my wife and I read nonanthropological books[5] aloud to each other by the fire) and so delayed consolidating notes until the warmth of the following day. I made two copies of everything: one was kept in a topological file (social structure, religion, etc., although the categories constantly shifted according to my changing perceptions of what the relevant local categories were), and the other was filed in a chronological sequence. I also kept a separate diary in which I recorded my more impressionistic feelings and reactions.

The standard methodological chestnut handed out to anthropologists about to embark for "the field" states that one must learn the local language. In the trilingual case of Tarangpur, this advice was not very helpful. To master all three languages—and acquire enough usable data at the same time—was beyond my linguistic competence (with one totally deaf ear, I have trouble enough understanding all the English I hear). Of the three languages, I already knew Nepali, had obtained a smattering of Tibetan in London, and of course knew no Kaike, which is spoken only in Tarangpur and two neighboring villages by about a thousand people altogether. The compromise I had to settle for was to collect extensive linguistic data in all three languages (see Fisher 1973, for example), but to rely primarily on Nepali as the main research tool.

My Sherpa assistant, Changchu, was fluent in Tibetan (he had been born in Tibet) and was able to assist in my difficulties with that language. My Nepali was about as good (or as bad) as that of the villagers, so we felt at home conversing with each other. I therefore worked without any interpreters or research assistants. I had planned to bring one research assistant from Kathmandu and so had engaged a young man who had just completed his M.A. in geography to spend the year with us. He unfortunately had to put his own affairs in order before he could leave, he told us, so we left Kathmandu with the understanding that he would join us in a few days. I gave him enough money for his plane ticket to Pokhara and his expenses until he could catch up with us on the trail or in Tarangpur. I never saw him again.

2

The Land and Its People

des ko bhes   Fashions of the country,   (When in Rome,
kapāl ko kesh   hair of the head.   do as the Romans do.)
   —Nepali proverb[1]

DOLPO DISTRICT

The Physical Setting

Like most of the rest of Nepal, the land that comprises Dolpo District and the areas adjacent to it in northwest Nepal is mountainous, stark, rugged, and remote (see maps 1–3). Pinning down the southeast corner of the district is the massif of Dhaulagiri, which climbs into the sky out of the west bank of the Kali Gandaki River, opposite Annapurna on the east bank. At 26,790 feet above sea level, Dhaulagiri is the sixth highest mountain in the world. This peak and its outliers dominate the topography and determine much of the climate of Dolpo. Within its rain shadow to the north and north-northwest lie many more peaks with relatively arid plateaus at their feet. There are several hundred square miles of such plateaus and valleys, separated from Mustang to the east by the bulge of Tibet which juts into the area in between, and from each other by scores of ridges and peaks in the 20,000-foot range.

Most of this northern part of Dolpo is drained by the Langu River and its tributaries, which empty through sheer, uninhabited, and normally untraversed gorges into the headwaters of the Mugu Karnali River beyond the northwestern tip of the district. Directly south of this drainage in the north and northwestern tip of Dolpo lie the Sisne and Kanjiroba massifs, the highest summit of which

15

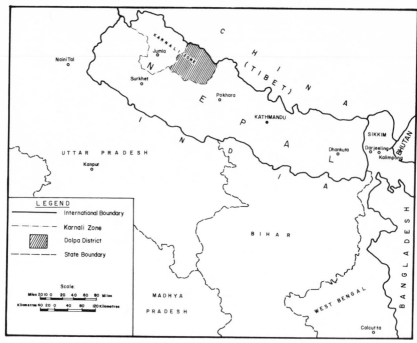

Map 1. Nepal and Neighboring Countries, 1979

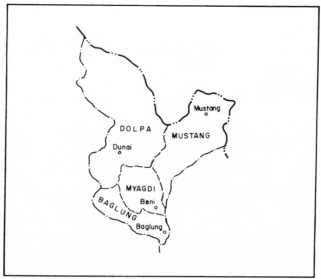

Map 2. Dhaulagiri Zone, 1969

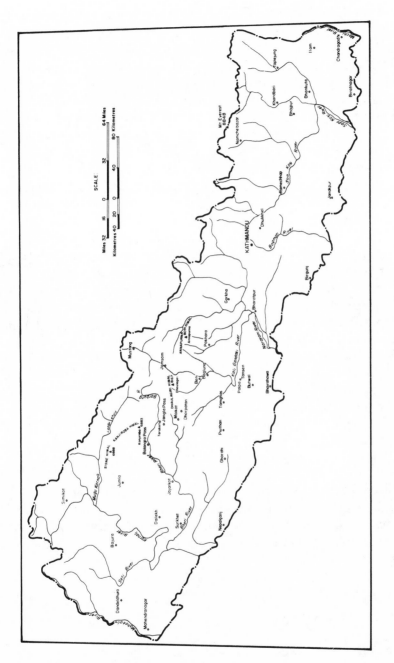

Map 3. Nepal

is above 22,000 feet, and to their south lie the relatively low and
hilly flanks above the streams that ultimately become the Bheri
River. Turning east again, one crosses the Balangra Pass (less than
13,000 feet) and descends to the Big Bheri River and the hilly
slopes above it. The Big Bheri here flows from southeast to northwest, so moving upstream puts one on a direct course back to
Dhaulagiri again, until a bend in the river moves the flow east–west
along the foot of the enormous ridge complex leading west from
the summit itself. After this twenty-five-mile east-west section, the
river—which by this time is called the Barbung instead of the
Bheri—takes a sharp turn north right under the nose of Dhaulagiri
and finds its headwaters in the glaciers north of the mountain, just
across the divide from the Langu basin.

There is nothing topographically homogeneous about Dolpo
District, and viable ecological adaptations range from irrigated,
riverine paddy fields to wind-swept alpine pasture suitable only
for brief summer grazing. The only common physiographic de-
nominator that gives the terrain any geographic unity is the inhospitable nature of the landscape to most forms of human livelihood.
One estimate (Thakali 1968) gives the following classification of
land surfaces:

    15 percent cultivated land
    20 percent forests
     3 percent arable wasteland
    12 percent grazing land, sloping meadows
    50 percent mountains, sharp stone ridges, and rocks

These proportions are very crudely calculated but are probably
roughly correct, although I suspect the estimate for cultivated land
is much too high. As will become evident later, different natural
features make for different ecological adaptations and different
ways of life.

The Cultural Setting

The political and administrative unit of Dolpo District is a culturally heterogeneous, ecologically plural, multilinguistic entity. In its

southern and southwestern sections, the occasional flat and fertile river valley bottoms and the hilly flanks above them are farmed for the most part by caste Hindus speaking Nepali, an Indo-European language closely related to Hindi and written in the Devanagri script. Pockets of so-called tribal peoples also inhabit this area, in their own villages as well as in predominantly Hindu villages. This Nepali-speaking area is called *Khasān* (literally, "land of the *Khas*").[2] The vast, high, cold and dry plateaus of northern Dolpo—separated from the People's Republic of China for well over 100 miles by the ridges and peaks which form the international border—are thinly populated by a farming, trading, pastoral people solidly within the Tibetan Buddhist cultural tradition: they speak Tibetan (a language belonging to the Sino-Tibetan family), dress in the Tibetan style, follow Tibetan Buddhism and/or Bon (the indigenous, shamanistic religion of Tibet), and have Tibetan institutions. In Nepali, these people of Tibetan culture and Nepalese citizenship are referred to as *Bhotias* (and the land they inhabit is called *Bhot*).[3]

Although its borders are constantly being redrawn (largely for gerrymandering purposes), at the time of the field research Dolpo District was distinguished by the largest geographic area (2,597 square miles) and the smallest population—estimated variously at 20,000 (Regmi Research Project 1968) and 22,075 (Ministry of Home and Panchayat 1966)—of any of the 75 development districts which make up Nepal. Given such a low population density (7.7 or 8.5 persons per square mile, depending on which population figure is used), it is not surprising that vast tracts of land are entirely without permanently settled people. A cluster of villages on the Bheri River in an area known in Tibetan as Tichurong[4] (there is no equally apt Nepali equivalent) lies isolated from other inhabited regions by just such barren areas.

Starting from Tichurong, it is at least a two-day walk up the Barbung River or its tributary, the Tarap River, to the nearest Buddhist,[5] Tibetan-speaking village, and it is a day's walk downstream to Dunai, the nearest Hindu, Nepali-speaking village and the administrative capital of Dolpo. Heading south over the two 15,000-foot Jangla passes that lie astride the principal trade and pilgrimage route connecting Tichurong with the rest of Nepal, it is a three-day trip to the nearest villages, which are inhabited by low-caste Hindus and by Magar farmers who speak Kham, a Tibeto-Burman language not closely related to Kaike (the language spoken in Tarangpur). These farmers constitute but one tribal variant of the hilly, Hinduized heartland of Nepal.

The Tichurong villages lie etched onto extremely steep slopes high above the Bheri River, which in its course chronicles the changing physical and cultural landscape. Its headwaters begin in the melting snows and glaciers north of Dhaulagiri and flow by yak and sheep pastures before reaching some of the Tibetan-speaking villages (where it is called the Barbung River) of upper Dolpo. It continues through an uninhabited stretch, then washes through the valley of Tichurong (where, after its confluence with the Tarap River, it becomes the Bheri River), inhabited principally by Magars, and winds down through the extensive Nepali-speaking hill regions and beyond them to the Hindi-speaking plains and jungle of the Terai. Finally it empties into the Ganges and thence into the Bay of Bengal.

TICHURONG

Internal Variation

The Tichurong villages, located at approximately 28° 53' latitude and 83° 00' longitude, are approximately as far from the equator as Cape Kennedy or New Delhi, but because of the altitude (between almost 9,000 feet and 12,000 feet above sea level), the climate is relatively severe. Temperatures in the summer are commonly in the 80s (°F), but temperatures during the winter are below freezing at night, even indoors. Not only the altitude but also the position of the villages vis-à-vis the sun determine different climates, growing seasons, and so on. Of the thirteen reasonably discrete villages (there are also a few small homestead clusters scattered here and there) that make up Tichurong, six villages, which constitute the Lāwan Village Panchayat, are on the right side of the Bheri; seven villages, which comprise the Tarangpur Village Panchayat, are on the left side of the river (see map 4).

The thirteen villages also vary considerably in size, ranging from 63 people in the smallest village to 365 in the largest, Tarangpur

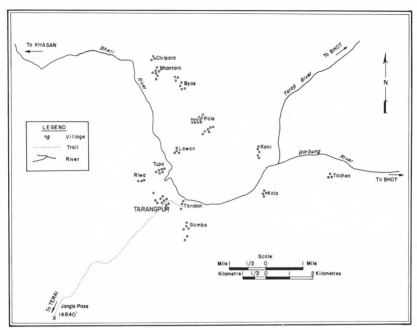

Map 4. Tichurong

(see map 5).[6] Tarangpur is in fact one of the largest villages in Dolpo District, and a political and economic center as well. As such, it cannot claim to be "typical" of Dolpo District, or even of Tichurong, not to mention all of Nepal. But from the perspective of economic and cultural change it is something more important, interesting, and arresting: it represents a cultural and commercial stage in which the forces and processes that are transforming this part of Nepal are silhouetted in a more conspicuous, compelling, and concentrated way than in the "typical" village.

Tarangpur's geographic remoteness and social isolation conjure up the image of a small, homogeneous, stable, or even static Redfieldian folk society. But a brief glance at the ethnographic facts compels an opposite conclusion. Linguistically, the village is complex. The mother language is an unwritten Tibeto-Burman language called Kaike, distantly related to Tibetan and other Tibeto-Burman dialects spoken elsewhere in Nepal.[7] In addition, all adults in Tarangpur speak the two other languages of Tichurong—Nepali and Tibetan. In nine of the thirteen villages, Ti-

Map 5. Tarangpur Village

Key to House Numbers

The following households (see map 5) had Tibetans living in them during the winter of 1968–1969: 9, 10, 13, 14, 16, 18, 18a, 19, 23, 25, 28, 30, 33, 34, 36, 41, 42, 43, 44, 47, 51, 55, 56, 57, 64, 66, 67, 68, 74, 75, 76, 77.

The following households patronize the gomba at house 5: 10, 11, 12, 14, 28, 50, 51, 52, 60, 63.

The following households patronize the gomba at house 18: 8a, 13, 15, 17, 25, 26, 27, 36, 41, 42, 43, 52.

The remaining households (except for the Tailors in 46 and the *dhami* (shaman) in 73) patronize the gomba maintained by houses 1–4.

The following households engaged in some form of long-distance trade during 1968–1969: 1, 2, 2a, 3, 7, 8a, 8b, 9, 10, 11, 13, 14, 15, 16, 17, 18, 18a, 19, 20, 21, 22, 23, 24, 26, 28, 29, 32, 33, 34, 35, 36, 38, 39, 40, 41, 42, 43, 44, 45, 47, 48, 49, 50, 52, 53, 56, 57, 59, 61, 62, 63, 64, 65, 66, 67, 68, 69, 71, 72, 73, 76, 77.

betan is spoken; one village (Riwa) is Nepali-speaking; in only three villages (Tarangpur, Tarakot, and Tupa)—and nowhere else in the world—is Kaike spoken. Fluency varies from individual to individual and from language to language, but all Tarangpurians (with the exception of very young children) feel free to express themselves without hesitation in either second language, and in the natural course of life they are required to do so.

Life-cycle rituals (name-giving at birth, funerals) tend to be Buddhist, though a boy's first haircut is Hindu, and marriage is neither; seasonal rituals (*Dasain, Saune Sankranti*) tend to be influenced by Hinduism, but strictly local deities are also worshipped in many rituals, the most notable being a nearly month-long religious festival in the winter with daily dancing—part of the cult of local mountain gods—which is neither Hindu nor Buddhist but entirely indigenous. The Hindu calendar (*Bikram Sambat*) is used for some purposes (to calculate the timing of Hindu festivals, auspicious and inauspicious months for marriage, school schedules, and other government-related activities), while the Tibetan calendar is used to calculate the beginning of the local New Year, which differs from the Tibetan and Nepali New Years (both of which are also celebrated, but in a much more minor key). At Lapsa, the indigenous New Year, the senior male member of each clan supervises raising a new "flagpole" on village houses—that is, the old flagpole is refurbished with a fresh juniper branch and white cloth flag (identical to Tibetan prayer flags but with no prayers printed on them) at the top. Celebration of the local deities (there are also household deities and spirits) should be managed by a quartet of ritual specialists: *barphun, narphun, sildin,* and *patum.* As villagers have become increasingly active traders, however, the number of men willing to perform these duties has declined, and there is now only a patum in Tarangpur. Other Tichurong villages have other of these specialists, but no village has a full complement of them. The many celebrations of the local deities throughout the year are held according to the lunar calendar.

Buddhist lamas and two distinct varieties of shaman live in the village. One is the animal-sacrificing *dhāmi* standard in this part of Nepal; the other is the patum, who is part priest and part shaman, for he both performs rituals in Kaike and Tibetan that guarantee purity and enters into states of spirit possession. Tarangpurians worship their gods at shrines and natural objects, such as trees, as well as at Buddhist and Hindu shrines and objects wherever they can find them. They acknowledge different gods as having different powers in different locations; hence the gods are not in competition with each other. They have accepted a local version of Pascal's wager: not certain of the limits of any specific deity, they hedge their bets by worshipping them all. Thus their religion is a complex syncretistic configuration of Buddhism, Hinduism, and their own autochthonous cult of village and mountain deities as well as household gods and spirits.[8] As one informant put it when I was trying to sort out all the different deities that seemed to impinge on Tarangpur life, "all the gods are the same." Tarangpur bears similarities to both its culturally disparate and far-flung neighbors, but it is identical to neither. Nor is Tarangpur typical of all Tichurong in this regard. Within Tichurong, the nearby low-caste Nepali-speaking village is entirely Hindu,[9] and some of the other Tibetan-speaking villages are more devoutly Buddhist (or Bon) than is Tarangpur.

There are a number of other important ecological and cultural differences within Tichurong. In several villages, for example, wheat is grown, whereas in Tarangpur it is not; corn is now grown in Tarangpur, but it has not yet spread to all Tichurong villages. Even such a basic fact of life as death is dealt with differently from place to place. Tarangpurians say that funeral procedures vary from village to village, although lamas conduct them all. In Gomba village, a three-day ceremony takes place during which lamas read and pray; in Bhantara, the ceremony takes seven days; and in Tarangpur, this ceremony is not held at all. When the body is burned in Gomba, one lama stands 30–40 feet away from the corpse, while the other lamas read and pray on the other side, and this again is not done in Tarangpur. The Tarangpur lamas do not touch the corpse with their hands, whereas in Gomba they do, and in addition the highest lama puts *prasād* (offering to a deity) in the mouth of the deceased. Tarangpur villagers consider their lamas less learned and expert than Gomba's village lamas, and they have fewer ritual implements, such as drums and thighbone trumpets. In Tarangpur, no care is taken over the position of the body, but in Gomba it must be burned in a sitting position. In Tupa and Tarakot, people stop working and return to the village if anyone dies, but in Tarangpur and Gomba they keep on working. Some differences may be doctrinal (Gomba has a Kagyupa as well as a Nyingmapa gomba), but many of the differences are more likely due to different degrees of education, dedication, and commitment. I cannot vouch for the accuracy of the above descriptions, which were all told to me by Tarangpurians, but the important point is simply that villagers themselves do not believe they share an utterly uniform culture within Tichurong. It is by no means a homogeneous area inhabited by ethnically identical people—hence the relative disutility of the term *Magar*. As will become clear, even the Kaike-speakers exhibit great variation among themselves. But because of its topographical isolation and somewhat ingrown social interaction,[10] Tichurong comprises a unit for analysis which is useful, convenient, and—within obvious limits—analytically viable. Taken as a whole it is, despite its internal diversity, a social system.

Transportation and Communication

To reach Tichurong from the capital, Kathmandu, one must first take the forty-minute flight west to Pokhara (or, nowadays, the

road, completed in the early 1970s, which connects the two
towns). From Pokhara it is a one-week walk via the Kali Gandaki
and Myagdi Rivers to the Swiss-sponsored Tibetan refugee settlement of Dhorpatan, and almost another week straight north from
Dhorpatan over the Jangla passes (almost 15,000 feet), which cut
through a relatively low western spur of the Dhaulagiri massif, to
Tichurong itself. Alternatively, it is a two-week walk from Pokhara
up the Kali Gandaki gorge and over the approximately 17,000-
foot pass north of Dhaulagiri into Tsharka, and then nearly
one more week walking south and west down the Barbung
River (which is called the Bheri by the time it reaches Tichurong). The administrative and commercial center of Jumla lies
almost one week's walk west of Tichurong, beyond two approximately 13,000-foot passes. There is a good grass airstrip at Jumla
(although because cloud conditions obscure the mountainous approach, it cannot be used during the monsoon), but no scheduled
flights land there. On the other side of a variety of 19,000-
foot passes to the north lie the plateaus and valleys belonging to
what is, culturally, Dolpo proper (Snellgrove 1967); beyond them
stretches the Autonomous Tibetan Region of the People's Republic
of China.

With the exception of the passes to Jumla, which are never
impassable for more than a week at a time in winter, all the passes
leading to Tichurong are snowed in throughout the winter—that
is, depending on the height of the given pass, for anywhere between
four and six months. Thus the region is quite inaccessible, the only
low-altitude route in or out being the long, difficult track down
the Bheri River, which—several weeks' march from Tichurong—
reaches the flat, alluvial extension of the Gangetic plain called the
Terai, with its roads and whatever means of modern transportation ply them. Not only is this river route twice as long as the pass
route, but during the monsoon it is frequently impassable because
floodwaters carry away the makeshift bridges. There is no single
guaranteed route to Tichurong open all year; in the winter, the
passes are not negotiable but the river is, and vice versa in the
summer.

Distances within Dolpo are equally imposing, and according to
one estimate, it takes ten or eleven days to reach the northern

boundary from the southern, and nine or ten days to reach the western boundary from the eastern (Thakali 1968). Compared with distances to villages outside Tichurong—not to mention the time and trouble involved in getting to any place that could be considered, however remotely, a part of the outside world—the region of Tichurong seems minutely shrunk and compact. Using one of the two bridges which span the Bheri in this area, the distance between the two most distant Tichurong villages can be traversed in a brisk five-hour walk.

EARLIER SURVEYS AND EXPLORATION

It is not surprising that there is virtually nothing known about such an isolated and inaccessible region. But it is a testimony to the vigor of ethnographic research in Nepal that no less than three other anthropologists had briefly visited Tichurong (although they had published nothing on the area) prior to my arrival there in 1968. My first publications (Fisher 1970, 1971—the latter reprinted in its present format in 1973) have been followed by Jest (1971, 1975), von Fürer-Haimendorf (1975), and Hitchcock (1978), so a clearer picture of Tichurong is beginning to emerge.

What had been published previously on the area by assorted travelers errant is so brief, misleading, or inaccurate as to be virtually worthless for scholarly purposes. Purna Prasad's *Mero Jumla Yātra (My Jumla Trip)*[11] has the merit of introducing the area for the first time to the Nepalese public,[12] and Snellgrove's *Himalayan Pilgrimage*[13] quite literally put Tichurong on the map, but in other respects these travelogue-diaries display the limitations of inaccuracy and superficiality characteristic of most examples of their genre. More recently, von Fürer Haimendorf (1975:204–222) has sketched a brief but useful overview of the economic and cultural characteristics of Tichurong, including trade. Despite his stay there of only a few days, the broad outline of his account (if not every detail) rings true.[14] For more detailed, accurate descriptive information, one must turn to various publications of the Nepalese government.[15]

HISTORY: DOCUMENTARY AND CONJECTURAL

The literary sources improve slightly but almost imperceptibly in an examination of the available historical documents. While it is reasonably unproblematical to portray the "betwixt and between" geographical position of Tichurong, halfway between the Tibetan highlands to the north and the Hinduized valleys to the south and west, the questions of how and when the people came to this valley, and of what historical forces have shaped their past, are far more vexing. It is uncommonly difficult to trace even the barest kind of historical sketch of Tichurong, which is much too far from Kathmandu and a little too far east of Jumla to be frequently mentioned in the inscriptions and documents concerning those places. Tichurong appears to have always been fairly independent of outside political influences and powers, but when it has been dominated by external *rājās* and petty chiefs, these rulers have usually, until relatively recent times, been from the west.

Although we can never know the details of the interaction between Tichurong people and those who have governed them—officially and unofficially—it is clear that both historically and within living memory, the people of Tichurong have deferred to power held by adherents of two entirely different cultural traditions. Just as Tichurong occupies a geographic position part way between the Dolpo plateau and the lower valleys, so it has been caught historically between two disparate cultural and political traditions; one or the other has always dominated, and often both influences have been at work simultaneously in different spheres. For Tarangpurians to be caught in the middle is nothing new. The historical details that follow—many of them discovered in previously unexamined documents in Kathmandu—demonstrate how Tichurong's cultural oscillation between Hinduism and Buddhism has developed over time.

From Tucci (1956, 1962) we learn that in the thirteenth and fourteenth centuries, west Tibet and a sizable chunk of western Nepal—almost certainly including the valley of Tichurong—were united under the Malla kings, whose two capitals were located at Sinja, northwest of Jumla, and at Taklakot, in western Tibet. For unknown reasons (perhaps related to political unrest on the plains), toward the end of the fourteenth century this kingdom rather suddenly collapsed. In the meantime, a succession of Rajput chieftains who were fleeing from Muslim invasions in India arrived in western Nepal, which they carved into petty principalities for themselves. By the beginning of the fifteenth century, one of these rajas, Balirāj, whose parents were from Rajputana (Regmi 1961:5), became king of Jumla and "enlarged his fief both to East and West. His glory was known as far as China; the Government of China promised to give him seven *dharnis* (= 17 seers) [between 34 and 42 lbs.] of gold, good horses, brocades, etc. A religious treaty was also signed between China and him and many kinglets both to the East and to the West of Jumla became his vassals and paid tribute to Jumlesvara" (Tucci 1956:122). By the latter half of the fifteenth century, Tichurong may have belonged to the principality of Parbat (also called Malaibam), which touched Jumla on the west and Kaski in the east. Parbat fell to Rudra Sen, who ruled over Palpa, to the south, between A.D. 1440 and 1475 (Regmi 1961:28). Possibly these princes in central and western Nepal owed vague, perhaps nominal, allegiance to the Moghul emperor in Delhi.

There were fourteen successors to Baliraj's kingdom (or twenty-one, according to less reliable documents) before the grandson of Prithvi Narayan Shah, the direct lineal Gorkha ancestor of the present King of Nepal, conquered Jumla from his power base in Kathmandu in 1788. Between Baliraj and the Gorkha conquest, various relatives of the Jumla rulers branched out and became petty princes in different parts of the kingdom, including Tichurong.

Tucci reports that the ninth successor of Baliraj was named "Vikram Sah, whose brother went to Byams Gan (?)" (1956:122), which is almost certainly the location known locally as Byas Gad (Nepali, Byas River), an uninhabited spot at the confluence of the Byas and Bheri Rivers.[16] This chieftain, still remembered in Tichurong as the Byas Gad Raja, was only one of a number of local rajas who were of the same lineage as the Jumla kings. Other brothers of rulers in immediately ascending and descending generations went to locations within a day's walk of Byas Gad, some of which were also unknown to Tucci, although they are clearly recognizable to anyone who knows local geography. Historians (e.g., Regmi 1961:7) call these rulers the Kalyal rajas, and it is by this term also that they are remembered today in Tichurong.[17]

The thirteenth successor after Baliraj was "Suratha Sah, whose brother went to Tiprkot Tara" (Tucci 1956:122). This undoubtedly refers to the village of Tarakot, or somewhere nearby—the village which, although it is one of the smallest villages of Tichurong, is listed on many maps, almost always to the exclusion of any other Tichurong village.[18] There is no evidence or remembrance now of his reign, but his residence (or that of his successor) may have put this otherwise tiny and obscure village on the map. According to Tucci (1956:127), another *tamapatra* (copperplate) dates Suratha Sah at Saka Eva 1646 (A.D. 1724), so his brother may well have been the father of Badri Sah, who was in turn the father (by his Magar wife) of Vikram Sah, who was eventually defeated by the Gorkhas and who is the only named historical figure generally remembered in Tichurong today.

According to local legend, Vikram Sah, the last raja of Tibrikot (one day's journey down river from Tarangpur, toward Jumla), was born less than 200 years ago[19] in Yelakot, which is now a flat, uninhabited piece of land overlooking the Bheri River below the Tichurong village of Gomba. Vikram's mother was a Magar woman named Agra Wati, but because his father's first, presumably high-caste wife in Tibrikot was without a male heir, Vikram was called there to be raja. He and the other Kalyal rajas were eventually defeated in 1786 by Gorkha troops commanded by Kazi Shiva Narayan Khatri and Sardar Prabal Rana (Regmi 1961:111), who were fighting for the grandson of Prithvi Narayan. Vikram said that rather than see his kingdom surrendered he would commit suicide, which he did. Vikram Sah is remembered in Tichurong now as blessed with an auspicious fate, because although his mother was of low caste, he nevertheless became an important king. It is believed that the *Gheru* plant, which normally bears fruit and no flower, bloomed when Vikram Sah passed by. After his death, Bhakti Thapa was appointed *subbā* (roughly, "governor") of the region.

Vikram Sah and his fellow rajas were probably subsumed under one of the *bāisi* ("twenty-two") raja states, which "were formerly in a certain degree tributary to the Jumlah Rajah; who annually received from one, as a token of homage and subjection a pair of slippers, from another fish, etc. The princes at the head of them are, without exception, I understand, of the Rajpoot tribe" (Kirkpatrick 1811:283). None of the baisi raja states except Jumla that are listed by Kirkpatrick, Hamilton (1819), Vansittart (1915), or Oldfield (1880) lie within Tichurong—or even near it—as far as I can tell.

The kingdom of Gaganiraj (who had given his territory to Baliraj) had been bounded on the east by "Tarikkot" (Tucci 1956:123)—perhaps a misspelling, or a spelling of the pronunciation current at the time (1393), of what is today known as Tarakot. After inheriting or usurping Gaganiraj's territory, Baliraj or one of his successors probably eventually expanded the Jumla kingdom to include Tichurong. By this account, Vikram Sah and the other Kalyal rajas were merely one of "a new aristocracy [which] came into being by the donation of fiefs, etc." (Tucci 1956:130). In any event, it is difficult to reconstruct more than the flimsiest outlines of what happened in a place as small, obscure, and remote as Tichurong, either from Tucci, who is "not interested in establishing the lists of these local chiefs; they ruled over a few villages and had little historical importance" (1956:128) or from Regmi, who prefers to "avoid details and also the description of less important principalities" (1961:5).

The point of this historical résumé is that for several hundred years prior to the Gorkha conquest in 1788 of this part of Nepal, the villages of Tichurong had been under the influence of a series of rajas to the west whose predominantly Hindu outlook displaced the Buddhism that had formerly prevailed. By the end of the eighteenth century, these same villages came under the authority, however loose and indirect, of the predecessors of the dynasty that sits on the throne at Kathmandu today. The grandson of Prithvi Narayan Shah, Ran Bahadur Shah, ruled from 1777 until 1799 (Wright 1877:290–291). During his reign, and during the regencies of his mother, Rajendra Lakshmidevi, and particularly of his uncle, Bahadur Shah, the *chaubisi* ("twenty-four") and *baisi* ("twenty-two") raja states were brought under the authority of Kathmandu (ibid., 260–261, 282).

Paradoxically, the rule from Kathmandu of the Gorkha conquerors, who were strict and uncompromising Hindus (they ex-

pelled Capuchin monks from Kathmandu, for example) resulted
in a cultural realignment of Tichurong back toward Buddhism. In
a Lāl Mohar—(a document issued by the royal court of Nepal and
recognized by its red (*lāl*) seal—dated A.D. 1790 (document 1), the
King of Nepal advised the Jumla subba that the Mustang Raja's
rule over Tsharka (in Bhot, up the Barbung/Bheri River from
Tichurong) was to continue. In another royal decree (document
2) of the same year, the King of Nepal directed the Mustang Raja,
whose family was of Tibetan ancestry with marriage ties to noble
families of Lhasa, to relay any information about Tarakot to him.
These two documents strongly suggest that toward the end of the
eighteenth century, the recently established Gorkha kings in
Kathmandu placed Tichurong under the general jurisdiction of
the Mustang Raja. Thus in place of the Hindu Jumla rajas, the
strongly Hindu Gorkha kings began to rule Tichurong. But they
administered the area through the equally strongly Buddhist rajas
of Mustang, who of course represented an entirely different cultural orientation as the effective ruling group.

Despite an administration mediated through Tibetan Buddhists,
by the beginning of the nineteenth century the government of
Nepal was already directly scouting its newly acquired domains
for whatever valuable economic resources might be found, particularly minerals. A royal directive issued in 1805 (document 3)
requested villagers in Tarakot (among other areas) to assist personnel from Kathmandu in locating hot springs and deposits of sul-
phur, palthar, lead, soda, iron, copper, and alum. In 1837 a land
settlement was made in Tarakot, and in 1838 taxes began to be
levied on salt, wool, cloth, goats, and woolen blankets (documents
4 and 5).

Royal edicts in the nineteenth century were quite explicit in their
detail. Porter rates were set (two annas per day), as were interest
charges on loans of food and money (25 and 10 percent, respectively). Fees were stipulated to *mukhiyās* (village headmen who
collected taxes in their villages), to priests for performing various
pujās (worship ceremonies), and for reading texts. District tax
collectors were authorized to sack incompetent mukhiyas and to
settle disputes over limited trade areas.

In remote country separated from external powers by such un-
accommodating terrain, central authority must have been directly

invoked only in matters as important as those involving remuneration to tax collectors and in disputes over commercial and administrative jurisdiction between different areas (document 6). There is no way to determine whether explicit directives of the kind just outlined were adhered to faithfully, but they could have been enforced only by local administrators of unquestioned loyalty to the king in Kathmandu. By the late nineteenth century influence seems to have swung back again to Hindu officials in nearby Tibrikot (Montgomerie 1875).

At higher levels, royal influence was mediated through princes and appointees who retained their positions of power at the pleasure of the king in Kathmandu. There were several devices the king could use to strengthen the bonds of loyalty between him and his underlings. Kirkpatrick noted that "the allegiance of all the tributary chiefs is secured either by hostages retained at Kathmandu, or by allegiances of marriage contracted between them and the reigning family. Thus Ran Bahadur [grandson of Prithvi Narayan Shah] is married to a daughter of the Rajah of Palpa and Bootoul, or, as it is sometimes called, Bootwal" (1811:274).

Without more documentation of the period prior to the elimination of the local Kalyal rajas in 1786, it is difficult to determine how life in a place like Tichurong would have changed with the transfer of ultimate political authority from Jumla to Kathmandu or from Hindus to Buddhists. Taxes seem to have remained constant, but the tax base established after the Gorkha conquest was not heavy. Government tax records show that the population of Tarangpur increased from sixty-one houses in 1846 to seventy-four houses in 1908.[20] In 1846 the salaries of chiefs, lords, and headmen were abolished, and Thakuris and other aristocratic groups were warned against taxing people to finance their trips to Kathmandu (document 7). Nevertheless in 1864 tax concessions were made to houses belonging to Thakuri rajputs, and fees were prescribed for temple priests (the reference is unmistakably to Hindu priests; document 8). Thus there was clearly an official bias toward Hinduism; moreover, contemporary local sentiment is strongly of the opinion that intermediary tax collectors and other officials were extremely exploitative and unfair.

Pervasive suspicion of Jumla officials may have been part of the reason for moving the principal government center for Tichurong

from Jumla to Baglung, a small bazaar town just two days west
of Pokhara, during a general administrative reorganization of the
entire country in the 1960s. Prior to that, disputes were usually
taken to Jumla for arbitration (and sometimes to other courts in
central and west Nepal), and justice dispensed from Jumla was
always suspect.

Beyond the haze of particularistic historical detail in these documents, cultural conclusions may be drawn. We know that from at
least the thirteenth century on, Tichurong (if it was inhabited by
then) was associated with kingdoms centered in or near Jumla.
Not only political power but also the cultural character of the
Jumla courts changed over the centuries. Initially the Malla kings
seem to have been both Buddhist and Hindu, but by Prithvimalla's
time in the fourteenth century Hinduism began to supersede
Buddhism, and Regmi concludes that by the seventeenth century
a metamorphosis had taken place and "Buddhism in any form
disappeared for good" (1961:6). This Hinduization also occurred
in attenuated form in Tibrikot District (Dāra) to which Tichurong
belonged after the Gorkha victory in 1786.

But Tichurong was always at the cultural periphery, under the
sway first of Buddhist, then of Hindu Jumla authorities, but with
traditional ties also to the Tibetan Buddhist regions of upper
Dolpo. In the late eighteenth and most of the nineteenth century,
Kathmandu administered Tichurong through the Buddhist rajas
of Mustang. Certainly itinerant and resident Buddhist lamas have
been—and still are—a regular and powerful feature of village religious life since the nineteenth century, and probably earlier.

In addition to the documented high-level, official relationships,
there have also been unofficial sources of power that administrative reports and royal edicts do not mention. Thus for a number
of years before his death in 1963, Nyima Tshering, a wealthy and
influential man of upper Dolpo, wielded vast personal power and
settled disputes at least as far away as Tichurong, though he held
no official political or ecclesiastical status or title (see Snellgrove
1961:82). Like all the permanent inhabitants of this part of Dolpo,
Nyima Tshering was culturally entirely Tibetan, although a
Nepalese citizen. Thus elimination of local Kalyal rajas after the
Gorkha conquest and the subsequent dependence on more remote
authority increased the scope for unofficial aggrandizement by

men with sufficient wealth or power. Such men then exercise regional leadership which, depending on the vagaries of local personalities, has been variously both Hindu and Buddhist. Historically, the Tarangpur Magars—neither a full-fledged Hindu caste nor unalloyed Tibetan Buddhists, but always at the mercy of outsiders who were one or the other—had to defer, serially or simultaneously, to both Hindu and Buddhist sources of power, prestige, and influence. Thus Tarangpur's aura of cultural marginality, which is so striking in the ethnographic present and which comprises the conceptual core of this book, is rooted in the historical setting.

Exactly how the people of Tarangpur reacted to and perceived these different cultural traditions and to what extent their own identities were forged between these two great traditions cannot be determined for the distant past reflected in Tucci's documents and government archives. But a study of Tarangpur's contemporary relations with the outside world reveals clues about the way in which Tarangpurians still accommodate themselves to these two powerful—and in so many respects opposed—cultural models.

HISTORY: MYTHICAL

The people of Tarangpur have quite clear notions of whence, how, and why (but not when) they came to Tichurong, but at the level of concrete detail, at least, local origin myths and what is historically known do not, by and large, overlap. The following story represents the Tarangpurians' own etiological perspective on their origin, arrival, and development in Tichurong.

During the time of the Kalyal rajas, political upheavals or fighting of some kind between warring groups forced a woman to flee from an unspecified village about two days' walk to the west, in the direction of Jumla. She successfully escaped from her village but two enemy soldiers were sent to pursue her, so when she reached Byas River, she begged the raja there to grant her protection in one of the two palaces standing there at the time. He was willing to help her by hiding her in one of the palaces and locking the door. Eventually the two pursuing soldiers arrived and asked the raja whether he had seen a woman on the trail. The Byas River raja replied that he had seen a woman traveling alone but that she had gone on up the trail. The soldiers did not believe him and asked if they could search the palaces to be sure she was not there. The raja agreed to this proposal, and they proceeded to look through all his rooms. As they neared the room in which the woman was locked, the raja said: "You can't go in there, because one of my daughters, who is pregnant, is inside." The soldiers did not believe him and demanded that he swear that the room contained only his daughter and not the woman for whom they were looking. The king was prepared to compromise himself (swearing falsely is considered locally to be an extremely grave offense against morality) for the woman's sake and swore accordingly. The soldiers took him to the trail and told him to swear on the sharp edge of a sword, which he did. The soldiers then returned in the direction from which they had come. After they were gone the woman continued on up the Bheri River to the site of what is now the village of Tarakot, although at that time there was no village there or anywhere else in Tichurong, which was then completely devoid of human population.

She had been pregnant when she fled her village, and she subsequently gave birth to her child, a son, while she was still living alone in what would later be called Tarakot. The boy grew up also on the site of Tarakot and looked after their gray cow, which he often grazed in the huge field around and above which Gomba village is now located. Through all these years the boy and his mother were the only inhabitants of the Tichurong area.

At that time there was a lake filled with milk near a large walnut tree on the site of Gomba village, and most of the area around the lake was covered by trees. While grazing the cow one day the boy saw seven goddesses[21] in the form of angels who came there every day to swim in the milk lake. The boy intended to tell his mother about this, but each day he forgot about it by the time he reached home. One day he put a stone in his pocket so that when he took his clothes off that night the stone would fall out and remind him.[22]

That night the stone did fall out, but when his mother saw the stone she was very upset because she thought he intended to kill her with it. She said: "I have suffered a great deal for you. All that I have done has been for your sake. And now you want to kill me?" Her son told her that she was badly mistaken and that he had brought the stone home only to remind him to tell her about the angels he had seen bathing in the milk lake every day.

His mother was delighted to hear about the angels, and the next day she accompanied her son to the milk lake. They hid behind a bush and watched the angels descend from the sky and undress to bathe. The mother wanted her son to catch a goddess, preferably the youngest, because she always flew away last. She told him to catch the angel by touching her with a cow's tail which, being impure, would destroy her special powers.[23] After the angels had been swimming for some time, the boy removed all their clothes from where they had undressed, and when they got out of the lake and saw him they were embarrassed by their nakedness. They demanded their clothes back, but the boy refused to hand them over. They demanded them back again and this time he returned the clothes of the older angels but not of the youngest one. In this way he was able to get close enough to catch her.

The boy and his mother took her back to their house at the Tarakot site, but she would not say anything because she could not speak their language, which was Nepali. So the mother and son made many different kinds of bread and worshiped her with bread offerings. She was surprised by all this activity and said: "Tai kenan?" which in her own language meant "What are you doing?" From that time on the mother and son began to learn her language so that it eventually became their primary conversational medium. This is the language now called Kaike,[24] spoken today in Tarangpur, Tarakot, and Tupa but nowhere else in the world.

As time went by, the son and his angel bride had three sons. The eldest one brought them great happiness and was named Quay, which means "smiling" or "happy." Since it is considered good to have two sons, the second was named Jei, which in Kaike means "suitable." More than two sons is considered too many, so the third son was named Ging, which in Kaike refers to a proud person who upsets people.

The three sons grew up and continued to live in their valley, which was still occupied only by themselves, so that there was no one for them to marry. The only way to acquire wives was to go outside Tichurong to find suitable brides where other people lived and bring them back to Tichurong. Thus Quay went to the Jumla

area where he found the daughter of a high-caste Thakuri from
Dailekh; Jei crossed over the Jangla passes out of Tichurong,
descended to the Maikot region to the south and brought back a
Magar girl; and Ging headed north to the area bordering Tibet
and returned with a Bhotia girl (see fig. 1).

When the three brothers had all returned with their brides, Ging
invited his two brothers and their wives to a feast. To provide
meat he killed a cow, since his Bhotia wife had no restrictions
against eating beef, but he hid the head and tail so that the others
would not know what kind of meat they were eating. As it turned
out the brothers discovered what he had done anyway and in
retaliation placed him under a curse, which stipulated that his
descendants should not multiply very greatly, but yet should not
die out completely either. His descendants are called Ghartis,[25]
and today the Gharti clan is, indeed, the smallest clan by far in
Tarangpur. The three brothers were Thakuris (their angel mother
fell outside the conventional caste categories, but their father
would have inherited his mother's caste, presumed to be Thakuri
since she fled from a Thakuri area), and by the marriage rules of
that caste, intermarriage among the children of siblings would
ordinarily be proscribed. But the father decided to make a rule
that his sons' children could marry, so that their descendants
would belong to three exogamous, intermarrying clans. Thus in
addition to the Ghartis, Quay's descendants are called Budhas,
and Jei's clan are the Rokayas.

The origin of the fourth major clan is different. One of the three
sons was a shepherd who kept losing the same female goat every
day, so one day he followed her when she wandered away from
the rest of the herd. He discovered that she was giving her milk
to a baby boy living in the hollow part of a bamboo tree near the
present village of Tupa. He came home and discussed what he had
seen with his family, and they decided to bring the baby home.
The boy grew up and became the ancestor of the Jhankri clan.
The Budha, Rokaya, Gharti, and Jhankri clans were of equal rank
and married among themselves, the offspring belonging to the clan
of the father. To this day Jhankris, unlike the other clans, do not
eat she-goats, because it was a she-goat who fed their ancestor in
the bamboo tree. They do eat he-goats.

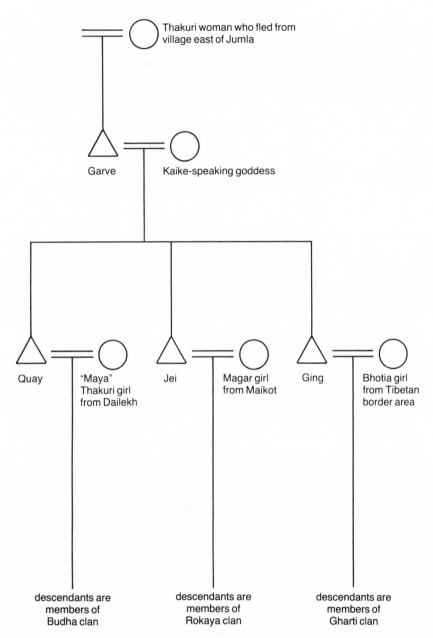

Figure 1. Origin of the Three Principal Clans in Tarangpur

Some more recent arrivals in the village have appropriated one or another of these ancestral clan names, so the clans are now further subdivided into lineages that may intermarry. For example, there are now two Jhankri lineages, Mapa and Topa. Mapa Jhankris are descended from the ancestor in the bamboo tree, while the origins of the Topa Jhankris are in Bhot. In Kaike and Tibetan, Topa means "above" and Mapa means "below"; these terms refer not to differences in social status but to altitudes of residents within a village—a terminological distinction common in Tibetan-speaking villages of west Nepal. Presumably, at one time there was such a terminological distinction in Tupa (no etymological connection with Topa), home of the greatest contemporary concentration of Jhankris.

Similarly, in addition to the "regular" Rokayas descended from the second brother, there are "three-eye" Rokayas who claim heroic origins. Once upon a time there was a wicked giant in Kola village. A Tibetan referred to now as the "three-eyed man" decided to do away with this giant, and so a contest was arranged in which their relative strength could be tested. To compare their power each had to swallow an entire male yak at once. Two yaks were produced, and the Tibetan swallowed his easily. He consumed the whole animal, but the giant's yak got stuck in his throat and he died on the spot. At that moment a third eye appeared in the Tibetan's forehead, like Siva's third eye, which appears when he's angry. Had the giant not died, the Tibetan could have burned him with his third eye. From then on the giant-slayer was respected as a king. He wore the fashions of the areas he visited, whether Tibetan or Nepalese, and the people of Gomba village imitated his clothes.

Different Budha lineages have multiplied in similar ways. The Palpali Budhas,[26] as distinct from the Budhas descended from the first brother, were originally of the Chhetri (i.e., Kshatriya) caste. In 1855, when Nepal was ruled by the first Rana Prime Minister, Jung Bahadur (1846–1876), a minor war broke out between Tibet and Nepal. A soldier from Palpa, due south of Tichurong and only one day's walk from the Terai, came through Tarangpur on his way to war. He fell in love with a local girl, who became pregnant by him. When he returned from Tibet she had married another man, a member of the Budha clan. The soldier was angry and threatened to kill him, but the man pleaded with him and said: "Don't kill me and I'll pass on all my fields to your son." The fields were Budha fields (all fields are associated with one or the other of the major clans who originally owned them, even if they are eventually inherited by a member of a different clan), so the soldier's son and his line became Budhas also, and his descendants are known as Palpali Budhas. But today they marry among themselves and are therefore distinct from the aboriginal Budhas.

There are a few other minor Budha, Rokaya, and Jhankri lineages which are prominent in one village or another in Tichurong, but they lack origin myths of the kind just recounted, and there is no need to become bogged down in further structural details at this point. The Lama families, for example, while visually indistinguishable from the rest of the villagers, form, like the Palpali Budhas, a largely endogamous group (see chap. 7 for a discussion of marriage classes). They generally call themselves "Budhas," although no one pretends that they are related to the primordial Budhas of the origin myth. There are also Bherba Budhas (so called because they at first lived in a section of fields called "Bher"), who are again distinguished from the so-called Arangba Budhas, the descendants of the ancestral Budha clan founder.

There is also an exogamous lineage of Thakuris (locally called "Thakula" to indicate the combination of high-caste origin and intermarriage with the Magar clans already mentioned), who emigrated from the Jajarkot region (several days' travel down the Bheri River) several generations ago. Since these Thakuris comprise a single exogamous lineage, they have always intermarried with members of the other Magar clans and hence are so thoroughly Magarized and absorbed into the society as to be indistinguishable from the rest of the villagers.

What is striking in all the myths is the unhesitatingly explicit and open acknowledgment of an ancestry that is so culturally and racially mixed. My census records from all Tichurong houses show that there is very little marriage into or out of the valley, and marriage with an outside group rarely occurs now or in the remembered past. Marriage of a Tarangpur Magar with a Bhotia would be unthinkable, for example, while marriage with a Thakuri or Magar from another part of Nepal would render the offspring of such a union ineligible as a marriage partner for another Tarangpur villager. Even the mere rumor of an illicit connection between a Tarangpur woman and a Bhotia man was the basis for one of the most sensational scandals of recent times. Genealogies are not written down or even generally remembered beyond four or five generations (informants had never thought about it before, but guessed that approximately ten or eleven generations had elapsed between the time of the original ancestor of the three clans and the present), yet the greatest importance is attached to the purity of one's descent so far as it is known. Paradoxically, by their own account, the clans were conceived and executed from the outset on disparate cultural foundations. These different groups still exist, and even surround the clans today, but acknowledgment of common kinship with them would be preposterous at best and irremediably scandalous at worst.

The boundaries that divide Tarangpurians from these other groups are partly ecological and partly reflexes of an ingrown social structure, but more than mountain passes and marriage rules are involved. There are shared elements with Tibetan culture, most notably the perennial presence of Buddhism; with Hindu culture, in concerns with pollution and hierarchy (see chap. 7); and even with Magar culture elsewhere in Nepal, in the partial overlapping of clan names (Hitchcock 1965).[27]

Whatever similarities exist between Tarangpur Magar culture and that of these other groups, it is emphatically the differences which matter most to the citizens of Tarangpur. Similarities are freely acknowledged, but differences are flaunted. From the Tarangpur point of view, the Thakuris to the west are in some sense "higher," the Magars to the south are of comparable status, and the Bhotias are "lower," although affinities exist in each case. Yet the rank of the three ancestral clans is unequivocally equal; the fact that one clan is descended from a Bhotia founder and another from a Thakuri does not in any way imply differential status today.

Thus the same persistent theme of cultural marginality suggested by both geographic and historical considerations is reiterated in these mythical origin stories. Whatever genetically and culturally mixed ancestry is historically involved, the myths charter (in the old-fashioned Malinowskian sense) the contemporary intermediate ethnic position of these people. Tarangpurians see themselves, by birthright so to speak, as an indeterminate mixture between distinct cultural poles, their physical and cultural isolation attenuated at the same time by mediating links with a complicated, powerful, and diverse external world. The specific social relationships of the mythical past cannot be reconstructed any more than those of the historical rajadoms can be, but the empirical study of contemporary Tarangpur which follows confirms the cultural miscegenation of those myths.

TARANGPUR AND THE WORLD BEYOND

Tarangpur is culturally convoluted, geographically isolated, and socially ingrown. For example, 41 percent of the marriages in Tarangpur were contracted between spouses born there, another 44 percent involved spouses from three villages less than an hour's walk away, and all but one (a marriage with a constable in the newly established checkpost) of the remaining 15 percent were all with Tichurong-born-and-bred marriage partners. The three Kaike-speaking villages of Tarangpur, Tupa, and Tarakot, plus Gomba village are, taken as a unit, relatively endogamous. If someone lives in Tarangpur, he was probably born there or in a nearby village or at least somewhere in Tichurong; conversely, if someone is born in Tarangpur, he will probably die there or some place not far away.[28] The same is true of all the thirteen villages of Tichurong (the exceptions are primarily the low-caste, Nepali-speaking artisans, and secondarily, the occasional Tibetan refugee family); there is very little leakage into or out of this social system.[29]

In Indian society, "the multiple interlacing of villages is primarily a function, not of polity or economy, but of jati and of family" (Mandelbaum 1970:114), but in Tarangpur just the opposite is true. The social structure is self-contained, but various trade and travel networks converge on Tarangpur, into, out of, and through which there is a large traffic of goods, accompanied by a concomitant flow of norms, values, and symbols. Despite the great distance and rugged terrain which seal Tichurong off from most of the rest of the world, an astonishing movement of goods and ideas does flow on a north-south axis through the hub of Tarangpur.

The economy is the dynamic subsystem which lifts Tarangpur out of its isolation; it does not "determine" the features of other subsystems, but it is a good place to make an analytical start, because a whole series of complex social and cultural changes have followed in the wake of distinctive quantum shifts (quantified in the following pages) in and among various economic sectors. Answers to questions asked of the opaque past can be discovered for problems phrased in terms of the present. How, in such a physically inaccessible place, do such totally different traditions as Nepalese Hinduism and Tibetan Buddhism simultaneously penetrate the peasant world of Tarangpur? What kinds of interaction link Tarangpur with the world beyond Tichurong? What are the mechanisms by which the people of Tarangpur model (or refuse to model) themselves on these two external cultural paradigms? How are ethnic borders maintained by such a mediating society? What kinds of transactions involve traffic out of, into, and through Tarangpur, and what status sets are manipulated in these transactions?

Only by understanding the whole series of transactions in which Tarangpurians are vitally involved can we understand the complexities of life in Tarangpur today and its place in interstitial Asia. Since all of Asia is changing, we will be able to clarify Tarangpur's changing role in the larger context by specifying the kind of transactional continuity that has persisted over time. Barth (1967:664) has described a way to study social change that can be built upon a transactional analysis:

> Imagine a situation where you stand looking into an aquarium, and you observe a fish. A moment later you find yourself looking at a crab in the same place where the fish was. If you ask yourself how it got claws instead of fins, you are implying a certain kind of continuity; this is the same body, and it has changed its shape. If, on the other hand, you say to yourself that this is the same aquarium, you are specifying another kind of continuity, implying a set of constraints that leads you to formulate other hypotheses about the dynamics of change in this instance. Different specifications of the nature of the

continuity that ties two situations together in a sequence of change give rise to very different hypotheses about the mechanisms and processes of change. For every analysis, it is therefore necessary for us to make explicit our assertions about the nature of the continuity.

Barth goes on to say that we can handle change if we look at behavior as an allocation of time and resources, and observe new allocations as concrete events with systematic effects that may constitute change. If we look at the remarkable shifts in transactional patterns over the last forty years in Tarangpur, we will be able to specify the nature of the continuity that ties together the contrasting scenes of the past and the heterogeneous present, and hence understand the mechanisms and processes of changes described.

An analysis of transactions and exchange patterns will also provide perspective on a different set of problems: how a nation as internally diverse and fractionated as Nepal manages to hold together at all. The situation seems comparable to what the Indian historian D. D. Kosambi described for northern India during the first millennium B.C.: "The bond that held so heterogeneous a society together, that made it a society rather than a set of tribes, was not so much common ritual and common language as a whole aggregate of common needs satisfied by reciprocal exchange" (1965:120).

In Nepal there is no question of common ritual or language,[30] even within as small and compact an area as Tichurong. Marriott (1955) has shown that in India a village cannot be studied as an isolated unit; in Nepal, a culture cannot be studied as an isolated unit. Deeply ingrained, highly traditional, exceptionally pervasive intercultural contact is the basis for Nepal's sociocultural system.

The nature of Tarangpur's intercultural contacts will be dealt with in due course through an analysis of the village's transactions with the world beyond Tichurong. However multifaceted Tarangpur transactions may prove to be, they all grow out of an economy which rests, as chapter 3 shows, on a solid agricultural base.

3

Himalayan Farmers

---

sya bilo patnai mothobnan   Meat cut into many shares is insufficient.
    —Kaike proverb

THE PROBLEM OF SURPLUS

Implicit in the notion of transaction is the existence of surplus—surplus goods and/or surplus time that can be transferred to a second party for something which is more desirable than the goods or time transferred. The stipulation is important because—assuming that transactions are interaction sequences systematically governed by reciprocity (Barth 1966)—people cannot be regarded as involved in transactions when their very survival depends on a course of action to which the only alternative, in this Nepalese situation, would be death by starvation. An exchange under duress, where there is no choice, is not a transaction.

In economic anthropology, the concept of surplus is much debated (Pearson 1957; Harris 1959; Dalton 1960, 1963), but Orans's useful refinement of the concept allows for Pearson's critical recognition that "a subsistence level is inextricably cultural and is not based simply on uniform biological species requirements" (Orans 1966:25). Adapting Orans's definitions to the agricultural circumstances of Tarangpur, what he calls the subminimal surplus—namely, food that is "left over" after expending enough energy to produce it and stay alive—would be formulated as follows:

Subminimal surplus = Crop yields − Input of food calories to produce the yield − Basal and intermediary metabolic activity − Reproductive activity

46

The usefulness of this concept is limited by the fact that it describes any agricultural community living off its own land without starving to death. Tarangpur of course transcends the conditions of this definition, which "allows one to know what is certainly not possible, but does not permit determination of what if anything is possible" (Orans 1966:26). The concept of subminimal surplus is thus not so much culture-free as cultureless. But culture is at the core of understanding Tarangpur's agricultural base and needs to be included rather than excluded.

An alternative way of proceeding is to examine indigenous concepts. From a Tarangpurian's point of view, what we have called here a subminimal surplus might keep someone alive and working in the fields, but that would barely count as living. Subsistence—in the inclusive, cultural sense—is defined locally as whatever is required to achieve the subminimal surplus level, plus some selected additional items the attainment of which constitutes a basic, inalienable right in the village. By this I mean that even people down on their luck should be entitled, beyond the subminimal surplus, to these things: meat, chili peppers, salt, beer/liquor, seed for the next crop, and new clothes.

This package of goods constitutes a top priority set, to be obtained before anything else. These goods represent culture at work—the first choice beyond the subminimal surplus. The list is flexible, in that quantities will always vary, and not even a wealthy villager could afford to eat meat every day. But everyone should be able to eat meat once in a while, or get a new shirt occasionally. Variations in amounts largely distinguish wealthy from poor and help maintain the relentlessly egalitarian village ethos (see chap. 7): since everyone has at least a little of these things, it is easy—rhetorically, at least—for anyone, no matter how poor, to assert equality with anyone else, no matter how high and mighty.

Just what constitutes a surplus is not something Tarangpurians think much about, but there was a broad consensus that the above list defines it. These items are not rank-ordered but are considered an irreducible set, even though salt and seed may be arguably more essential, over the long run, than new clothes and beer/liquor. Armed with these definitions, surplus can now be defined as what is left over for commercial and cultural activities after subsistence

needs (as Tarangpurians tend to think of them) have been met—
that is:

Surplus = Cultural and commercial expenditures − Subsistence

The actual measurement of these kinds of goods and services is
one of the more fractious dimensions of empirical research in
economic anthropology, and time is often an equally useful—
and certainly more easily measured—quantity. Firth, summarizing
Belshaw's position, points out that time has two advantages: it is
measurable and must be used in the satisfaction of any ends whatsoever (Firth 1967:20). Surplus time, then, is time left over after
an adequate allotment has been made to produce the food necessary for each step of the subsistence equation.

Conceived in these terms, the elaborate series of transactions in
which Tarangpurians participated is built upon a pile of surplus
grain, which is traded during surplus time (the winter) and which
for ecological reasons can be utilized in no other important
economic activity. Unlike some trading villages elsewhere in Nepal
(e.g., in Namche Bazaar in the far east, in the upper Mugu Valley
northeast of Jumla, or in the upper Kali Gandaki's Thakkola
region north of Pokhara and just the other side of Dhaulagiri from
Tichurong), Tarangpur has a full complement of agricultural activities at the base of its economy. This lends to trade patterns
distinctive qualities different from those that characterize trading
activities which depend on something other than an agricultural
base. As in any agricultural community, an understanding of the
use and control of land is critical to any analysis of the economy.

I attempt to quantify as much as possible the description of
agriculture and trade in this and the following chapters, exasperat-
ingly difficult though that job is. I do so not because I believe there
is magic in numbers, since Whitehead pointed out long ago that
"apart from a presupposed pattern, quantity determines nothing"
(1968:195). In any case, my numbers are quite thin in spots. The
data on time allocation (table 10) and field measurements (appendix E) are all drawn from single households, but I think some
numbers are better than none. These weaknesses in the data follow
in part from the difficulties in collecting them (see chap. 1), but
here I seek not to defend or criticize the data but simply to charac-

terize them. Claims that such data are "typical" can be supported only by my assertions, based on protracted experience of the culture (see also chap. 3 n. 4).

Yet even such crude measurements as those employed in the following pages are preferable to vague impressions, especially in an ecological-economic study of this kind. The monumental difficulties of quantifying such variables as size of landholdings, crop yields, and profit margins in trading in a place like Tarang-pur—where written records of such things do not exist, have never existed, and in most cases have never been thought of—mean that most of the dimensions recorded here can only be very rough estimates.[1] This is certainly the case with respect to almost anything concerned with land.

THE LAY OF THE LAND

The villagers of Tarangpur classify land surfaces into seven basic types:

1. Fields (cultivated or fallow, and including within them non-arable sections composed of boulders too huge to move)
2. Grassy or forested areas
3. Land along a river bed, whether arable or not
4. Rock cliffs
5. High mountainous land, including passes
6. Pasture land
7. Gardens

Of these, the most important economic category by far is that of fields. Different varieties of fields in different parts of Nepal, and even within a single village area, are classified by different government agencies according to fertility, topography, water source, cultivating technique, and so on. Tichurong people call all their fields *kodale*—unirrigated hilly land too small to be plowed by oxen (Regmi 1976:234), although, inconsistently, in Tichurong a distinctive plow pulled by a single bullock is used (see section on technological consequences below). All Tichurong land is now classified by the Central Bureau of Statistics as *pākho*—unirrigated

hill land (Ministry of Economic Planning 1966:11).[2] Fields in
Tarangpur are not only hilly and unirrigated, but also steep, rocky,
and limited to a single growing season. They face a generally
northeastern direction.

All land utilized by Tarangpurians for agricultural or pastoral
purposes extends several thousand vertical feet over an enormous
hillside. Given an economy based on such topographic considerations as these, it is simplistic and misleading to ascribe a specific
altitude above mean sea level to a village like Tarangpur; even
excluding fields, the village houses themselves are spread out over
almost a thousand vertical feet.

According to the most recent (1963) Survey of India map, which
is by no means a paragon of accuracy, the lowest millet fields next
to the Bheri River are at 7,600 feet, and the village of Tarakot
stretches from 8,000 feet to 8,200 feet. The lower edge of
Tarangpur begins at 8,700 feet, and the uppermost houses, belonging to lamas and their families, lie at about 9,600 feet. Fields are
cultivated to virtually the same altitude, and beyond that stretch
fairly dense mixed jungle, mainly coniferous, and alpine grazing
pastures that extend to the Jangla pass, at 14,840 feet, which cuts
through the enormous western spur leading from the Dhaulagiri
massif.[3] The land between the river and almost 10,000 feet is
cultivated extensively except, of course, where houses are standing
or where natural obstacles such as trees, boulders, or sheer cliffs
obtrude.

SIZE OF FIELDS AND TERRACES

Cultivated fields lie on hillsides with a general slope sometimes
approaching 35 degrees. By extensive terracing Tarangpur farmers
have reduced the angle of fields under cultivation, although even
these run as high as 25 degrees. Thus the entire hillside is laced
with low stone-wall embankments (made from stones dug up
while preparing and plowing the land), which hold back the soil
during the monsoon and render the land level enough to be plowed
and planted.

A consequence of cultivating such steep slopes is that the size
of any given terrace is usually quite small, or at least narrow.

Because of the cliffs, boulders, shrubs, and trees liberally sprinkled over the hillside, many fields are not rectangular, so measurements in square area are difficult to make. But of forty-one fields belonging to a man of average landholdings,[4] almost two-thirds are less than 35 feet wide. Thirty-eight reasonably rectangular fields (out of the forty-one) have a mean length of 98 feet and a mean width of 39 feet; the average "side" of a field is therefore about 68 feet long. The mean number of cultivated square feet per field is 4,415. Appendix E summarizes the dimensions of all forty-one fields. A field is defined as a cultivated piece of land usually owned by a single family, completely surrounded by unowned land or by land owned by someone else. Thus a field is not normally a continuous piece of land but an expanse of owned territory divided by stone walls into a series of sloping terraces. The number of terraced sections is therefore much greater than the number of fields.

Not only are the fields themselves small but it must be reiterated that each of the forty-one fields in appendix E is broken up by a succession of stone retaining walls as little as four feet apart. It is these terraces that constitute the minimal plowable unit—the amount of continuous land that can be worked at one stretch. These small plots average only about 10 feet in width. Anthropologists frequently make much of fractionation of fields through inheritance, but the lay of the land can be an equally important factor in determining field size. In Tarangpur the number of fields is largely a reflection of fractionated holdings, while the size of any strip of continuous arable land—that is, land which is not broken up by boulders, stone walls, cliffs, or other obstacles—is sharply limited by what are essentially geographic variables. In other words, land use patterns are determined by constraints which are as much ecological as social. Figure 2 sketches the dimensions and obstacles of a typical field.

Nor is the size and even location of terraces immutable. Because the stone walls that divide the terraces deteriorate over time, every year a number of them are torn down and rebuilt a few feet below their former locations. Then the earth of the former terrace is dug up and piled against the back of the new wall. This brings to the surface earth which was formerly buried and unused and which is hence more fertile than the old, worn-out topsoil. Any individual can move his walls in this manner as he sees fit. No one objects if

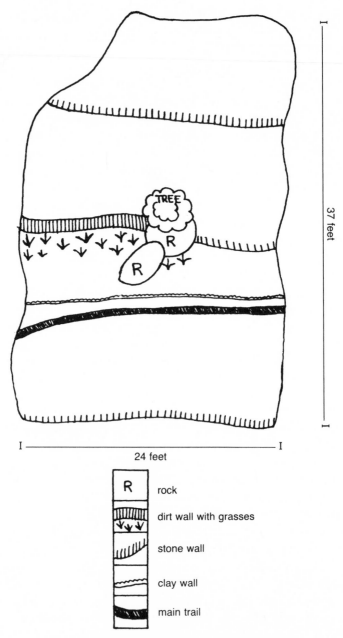

Figure 2. Sketch of a Typical Field*

*See Appendix E, field 31.

he finds that a wall bordering the top of one of his fields has been moved two or three feet into his field, making it that much smaller, because he will have done the same thing to someone else. This agrarian calculus is thought to work out in such a way that nobody ends up with any more or less land than he had before. A sense of reciprocity pervades all this earthwork tinkering, so that it is not regarded as zero-sum machinations at all. Pieces of the pie are not equal, and they do get shoved around, but in the long run each piece does not change size—at least not by these maneuvers. Farmers claim that the more frequently walls are moved the more fertile land will be, but since this is time-consuming, backbreaking labor, relatively few walls are moved in a given year.

LAND MEASUREMENTS

Nominal land taxes are paid, but the land itself has never been surveyed.[5] The hillside is divided into such a multiplicity of plots, and each household's fields are scattered in so many different locations and directions that, according to villagers, a government land reform survey team that arrived recently to assess the situation looked at the mountainside, regarded a scientific survey as hopeless, left the village in despair, and never returned.

Land belonging to a household is demarcated from adjacent land belonging to another household by a large natural or man-made feature, such as a boulder or rock wall, or by a relatively small rock planted intentionally in the earth as a boundary marker in an otherwise undifferentiated field. It is always clear who owns a piece of cultivated land, but there is no abstract unit in common use by which the area of specific fields may be totaled. Tarangpurians do not normally measure their land by feet, by a local linear equivalent, by yield, or by any other quantitative unit.

If villagers need to use such a unit (in order, for instance, to answer the queries of an anthropologist), they speak of the *hul*. A hul is the amount of land a bullock can plow in a single day, just as an acre was originally defined as the amount of land a yoke of oxen could plow in a day. The term may be used either to denote the land a bullock can plow for the first time in a plowing season, or it can refer to the amount of initially plowed land a bullock can replow. The second referent is about twice as much land as the first. I use the term exclusively in the first sense, as the Tarangpurians tend to do—namely, to refer to the amount of unplowed land a bullock can plow in a single day. Although this amount varies somewhat according to the lay of the land and the size and strength of the bull, in general, a hul is about 12,231 square feet, or about 28 percent of an acre. According to this calculation there are 3.6 huls in one acre.[6] Since there are about 1439 huls (roughly 400 acres) under cultivation (see table 6 and appendix E), there is more than one acre of cultivated land for each man, woman, and child in Tarangpur.

These terraced, cultivated fields lie in seven large, named regions that surround the village. The names identify general areas, so that one can locate a particular field (to find someone who is working there, for instance), and each of these seven areas is subdivided into smaller named units that pinpoint a group of fields even more accurately. Sixty-three of these smallest units are scattered over the mountainside. A few of the names derive from some obvious geographic feature nearby (tree, river, etc.), but most are simply names with no intrinsic meaning of their own.

SOIL

Even though the rock walls are made entirely from stones that have been removed from the cultivated fields, the soil is extremely rocky, and stones the size of cantaloupes are frequently seen lying in the middle of a growing crop. Despite its ostensibly inhospitable appearance, the soil is well suited to the crops which grow there. A complete soil analysis has not been performed, but a limited sample indicates a slightly acidic to neutral pH level, medium to high percentages of nitrogen, very high amounts of phosphorus and potash, and medium amounts of organic matter. Since the sample was taken from a field not too far from the village houses, where it is likely to have been fertilized more adequately than other, more distant fields, only limited confidence can be placed in this analysis.

The practice of periodically moving the stone walls undoubtedly contributes to maintaining the quality of the soil. Tarangpurians believe that moving a wall will double the crop yield the following year. The quality of the soil then deteriorates progressively for the next ten to fifteen years, until the wall is moved again. After a wall is moved it is not considered necessary to apply manure to the field for six or seven years. Otherwise, fields are manured every other year, in coordination with the millet/buckwheat alternate-year crop rotation cycle described shortly in the section on crops.

CLIMATE

Climate and weather conditions are also critical factors constraining productivity in this alpine agricultural area. Since the ground is frozen during the winter months, the agricultural cycle is limited to a single (summer) season, and consequently to a single crop— except for barley and sweet buckwheat, which are grown serially in the same ground. Winter crops are grown at lower elevations elsewhere in the hills of Nepal, and Nitzberg (1970) reports double cropping also in the western Himalayas. Total production at higher altitudes cannot equal that of warmer climates where winter crops are planted. But since Tarangpurians cannot farm all year, they are never caught in the time-bind of having to harvest one crop before it is completely ready in order to make room for the next one.

Although much of the rest of Dolpo presumably lies in the rain shadow of Dhaulagiri, the Tichurong villages receive regular monsoon rains. No meteorological data are available, but during the growing season of my residence in the area, monsoon rains fell on 93 days during the 225-day period between March 17 and October 27. Excluding the month of October, when the growing season was largely over, it rained 89 days out of 198, and during the critical month of July, it rained all but three days. Considerable snowfall during the winter also adds to the moisture content of the soil.

The villagers of Tichurong consider themselves fortunate to have such ample rainfall, as opposed to the Khasan villages only a few miles down river, which sometimes suffer grain deficits because of drought. Similarly, the Bhotia villages up river receive relatively little moisture and must resort to irrigation for the same crops that are cultivated in Tarangpur with available rainfall. Tarangpurians say that they have never suffered a drought-induced famine, although there are mythical references to a famine during remote ancestral times.[7]

CROPS

A diverse habitat, created by differences in altitude, exposure to sun, degree of slope, and the quality of the mantle itself—which includes open fields and extensive forests—gives rise to a diversity of crops and other food sources. The difficult terrain and climate constrain total production, but whereas the quantity of food produced per land area is small relative to the Terai, the variety of grain crops is considerable.

The two staple crops grown in Tarangpur are buckwheat (*Fagopyrum tataricum*) and a buckshot-sized grain called *la* in Kaike, *chiji* in Tibetan, and *chinu chamal* (*chinu* rice) in Nepali. This grain is prepared the same way as paddy rice and tastes something like it; it is actually not rice but a kind of millet (*Panicum miliaceum*). Because of the extreme variation in height of the different fields, three different strains of this millet (classified by identical botanical terms but distinguishable by color) are grown at different altitudes. These two crops constitute the bulk of the diet, and most fields are planted to these two grains, generally in alternate years on the same field. If in a given year a field is planted to buckwheat, the following year it will be planted to millet, and vice versa.

The manure cycle is tied directly to this crop rotation. If millet is planted, the field is manured (before plowing); the buckwheat fields are planted and harvested without any fertilizer. The following year, when buckwheat is planted in the millet field and vice versa, the pattern is reversed: the same crop, millet, is manured each year, and with this crop rotation a field is fertilized every two years (excluding fields with walls that have been recently moved, as already mentioned). A disadvantage of the remote setting of Tarangpur is that imported fertilizers are of course not available, as they are in the plains to the south; yet in one respect Tarangpur has an adaptive advantage over the plains: extensive forests above the village provide plentiful firewood, so that all dung can be used for fertilizer instead of for fuel. The forest also provides leaves and grass for cattle fodder, as well as bedded leaves, all of which ultimately increase the available manure.

In addition to these staples there are a number of other, supplementary crops. Another kind of buckwheat (*Fagopyrum esculentum*), which in Nepali is called sweet buckwheat, is grown in seasonal variation with hull-less barley (*Hordeum vulgare*). These two quick-growing cereals are planted in the same field in the same year. The very first crop to be planted in the spring is barley, which is harvested in midsummer. As soon as the barley has been cut, the field is sown again with the sweet buckwheat, which is the last crop to be harvested in the fall. This is the only example in Tarangpur of anything approaching a double crop. The barley is used primarily for brewing beer, and the sweet buckwheat is used primarily for breads prepared and distributed during festive or ritual occasions such as marriage feasts, a firstborn male's first haircut, and funerary periods. It is often offered to guests regardless of the circumstances.

Another kind of millet, known as Japanese millet (*Echinochloa frumentaceum, kodo* in Nepali), is grown in alternating years with chinu millet, but unlike chinu millet it is used in the preparation of a flat, pancake-type bread similar to that made with the coarser buckwheat. These are the major kinds of cereal grains cultivated in Tarangpur, but a species of amaranth (*Amaranthus caudatus*) is sown around the edges of chinu millet fields. There are two different varieties of this plant, one bright crimson and the other yellow, but they are prepared the same way: the seeds are fried in a dry pan and then mixed with honey and eaten as a snack. A third kind of millet is also grown (*Setaria italica*), but it is the least important of the millets.

In addition to these cereals and grains, which provide the bulk of the Tarangpur diet, there are other crops of varying importance. French beans (*shimi* in Nepali, Kaike, and Tibetan) are grown mixed in with chinu, but are never eaten Western-style in the pods. Instead the beans are dried, then ground into *dal,* which is poured over boiled millet (usually *Panicum miliaceum*). This is the major source of protein and is the standard meal once a day, buckwheat cakes being the other. There are two varieties of these beans, one more elongated than the other; they are planted haphazardly in the millet fields. Relatively insignificant in comparison are soy-beans (*Glycine max*).

Of increasing importance in recent years are corn and potatoes. Farmers in other villages of Tichurong have been planting corn for some time, but Tarangpurians have been planting it only since the late 1950s. About that time a village meeting was held and it was decided that it was all right to grow corn, which is thought to yield about five times as much grain as chinu millet (*Panicum miliaceum*). But corn is confined mostly to gardens near houses, because of the fear that animals will eat corn planted in the millet and buckwheat fields. By now every household grows some corn, although a few families have been planting it for only two or three years.

Until forty or fifty years ago, potatoes were not planted in Tarangpur. Then a lama from the upper part of the village brought back some potatoes from the village of Rimi to the west (near Kaigaon, between the two passes on the route to Jumla). He first planted them in a dirt-filled basket indoors but did not obtain very good results. Then he planted them in a garden, and finally in a field. By then there were potatoes in abundance and they spread around the village. Nowadays people so poor that their grain stocks do not last from one harvest to another do not have to beg for food from wealthier villagers, for which they traditionally had to give several days labor per *muri* (ca. 2.4 bushels) of grain.[8] Instead, they get by on potatoes, which grow well in any of the fields.[9]

In addition to corn and potatoes, which are grown in gardens and fields, there are a few crops that are grown exclusively in gardens—that is, in "fields" located around and between the houses. The most important are squash and pumpkin, both of which are boiled until soft. There are also two varieties of radishes and a turnip-type vegetable. Tobacco is also grown.

There are a few crops which are grown by certain households and not by others. Green peas are grown only by some of the Lama families, and two houses plant another kind of bean; flax (*Linum usitatissimum*) is grown by only a single household.

Two other important domesticated crops are eaten as oil. Both mustard (*Sinapis arvensis*) and marijuana (*Cannabis sativa*) are grown mixed in with cereals, and in both cases the seeds are ground and kneaded to extract the oil, which is used for cooking. Marijuana seed oil is the most common source of cooking oil.[10]

In addition to all of these cultigens, there are a number of wild food sources. Three varieties of peach tree grow in and around the village, but the fruit of each is small and not abundant. There are only a few examples of each kind, and one species is represented by only two trees. There are also several walnut trees that produce nuts with more shell than meat.[11] And there are at least nine types of wild berries and fruits, ten kinds of wild greens and vegetables, and fifteen varieties of mushroom. These wild plants grow by stream beds, in the forests, on rock walls, and in other nooks and crannies around the mountainside. None are eaten regularly, even when they are in season, and they do not detract from the primacy of the millet and buckwheat crops, which constitute the overwhelming bulk of the diet.

LAND USE AND YIELDS

The percentage of land allocated to each crop depends partly on dietary preferences and partly on differential yields among the different grains. Table 1 shows the average amount of grain produced on one hul or one acre for each of the major crops.

To meet the requirements of subsistence as defined in Tarangpur, it is generally agreed that an adult needs about four hul, or a little more than an acre. Since land is owned and operated by family units, household holdings are rarely that small. Table 2 produces the dimensions of a hypothetical subsistence for one adult, as estimated by informants. These figures represent the land and grain an adult would need to sustain himself for a full calendar

TABLE 1
ESTIMATED TYPICAL YIELDS OF FIVE MAJOR CROPS

Name of crop	Muris/hul	Muris/acre	Bushels/acre
Chinu millet	3	10.8	25.9
Buckwheat	5	18.0	43.2
Sweet buckwheat	3	10.8	30.2
Japanese millet	3.5	12.6	25.9
Barley	2	7.2	17.3

TABLE 2
HYPOTHETICAL ALLOCATION OF FIVE MAJOR CROPS
ON FOUR HULS (1.12 ACRE) AND THEIR YIELDS

Name of crop	No. of huls	No. of acres	% of total crops planted	Total yield in muris	Total yield in bushels
Chinu millet	2.00	.56	48	6.00	14.40
Buckwheat	1.40	.39	33	7.00	16.80
Japanese millet	.40	.11	10	1.20	2.88
Sweet buckwheat[a]	.20	.06	5	.70	1.68
Barley[a]	.20	.06	5	.40	.96
Total	4.00	1.12	101	15.30	36.72

[a]Since sweet buckwheat and barley are double-cropped on the same land, the 1/5 hul allotted for these crops is counted only once.

year. Land devoted to garden crops and potatoes are for the moment ignored.

The figures in table 2 are artificial in that they are arithmetical derivatives from greater amounts of land for more people rather than empirical descriptions of the way a single adult lives. Planting strategies change with the quantity of exploitable land, and if an individual did own just four huls, he would maximize his output by planting only chinu millet, buckwheat, and potatoes, foregoing the luxury of barley and sweet buckwheat, neither of which would be planted at all under such poverty-stricken circumstances. Diversification of crops is necessary, since high-yield crops are more apt to fail completely when conditions are not quite right than are poorer yielding crops, which will almost always yield something even under the worst conditions. Still, the fact that farmers plant any relatively low-yield crops at all points to—and is a measure of—surplus.

CONSUMPTION: IDEAL AND REAL

Direct personal consumption of food is difficult to estimate because of the difference in what Tarangpur people think (or at least what they say they think) they eat and what they actually do eat. They say that they eat a *māna* (a little less than a pint)[12] of grain per meal, three meals a day, or three manas of grain per day. Were they to eat three full meals a day they could, in fact, eat this much, and they sometimes actually do so. But they do not do so regularly, day in and day out. Depending on their work schedule, appetites, general health, and social life, they may eat considerably less. Three manas per person per day actually represents the near maximum amount of grain an able-bodied adult farmer might eat in a day. Such a person will rarely eat more and usually eats less.

As a corrective to this ideal consumption, I recorded the amount of grain in each meal eaten by a relatively well-to-do family for a month during the agricultural season, when calories are presumably in peak demand. The results, shown in table 3, reveal daily consumption well below the ideal.

What then is the average consumption per person per day? The average of all four of these household members is only 2.12 manas per day, but there is reason to think that this is an unrealistically low figure. First, the mother suffered from rather severe stomach discomfort and ate much less than she would when in good health. Second, the son was still prepubescent and therefore should not be counted as an adult. If we exclude the son but include the mother, the average is 2.29 manas a day, and if we include only the two adult, healthy individuals, the average is 2.48 manas (less than 2.5 pints) per day. Since our hypothetical subsistence adult is a healthy one, we can use 2.48 manas (pints) per day to represent

TABLE 3

ONE FAMILY'S AVERAGE DAILY FOOD CONSUMPTION
DURING ONE MONTH OF THE AGRICULTURAL SEASON

Person	Age	Average daily consumption in manas (or pints) of uncooked grain
Father	53	2.35
Mother	46	1.91
Son	15	1.57
Son-in-law's sister	20	2.60
Total pints or manas/day		8.43

the average adult consumption. Projected on an annual basis, this adds up to 905.20 manas, or about 13.5 bushels of grain for an adult each year.

But we cannot directly compare crop yields,—which are given in volume measures of grain that is unprocessed except for the removal of stalks and stems,—with household consumption figures, which are given in volume measures of ready-to-cook grain from which the chaff has been removed. Instead, we must convert by a factor of 30 percent, a weighted average difference that roughly represents the chaff percentage of a volume of grain before it is beaten (dehusked) and winnowed. Using this figure to calculate the consumption in unprocessed grain gives 1,293 manas of grain per year, or 8.08 muris (ca. 19.3 bushels). This is in contradistinction to the ideal figures (based on three manas a day) of 1,095 processed manas, which is the equivalent of 1,560 unprocessed manas, or 9.75 muris (ca. 23.3 bushels) per year. To summarize, there is a difference of four bushels, or 8.3 percent, between what people say they eat and what they actually do eat.

OTHER HOUSEHOLD EXPENDITURES

In addition to the grain consumed, Tarangpurians like meat, and even a poor man can afford to eat some occasionally. To provide meat, sheep and goats are acquired from Bhotias in the fall. The traditional rate of exchange for a sheep or goat is two muris (4.8 bushels) of buckwheat or one muri (2.4 bushels) of chinu millet; so to acquire one sheep, one and a half muris (3.6 bushels) of grain (using equal amounts of each) must be allocated by our hypothetical subsistence adult.

Like sheep, salt is also obtained through barter with Bhotias. The exchange rate varies according to supply and demand, which is a shorthand way of referring to the time of year. Chinu millet is traded for salt at a more favorable rate than is buckwheat, but on the average, about three-quarters of a muri (1.8 bushels) of grain must be traded for about 75 percent that amount of salt. Red peppers are used as commonly in the Tarangpur diet as salt is (they are used in dal). Like salt, the peppers have to be imported, though from the south and west rather than from the north. These peppers sell at the rate of three manas (pints) per rupee (equal to $0.10);[13] thus forty manas (pints), or 0.25 muri, can be bought for Rs. 13.33 ($1.32). Grain can be sold as well as bartered, and the going rates are Rs. 80 ($7.92) for a muri (160 manas or 2.4 bushels) of chinu millet and Rs. 40 ($3.96) for a muri (2.4 bushels) of buckwheat. If equal amounts of chinu millet and buckwheat are used to generate Rs. 13.33, a total of 35 and 5/9 manas (pints) of grain will be sold. This is approximately 22.5 percent of a muri or, in rougher terms, about a quarter of a muri, or 0.6 bushel. About half a muri or 1.2 bushels (i.e., the total production of barley) would be used for manufacturing beer or distilled liquor.

Some grain must be set aside for obtaining clothes to wear. Calculating equal measures of a total of three muris (7.2 bushels) of buckwheat and millet, Rs. 180 ($17.82) would be realized from the sale of such an amount of grain. This is the approximate minimal sum required to purchase enough new clothes to last an entire year.

Then from each crop a portion must be set aside as seed for the next spring's planting. This varies from crop to crop, as the estimates by informants presented in table 4 show. Thus 228 manas (pints) or 1.43 muris (3.43 bushels) must be reserved for planting the next year's crop.

Finally, to balance the books, a miscellaneous fund of 1.49 muris (3.58 bushels) covers such items as loss to rodents, annual payments in kind to Blacksmith/Carpenter clients, or possibly an

TABLE 4

AMOUNT OF SEED NEEDED FOR PLANTING
PER HYPOTHETICAL ADULT (at subsistence level)

Name of crop	Manas (or pints) of seed needed for planting
Chinu millet	38
Buckwheat	60
Sweet buckwheat	38
Japanese millet	50
Barley	42
Total	228

annual payment to a Tailor client, feeding of guests, and so on. Table 5 represents this total annual consumption or expenditure budget. Total consumption and expenditures at a subsistence level total slightly more than the hypothetical yield from four huls (15.3 muris or 36.72 bushels) shown in table 2. Ignoring for the moment all the many possible errors in estimating and measuring these variables, the difference would be easily made up by garden crops, especially potatoes.

All of these figures are contrived because of the caveat mentioned earlier about the actual size of any given landholding and the group controlling it, and also because these figures do not take into account past capital formation or income generated in other sectors of the economy. They should be regarded as fictions, in the ideal-typical sense. For example, very few families actually sell any grain at all. Instead they use cash revenues, left over from the previous year, which have been generated in other sectors of the economy, from the sale of sheep, goats, beer or liquor, or woolen goods. Furthermore, there are great variations in productivity rooted in the differential skill, industry, and interest of individual

TABLE 5

TOTAL ANNUAL CONSUMPTION AND EXPENDITURES
OF GRAIN PER HYPOTHETICAL ADULT
(at subsistence level)

| | Amount of grain required | |
Type of expenditure	Muris	Bushels
Personal consumption	8.08	19.39
Barter for sheep/goats	1.50	3.60
Barter for salt	0.75	1.80
Sell for money to buy clothes	3.00	7.20
Reserved for next year's planting	1.43	3.43
Sell for money to buy red peppers	0.25	0.60
To make beer or liquor	0.50	1.20
Miscellaneous	1.49	3.58
Total	17.00	40.80

farmers. Some villagers are excellent cultivators, others are indifferent ones.

But given all of these qualifications, such figures do give some idea of just what subsistence means in such an area—as defined culturally and as produced and measured as already described. This is important, because the elaborate transaction circuits (some of which have already been implied in the barter and sale of grain for the items in table 5 that are not available locally) are all built upon and depend on the existence of an agricultural surplus beyond these subsistence needs. Not all households are able to produce a surplus every year, but most of them do so during most years.

EXTENT OF THE SURPLUS

To calculate the size of the surplus for all of Tarangpur, it is necessary to determine how much land is owned by each family. Then total production of the agricultural sector of individual households and of the entire village can be determined.

The lay of the land and fractionation through inheritance that defeated the government land reform team also made an adequate survey of the village fields impossible for a lone investigator, so I had to rely on estimates given by a representative of each household, which were then reviewed and sometimes corrected by a knowledgeable informant. Since villagers have never had to think about the total area of their holdings, they frequently do not have a very good idea of how much land they own. Nevertheless the estimates give a reasonable approximation of the total amount of land held, as well as the amount of land cultivated relative to the amount of arable land left uncultivated. Appendixes E and F summarize these holdings.

Of the eighty-three households listed in appendix F, two have no fields at all. One of these houses was inherited by a wealthy man who already owned his own house; for the present, this extra house is inhabited by a poor immigrant from Thak Khola, east of Dhaulagiri. The fields that were inherited with the house are counted with the wealthy man's other fields (hence the landless immigrant). The other landless house (or, in this case, shack) is occupied by a family of low-caste Tailors—also immigrants, albeit long-terms ones—who secure a major portion of their livelihood from the practice of their craft. This leaves eighty-one land-owning, permanent households from a total of eighty-three houses.

Applying the subsistence formula of four working, cultivated huls (1.12 acres) for each first adult, three and one-half huls (0.98 acre) for each additional adult (assuming some economy of scale), and two huls (0.56 acre) for each child between three and fifteen, fifty-seven of the eighty-one landowning households are at or above the subsistence level as defined above, and twenty-four are below it (see figs. 3 and 4).

Of the twenty-four below-subsistence houses, which constitute 29 percent of the village households, nine are Lama families. The Lamas arrived in the village only four or five generations ago and received donations of land from each of the three original clans, who had requested them to come. As a group they are still relatively poor, although there is one wealthy exception. But as practicing lamas they have access to outside employment—officiating at name-giving ceremonies after birth, funerary rites, and so on—for which they are always paid in kind. Thus by virtue of religious competence, six of the nine Lama households have resident lamas who supplement the income from their landholdings with compensation for the ritual services they provide; in five cases this is enough to put these families over the subsistence level. The ritual specialist for the religious festivities of the cult of local gods, which take place each winter, lives in another of the grain-deficit households, and payments for his ritual services each year are considerable; unlike the lamas, he has no competition, so the demand for his services is high and inelastic.

Six cases are anomalies. One involves a brother who before his land was divided among himself and his brothers was relatively well-to-do. He is able to utilize his former wealth to provide a standard of living which, though not as high as previously, is nevertheless considerably above subsistence level. One is a single woman who has considerable wealth but in a form other than land, which would be difficult for her to work by herself. Two cases involve aged parents who, though technically still a household, have given most of their property to their children, who help support them. Two households are families not of wealth but of

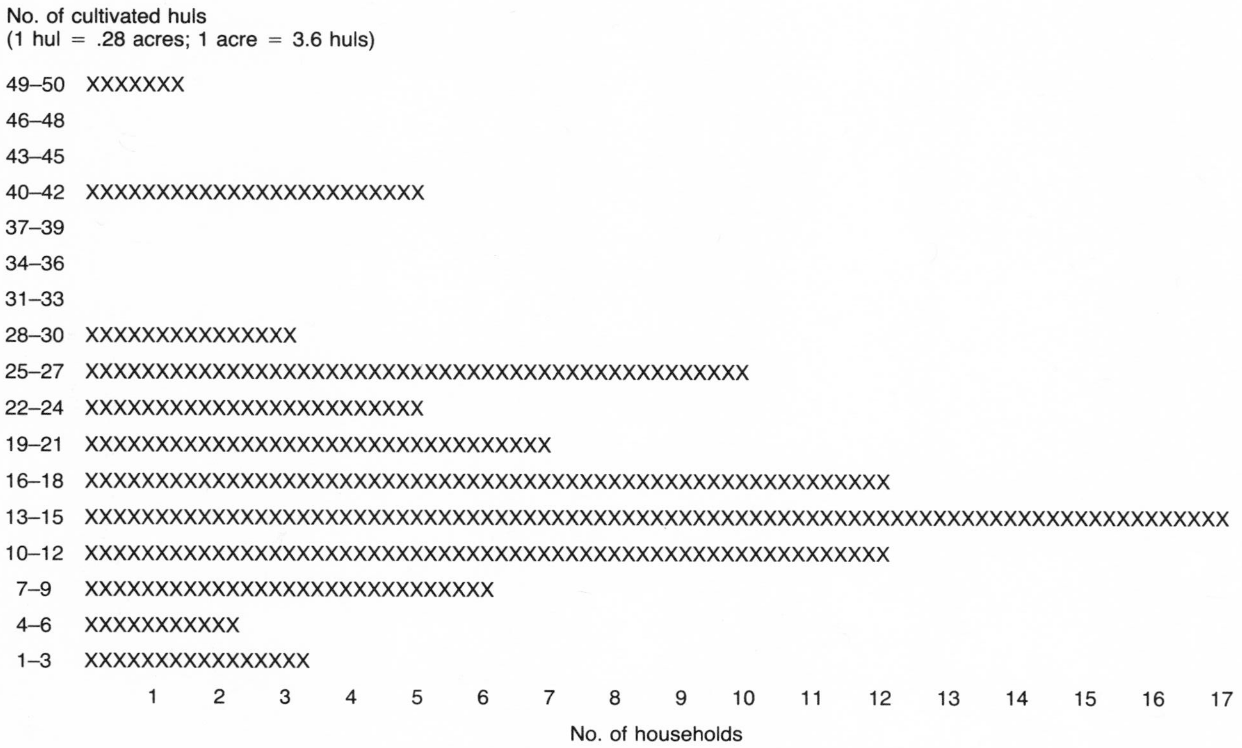

No. of cultivated huls
(1 hul = .28 acres; 1 acre = 3.6 huls)

```
49–50  XXXXXXX
46–48
43–45
40–42  XXXXXXXXXXXXXXXXXXXXXXX
37–39
34–36
31–33
28–30  XXXXXXXXXXXXXX
25–27  XXXXXXXXXXXXXXXXXXXXXXXXXXXXXXXXX
22–24  XXXXXXXXXXXXXXXXXX
19–21  XXXXXXXXXXXXXXXXXXXXXXXXX
16–18  XXXXXXXXXXXXXXXXXXXXXXXXXXXXXXXXXXXXXX
13–15  XXXXXXXXXXXXXXXXXXXXXXXXXXXXXXXXXXXXXXXXXXXXXXXXXXXXXX
10–12  XXXXXXXXXXXXXXXXXXXXXXXXXXXXXXXX
 7–9   XXXXXXXXXXXXXXXXXXXXXX
 4–6   XXXXXXXXX
 1–3   XXXXXXXXXXXXX

        1   2   3   4   5   6   7   8   9   10  11  12  13  14  15  16  17

                              No. of households
```

Figure 3. Distribution of Land among Tarangpur Households

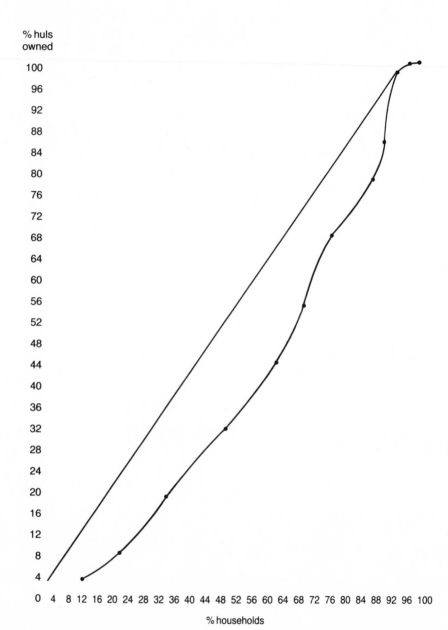

% huls
owned

% households

Figure 4. Distribution of Land Ownership in Tarangpur (Lorenz Curve)

an economic level above others in this less-than-subsistence category. I cannot account for this discrepancy except by inaccurate data; since there is a fear that responses to my questions would result in higher land taxes, the general tendency to underestimate the amount of land owned may account for these two statistically deviant cases.

Finally, there are eight grain-deficit households clearly poorer than the others, and the reason for their poverty is straightforward: they do not own enough land relative to their numbers to grow enough food to feed themselves. No Tarangpur family, rich or poor, has a Gurkha Brigade pension or salary to draw on, unlike the well-documented situation in many Nepalese villages (see Hitchcock 1961; Macfarlane 1976). One villager served a few years in a Gurkha unit, but not long enough to qualify for a pension.

In summary, 71 percent of all the households in Tarangpur produce a grain surplus. Of those with a grain deficit from their own lands, six are anomalous cases with income from a variety of other sources, and ten support themselves through a combination of income from land and remuneration for ritual services. Only 12 percent of all households are either landless (two households) or have no alternative sources of income (eight households) other than working for wealthier villagers, for example, by carrying loads. But this strikes at village solidarity, since it is considered exceptional, unfortunate, and demeaning for one villager to be in the employ of a fellow villager.[14]

WORKING CAPITAL

Every farmer must allow for working capital requirements, not to enter farming, since that is done gradually and with a certain amount of inherited working capital, but to meet depreciation over the years as old equipment wears out or energy sources die off. The following list includes most items for which capital must be expended to practice farming:

1. *A plow:* this can be made by oneself, bought from any of five village men who are particularly skilled in making plows

and who are therefore occasionally asked to do so, or bought
from a Carpenter/Blacksmith for Rs. 6–9 (between $0.60
and $0.90) or its equivalent in grain.

2. *A hoe-like instrument* for breaking up clods of earth after a
   field has been plowed: this is made by one's Carpenter/
   Blacksmith client for a meal on the working day plus the
   annual payment.

3. *A hand-held weeder:* this is also made by the Carpenter/
   Blacksmith client on the same basis as the hoe-like instrument.

4. *A bull:* a bull can be bought full-grown for about Rs. 240
   (less than $24). Since there is not enough feed to support
   herds of cattle, few households keep cows in Tarangpur,
   although the total number of cows almost equals that of
   bulls. Villagers say they import most bulls from villages
   outside Tichurong. Appendix B summarizes the livestock
   population of Tarangpur.

5. *Land:* land prices vary according to fertility, location, slope,
   and general quality (size, number of boulders, brush, etc.).
   Proximity to forests is undesirable because crops are more
   subject to marauding bears, and fields at the far edge of a
   cultivated area are undesirable because cattle which enter
   such an area will devour the crops closest to the edges before
   they are discovered and driven off. The prices for most land
   range from Rs. 200 to Rs. 500 per hul (between roughly $71
   and $178 per acre), but in one river-bottom area, fields
   command a price of up to Rs. 1,000 per hul (about $356
   per acre).

The first three items represent such small expenditures that
anyone can afford them. A bull is highly desirable, but families
can and do farm sizable holdings without them, by exchanging
their labor for that of someone else's bull. Land, of course, is the
sine qua non, and it is difficult to acquire because it rarely comes
onto the market. The requirements of working capital are so small
that they are never a barrier to entering farming for a villager with
land, and 98 percent of all village households own some land.

THE SURPLUS AND ITS USES

Since working capital is a prerequisite to farming and not a dimension of annually measured subsistence, the central point established earlier is still valid: most villagers produce more grain than they need for subsistence purposes. More importantly, for its relations beyond Tichurong, Tarangpur as a whole is a net grain surplus area. That this is so can be shown by subtracting the total amount of grain consumed (allowing for secondary adults and children, as before) from the total amount of grain produced. Table 6 shows the total number of muris and bushels produced annually, and table 7 shows the net surplus.

The surplus figure of 412 muris (991 bushels) in table 7 is probably low, for several reasons. First, the subsistence figure is based on normal, healthy consumption. Since people frequently fall sick with a variety of maladies, especially gastrointestinal problems, the average consumption over the course of a year would be reduced. Second, four or five children are away from the village studying in schools elsewhere in Nepal and, in one case, in India. Third, crop yields are based on the "typical" farmer; while few farmers produce less than this, some of the more conscientious farmers (those who move their terrace walls often, for example) produce much more. Finally, the existence of other, minor crops has not been included in the calculations. Nevertheless, the figure of 412 muris or 991 bushels—slightly over 7 percent of the total harvest—though it is undoubtedly low, does show that there is a surplus even after every poor inhabitant has been taken care of. Since the surplus is not distributed evenly, a few families have sizeable resources to put to other ends. Grain surpluses are not typical or even common in western Nepal (McDougal 1968), and deficits are often casually assumed (Jest 1971) even when surpluses are present, so it is important to establish that a surplus does exist and to analyze what available options are exercised in disposing of the surplus.

One way to dispose of the surplus grain is to bury it. After the fall harvest, much of the grain is stored in enormous earth pits, 12 to 15 feet deep and about 4 feet in diameter. The pits are lined

TABLE 6

TOTAL ANNUAL GRAIN PRODUCTION BY TARANGPUR HOUSEHOLDS

Type of grain	% huls (or acres) planted	Huls planted	Acres planted	Muris/ hul	Bushels/ acre	Muris harvested	Bushels harvested
Chinu millet	50	719.50	200	3	25.9	2,159	5,180
Buckwheat	35	503.65	140	5	43.2	2,518	6,048
Japanese millet	10	144	40	3.5	30.2	432	1,036
Sweet buckwheat[a]	5	72	20	3	25.9	252	604
Barley[a]	5	72	20	2	17.3	144	346
Total	100	1,439	400			5,505	13,214

[a]See table 3.

TABLE 7
ESTIMATION OF ANNUAL NET GRAIN SURPLUS
FOR TARANGPUR

Grain consumption:

83 adults @ 17 muris	1,411 muris
40.8 bushels/adult	3,386 bushels
182 adults @ 16 muris	2,912 muris
38.4 bushels/adult	6,989 bushels
77 children between ages 3 and 15 @ 10 muris	770 muris
24 bushels/child	1,848 bushels
Total grain consumption	5,093 muris
	12,223 bushels
Total grain production	5,505 muris
	13,214 bushels
Net grain surplus	412 muris
	991 bushels

with large sheets of bark to keep out dampness, and an earth-covered flat stone "lid" protects the top from animals and surface moisture. As the grain is needed, it is dug up and temporarily stored indoors in large wooden grain chests or earthen jars, from which it is taken every few days, beaten, winnowed, cooked, and eaten. Those with more than they can eat or utilize in other ways keep the surplus grain in such pits, which can accommodate between 15 and 20 muris (between 36 and 48 bushels) each. Two households have vast quantities of such grain; one has about 15 pits and the other has 30. Calculating an average of 17.5 muris (42 bushels) per pit gives a life-savings surplus of over 500 muris (1,200 bushels)—an astonishing total considering that this grain would feed the family of five adults and one child for 23 years. This case is obviously exceptional, but even the average family has between 3 and 6 muris (between 7.2 and 14.4 bushels) of grain left over at harvest time. Even if each family had, on average, only three muris (7.2 bushels) surplus, the total for the village of 83 households would be 249 muris (597 bushels). If each household averages 6 muris (14.4 bushels) surplus, the village total would be 498 muris (1,195 bushels)—a more likely figure, and quite close to the surplus (412 muris or 991 bushels) calculated in table 7. Those who have excess grain in pits use the oldest grain first so that the problem of rot is reduced.

This hoarding in the ground is the easiest, least imaginative, and by Tarangpur tradition one of the first methods used to dispose of excess grain. Buying grain is good insurance against crop failure, which is always a possibility even though villagers express great confidence in regular rainfall. But the expenditure budgets suggest that grain can also be bartered or sold for other requirements of life that are not available locally. If there is a surplus beyond what is needed to satisfy these requirements, it can be invested in several ways: in jewelry, political or religious activity, or trade. Grain as a surplus is not always very marketable in the hills. It is heavy, bulky, and profits are literally eaten up by porters. Many Nepalese hill people deal with this problem by converting the grain or grain potential into products with a higher per pound value. This is usually done by purchasing animals, which produce ghee, wools, meat, eggs, and so on. It can also be done by planting fruit and nut trees on good land or by employing artisans to make salable manufactures. But unlike other hill people, Tarangpurians have traditionally traded in grain, as chapter 4 demonstrates.

Since they speak both Tibetan and Nepali, Tarangpurians are able to transport and market goods, including grain, from the south to the north and vice versa. Their linguistic competence—unique along this north-south trade axis—gives them a great competitive advantage, since Bhotias along the Tibetan border do not generally speak Nepali, although they need goods from the Nepali-speaking area, and Nepali-speakers to the south need goods from the north but do not speak Tibetan. In this way trade networks pass through and spread out from Tarangpur and neighboring villages, where over the years individuals have parlayed their excess grain into diversified exchange systems that generate profits and more capital to invest in still other commercial endeavors.

Tarangpurians are able to convert resources in this way partly because of the surplus time which their alpine ecological adaptation thrusts upon them. The time between the fall harvest and the spring planting, a period of at least four months, can be devoted to only three pursuits: religion, rest and relaxation, and trading.

The month-long indigenous religious festival is celebrated in the middle of winter. This fulfills religious and social needs, but no economic needs except for those of the ritual specialist, without which there could be no ritual at all. Winter is also a time of rest and relaxation, and there is much house-to-house visiting and drinking to while away the days. People often spin wool or knit scarves and sweaters while socializing, and these periods are to that extent economically productive, but spinning and knitting are done at other times, too, and the production of woolen goods does not depend on casual winter production. The third use of winter surplus time is to engage in long-range trading expeditions to southern parts of Nepal and to India. As a rule, those who have the material resources, commercial skill, and physical strength to engage in trade do so, and those who lack one or more of these characteristics do not.

DIVISION OF LABOR

Allocation of personnel to perform these agricultural and commercial tasks is not random but determined by a specialized division of labor which is a behavioral unfolding of certain norms dictated in part by religious belief. The division of labor can be discussed on two levels: the permissive (who may and may not do certain tasks), and the statistical (who does or does not do certain tasks). There is no need to abstract a normative level (who should or should not do what work) because in this still traditional society, villagers do not do what they may not do in matters pertaining to the organization of work. Whether they actually do what they may do is a legitimate but still statistical question.

The general, permissive rule is that women may not do men's work, but men may do women's work, unless it is polluting.[15] In this context, polluting refers to work involving direct contact with excrement, whether human or animal. There are other pollution concepts in other spheres of life, but this is the only instance relevant to the division of labor. This differentiation along sexual lines breaks down with the inclusion of Buddhist priests, since women and lamas are equivalents in the labor force. Neither can do certain kinds of work, such as plowing, which is considered sinful because of the pain caused to the bullock. Thus Lama families with multiple sons often purposely keep one son as a layman so that he can plow the family fields. The roles of woman and lama both require abstinence from sin, so defined. To put it another way, men (except for lamas) may perform sinful and most other kinds of labor, but not work that is polluting. Women and lamas may work at any task that is not sinful (see table 8).

But between the sin of plowing and the pollution of manure-carrying there is a wide range of tasks to which no strictures apply—that is, they are morally neutral. Although men may do any kind of agricultural labor (except for carrying manure), they in fact do relatively little farming, except for plowing, which they do exclusively. Thus from the very beginning of the agricultural cycle, when women start carrying manure from the barnyards to the fields, agriculture is largely women's work. The men return from the winter's trading trips in time to do the actual plowing, and they help cut the grain and carry it from the fields to the village during the harvest, when demand for labor is at a peak; but the sowing, harrowing, weeding, thrashing, winnowing, and grinding is done generally, though not exclusively, by women.

Because women do the actual bulk of the agricultural work, they are more knowledgeable about it and are therefore the locus of authority in agricultural matters. In day-to-day farming operations, a large number of decisions and judgments must be made: which field to work, what priorities to establish, when to begin

TABLE 8
DIVISION OF LABOR
(permissive)

May (+) or may not (−) be done by	Type of work		
	Sinful	Polluting	Neither sinful nor polluting
Men	+	−	+
Women	−	+	+
Lamas	−	+	+

weeding, when to start harvesting, how to deploy the labor force when labor is exchanged, with whom to exchange labor, and so on. These decisions must often be made simultaneously and require carefully considered judgments. Generally it is the women who make these decisions. Even when the participation of men is essential, as in plowing, for the most part the overall strategy is conceived and planned by women.

In contrast to the female-oriented agricultural division of labor, the world of commerce is essentially a man's world. In the fall, men (occasionally accompanied by their wives and sisters) cross over the passes before they are closed with snow and ice for the winter, taking with them woolen goods (scarves, blankets, sashes, sweaters), sheep, goats, and sometimes horses, to sell in the middle hills. Their ultimate destination is usually Butwal in the Terai (though some go as far as India—to places such as Kanpur, Kalimpong, and Calcutta), where they use the proceeds of their sales to buy manufactured commodities, such as cigarettes, cloth, and tea, which they carry back and sell to villagers in Khasan and Bhot. They make this return trip from the Terai to Tichurong in the spring, when the snows have melted again. All these transactions— and others involving exchange of goods with the world beyond Tichurong—are made by men, and men alone. Women may accompany men on the trading expeditions and, on rare occasions, help out by distributing goods and collecting debts, but the actual negotiations and strategy are entirely in men's hands. Table 9 summarizes who does what kinds of work for the most part.

ALLOCATION OF TIME

This unequivocally sexual basis for the division of labor can be quantified by observing the actual pursuits of the members of a given economic unit (i.e., a particular household) on a day-to-day basis. In other words, by describing the way people allocate their time—both that which is needed to produce food for subsistence and that which is "surplus"—we can assess the strength and importance of the division of labor and give it an empirical base that transcends impressionistic feelings.

Because the ways of spending time vary so widely over the

TABLE 9

DIVISION OF LABOR

(statistical)

Type of work	Performed mostly or entirely by		
	Men	*Women*	*Lamas*
Plowing	+	−	−
Carrying manure	−	+	+
Harvesting	+	+	+
Sowing	−	+	−
Harrowing	−	+	−
Weeding	−	+	−
Thrashing	−	+	−
Winnowing	−	+	−
Grinding	−	+	−
Trading	+	−	+
Spinning	+	+	+
Knitting	+	−	+

course of a year, I chose to follow the activities of one family through as much of an entire year as possible, rather than observe a sample of several households for a shorter time. Since I was occasionally outside the village and sometimes preoccupied with other tasks while in the village, there are gaps in the work calendar, but the trend seems sufficiently clear nonetheless. The family consisted of only one old woman and her two grown but unmarried sons. Thus this is a limiting case: If there were any exception to the tendency for women to do a disproportionate amount of the agricultural labor, this would be it. That this single old woman still does most of the agricultural and household work makes the argument more convincing than a more typical case would. Table 10 presents the daily activities of this family.

These figures substantiate the impression that during the working agricultural year, women spend a much greater proportion of their time in agricultural production and processing than men. In this case, one old and often ailing woman spent almost as much time (151.50 days) in farm-related activities as her two healthy sons combined (180 days). Conversely, the sons spent a total of 171 days away from the village while trading, largely during the winter months. Their mother engaged in no trading activities at all and never left the village or its environs. Nor was she immobile only because of her relatively advanced age; in her entire life she had never been to either Bhot or the Terai.

The figures for rest days are somewhat misleading, in that many of the winter days counted as rest days for the mother were spent in assorted household jobs of such short duration (grinding flour, cooking, washing dishes) that these days are assigned to the rest category rather than the "other" category, which includes housework. The winter days devoted to trading—while spent in pursuit, directly or indirectly, of economically productive ends—are not all really working days any more than all the days spent by traveling salesmen anywhere else are. Much of the time is spent in simply traveling (carrying a heavy load, it is about two weeks' walk—each way—to the Terai from Tichurong) and resting at various way stations and bazaars. None of these winter activities can be readily sorted into the "work" and "rest" pigeonholes of table 10, and if the months of January and February, for which complete figures are unavailable, are subtracted, the mother is left with only 58.50 rest days, compared with 78.25 for one son and 74.50 days for the other. This bears out the generalization that if there is work to be done around the house or fields, women will do it; and if trading expeditions are undertaken, men will organize and lead them.

SOCIAL AND TECHNOLOGICAL CONSEQUENCES OF THE DIVISION OF LABOR

There are three sociocultural consequences of this division of labor. First, men retain ultimate jural command over the disposition of the household's resources, but the effective manager and local economic decision maker is the woman of the house. If time has to be invested in the management of the affairs of a household, women will in the first instance supply the time and energy required. "Surplus" time is spent in minor household errands, caring for children, gossiping, visiting, and observing and participating

TABLE 10
ANNUAL ALLOCATION OF ONE FAMILY'S TIME
(in days)

Person	Age	Month	Agriculture	Trade	Rest	Other (Religion, etc.)	Total days recorded
Mother	51	January	0	0	31	0	31
		February	2	0	26	0	28
		March	7.5	0	1.5	1	10
		April	6.5	0	3.5	0	10
		May	18.5	0	3.5	7	29
		June	24.5	0	1.5	0	26
		July	28.25	0	2.75	0	31
		August	17.25	0	11.75	1	30
		September	1.5	0	20.5	7	29
		October	27	0	2.5	1.5	31
		November	14.5	0	10.5	4	29
		December	4	0	.5	14.5	19
	Total		151.5	0	115.5	36	
Son	28	January	0	31	0	0	31
		February	0	28	0	0	28
		March	4.5	1	4	.5	10
		April	6.5	0	3.5	0	10
		May	12	0	9.5	7.5	29
		June	14.5	0	9	2.5	26
		July	15.25	0	8.75	7	31
		August	3	0	23.75	3.25	30
		September	14	0	4.75	10.25	29
		October	11	10.5	8.5	1	31
		November	0	17.5	6.5	5	29
		December	0	19	0	0	19
	Total		80.75	107	78.25	37	

TABLE 10 *(continued)*
Annual Allocation of One Family's Time
(in days)

Person	Age	Month	Agriculture	Trade	Rest	Other (Religion, etc.)	Total days recorded
Son	26	January	0	31	0	0	31
		February	0	28	0	0	28
		March	5.5	0	4	.5	10
		April	3.5	0	3	3.5	10
		May	19	0	4.5	5.5	29
		June	11.5	0	8	6.5	26
		July	14.75	0	10.25	6	31
		August	3	0	24.25	2.75	30
		September	13.5	0	5.5	10	29
		October	25	0	4	2	31
		November	3	0	6.5	19.5	29
		December	.5	5	4.5	9	19
Total			99.25	64	74.5	65.25	
Grand total			331.5	171	168.25	138.25	303[a]

[a]This is equivalent to 83 percent of a year.

in religious rituals. Most of the winter "rest" days are spent in minor preparations for or observance of the ritual and dancing which continue daily for several weeks during the coldest months. From their mid-teens until their forties, men rarely see this annual festival.

During the agricultural season, men devote their time to agriculture when necessary, and to resting, gambling, drinking, and trading when possible, while women devote almost all their working time to agriculturally oriented tasks and little else. During the winter women spend the bulk of their time in economically unproductive activities—"just sitting around," as they say—while men procure clothes and other manufactured goods for their families.

Surplus time and resources are allocated differently for men and women; men spend their surplus time and surplus resources—if they have them—in trade; if they lack resources, they can do little more than purchase a minimum of cloth for domestic needs and putter around the village or visit friends. Women spend their surplus winter time primarily in religious activities.

Second, most of the activities which link Tarangpur with the world beyond Tichurong are male-linked. Men spend the agriculturally unproductive winter months in trading or just personal shopping to acquire enough cloth to clothe their families. Even beyond that, men can and do spend other parts of the year trading; the only time when their presence is vital is during the spring plowing and the fall harvest. In all families men do play a vital role in the agricultural cycle, but if they can so arrange it, they tend to work mainly during the two critical periods of plowing and harvesting. In the winter they combine a surplus of goods—including goods convertible into cash—with surplus time to engage in exchange activities of various kinds.

Third, the technological adaptations in each sector (i.e., agricultural and commercial) are of a quite different mode. The technology used to accomplish the round of agricultural tasks is simple, and nonhuman energy available in the forms of water and animal power escapes relatively untapped. To begin with, manure is dumped into baskets and carried on the human back—never by idle horses that could do the job quicker and more easily (not all Tarangpur families own horses, but many do; there are over 100 horses in the village). The plow used in Tichurong[16] is found nowhere else in Nepal, not even a few miles away (see Aitken 1963), nor anywhere else in South Asia. It is drawn by a single bullock, never by two, and never by a horse. The plowman stands beside the plow (not behind, as elsewhere) and bends nearly double over it, using his body weight to force the plowshare into the hard and rocky soil while the bullock provides traction. Virtually everyone has seen other plowing techniques in Bhot, Khasan, and the middle hills and Terai—horse-drawn plows, plows drawn by two bullocks, iron-tipped plowshares, and stand-up plows; but villagers never experiment with any of these features themselves. They argue that because of the difficult terrain under cultivation, and because individual terraces are generally very narrow (often only 5 or 10 feet wide), it is not possible to use more than one bullock. Similarly, since there is plenty of wood in nearby forests, there is no need to use iron-tipped plowshares (they do use iron for other implements).

There are several sources of water surrounding the village—mostly fast-flowing streams—but water is not harnessed as a power source or used for agricultural purposes. All grinding of grain into flour, which is almost always by women, is done by a laborious, hand-powered grindstone. Several of the surrounding streams, not to mention the Bheri River itself, provide sufficient water power for a grinding mill. Mills, like other varieties of plows, are well known, since they are commonly used a few miles down the river in Khasan.

Traditionally, the movement of commodities has depended on the backs of the traders themselves, and wicker basket loads of 100 to 150 pounds are standard. For those who bring goods to sell in addition to those goods intended for family use, extra loads are transported on the backs of hired porters. One wealthy trader innovated about four years ago by deciding to use the horses he already owned to carry loads. His experiment succeeded, saving him several thousand rupees in porter fees, and his example has already been emulated by one other Tarangpurian, and by another Tichurong trader. Another man in a neighboring village bought six mules in order to go into the transportation business himself. Neither mules nor the idea of moving goods as an economic enterprise in itself (i.e., apart from moving one's own goods) had ever existed in Tichurong before. Why the innovation in commercial transport versus the completely static technology of the agricultural sector?

The reason, in my view, is inextricably bound up with the division of labor itself. The men, on their annual trading trips both north and south, have a wide acquaintance with different ways of life and different means to accomplish ends. They have established social relationships of a distinct kind (which will be examined later) with people in various parts of Nepal, and through them receive annual exposure to different life-styles. Since it is they who carry the heavy loads from the Terai to Bhot or Khasan, or pay the wages of those who do, they are ripe for any innovation that makes their trading trips easier or more economical.

The women, though they sometimes accompany their husbands or uncles on trading trips, do not do so regularly, and most do not have the special relationships which the men have developed far from home. When they do leave Tichurong, they go with men who handle the relationships and arrangements in these far-off places. The women are thus more isolated, more conservative, and in any case less capable of carrying an innovation through to fruition. They do not handle or work with animals, so they are incapable of training horses to carry manure. Even if the horses were trained, using them is mildly sinful and therefore proscribed to women, because carrying loads causes the animals pain.

Since the men do not carry manure at all (because it is polluting), and since the workload of their wives, sisters, and mothers is not a central concern for them, there is no incentive for them to load the horses with manure. Similarly, since women do almost all the grain grinding—between two laboriously hand-driven stones— there is no particular reason why men should be interested in harnessing water to do the job. Women do not possess the mechanical skills to build a mill, or—since men control the household and village financial resources—the wherewithal to hire a craftsman to manufacture one. So stasis in the agricultural sector persists,[17] with nothing and no one to knock it off-center. In general, innovations which are merely labor-saving are not adopted. With plenty of labor available, Tarangpurians see little point in saving it, but profit-making innovations are eagerly tried and adopted.

SURPLUS AND DEMOGRAPHY

The existence of surplus grain in part generates the surplus time available to men. Men take some food with them on their trading trips, but for much of the time they must buy food wherever they are. Thus some of the "subsistence" grain a man would eat in the course of a year is not consumed by him. But because of a peculiar north-south demographic shift, it is consumed by Bhotias who come to villages like Tarangpur during the winter months and "take the place" of Tarangpur men who have gone still farther south to trade. Since Tarangpur is a grain surplus area and Bhot is a grain deficit area, large numbers of Bhotias come south during the winter to the relative warmth and prosperity of Tarangpur.

In the winter of 1968–69, for example, 101 Tarangpurians, well over 25 percent of the entire village (38 percent of the adult population) left the village for several months, while 151 Bhotias came and lived in the partially empty houses of Tarangpur (see map 5). They are able to sustain themselves by doing odd jobs, such as carrying water or beating millet, or specialized work, such as blanket weaving, which requires skills most Tarangpurians lack. For this labor they receive food on the day they work plus six manas (pints) of unprocessed grain for hard work (bringing firewood, carrying manure) or three manas (pints) of grain for work such as weaving or beating millet, which is not so strenuous. Thus the subsistence grain has a second economic use: to hire seasonal labor on a grain payment for piecework basis, which fills the gap created by the long absence of the Tarangpur men. The Bhotias thus contribute goods (e.g., blankets) which the Tarangpurians use in trade. The fact that the Tarangpurians in exodus during the winter are outnumbered by the incoming Bhotias is balanced by the fact that Tarangpurians who leave are all adult, while the Bhotias who replace them include many children, so that the total amount of grain consumed would be roughly the same for both groups.

SURPLUS AND CHOICE

The distinctive ecological adaptation of Tarangpur sketched in the previous sections, involving a single-growing-season agricultural year and a grain surplus beyond subsistence needs, provides most villagers with at least the possibility of choices to make. This is shown not only in the data and analysis of the agricultural system presented in this chapter but also in Tarangpurians' own perceptions of their situation. Villagers spend a lot of time discussing options. Some deal with mundane questions: whether to plow this field today or help in another family's fields in exchange for their help the following day; whether to refurbish a house; how much to give on the occasion of a sister's son's first haircut; or who to support in a quarrel. Others deal with more fundamental strategies for coping with the environment: whether to go trading this year, and if so, when, with whom, by what route, and to sell and buy what, or whether to spend several months on a pilgrimage; whether to plant some uncultivated land to produce more grain, or use grain already in hand for trading; even whether to work or to relax, since with the exception of plowing and harvesting, almost any task can be delayed for months and even years.

There are not many options involved in eking out a living in this environment, but what to do with surplus time and resources is not socially or culturally stipulated or economically dictated, and permissible latitude for deploying these surpluses is very wide. Throughout other mountainous sections of western Nepal there are no choices in this sense. As in generally grain-deficient Bhot to the north, mere survival in the western hills demands seasonal movement to another region where sufficient food can be obtained (Caplan 1972), either by working or by exchanging a product of the hills—such as ghee—for food (McDougal 1968). But in Tarangpur, most villagers can exercise choice in the way they utilize their excess time and resources. The choices that are made— by men and by women, now and in the past—vitally affect the direction in which Tarangpur society and culture is moving.

At the core are the women, who conserve traditional life-styles and oversee the maintenance of institutions and symbols which have long dominated life at the village level. Geographically and socially, they form the immovable if not immutable core of Tarangpur life, pouring their surplus time into religion and the maintenance of tradition.

But at the changing, innovating periphery, linked with external models, are the men. As will become clear in chapter 4, for however long the people of Tarangpur have inhabited their valley, they have been part of vital networks that link Tarangpur with areas much farther afield than Tichurong. The nature and scope of these networks have been undergoing slow but steady change over the last forty years, with repercussions which are felt throughout the entire society. The next chapters will deal with these links, the choices that result in different kinds of links, and the consequences that follow from the different choices that are made.

4

Transactions:
The Salt Circuit

ra rana nyabo
lu luna nyabo
   —Kaike proverb

Goats with goats,
sheep with sheep.

THE DEMAND FOR SALT

Although we will never know exactly how long the site of Tarangpur has been inhabited, we do know that despite their geographical isolation the people of Tichurong have been linked with other places and peoples from primordial times. However much grain is produced and however few people are available to eat it, Tarangpur shares with all other Nepalese villages a common and irreducibly basic lack: an indigenous source of salt. And like villagers elsewhere in Nepal—and indeed, like most people of the world except those who live mainly on milk and raw or roasted meat (so that its natural salts are not lost)—Tichurong people must supplement their predominantly cereal diet with salt. I am unable to say whether Tichurong people eat more salt than they biologically require (my impression is that they do not, since their food, while very spicy, never tasted particularly salty to me), but at some undetermined minimal level, the demand for salt is inelastic. Given the long, grueling trip to India and the relative proximity to Bhot, Tarangpurians must have always depended on the place on which they still depend for their salt needs—Tibet. Contemporary villagers know of no way to produce or extract salt from their environment, nor is there any reason to suppose that their ancestors did.

EXCHANGE RATIOS

Tarangpur villagers never cross the Tibetan border to acquire salt, and apparently never have. Instead they rely on Bhotias who enter Tibet, where they exchange grain for salt at villages and entrepôts just over the border. Before the Chinese exerted their full authority, one measure of grain would generally bring three of salt in Tibet. Then, as now, exchange rates varied somewhat—by perhaps one-fourth or one-third—according to seasonal supply and demand. But since the Chinese have established their incontrovertible presence in all of Tibet, salt has become more expensive, and Bhotia traders who used to rely on commercial ruses such as mixing the residue of grain which has been used for making beer with unused grain must now engage in such deceptive practices at the risk of discovery by the Chinese. At present a measure of chinu millet brings only two of salt, and a measure of barley brings between one and a half and two measures of salt, depending on the quality of the barley. In pre-Chinese times, Nepalese money was accepted in some of these Tibetan border posts, but now all exchanges are strictly in barter terms—an exception to and reversal of the almost universal process of monetization which has taken place in other parts of the world where trade by barter has been traditional.

The Bhotia traders then carry the rock salt south to villages like Tarangpur, or wait for Tarangpurians to come to Bhot to get it, typically in the fall or spring. The exchange ratios in the two areas are almost the exact inverse of each other: in Tichurong, 13 measures of chinu millet (15 of buckwheat) bring 10 measures of salt, and in Bhot 10 measures of chinu millet (12 of buckwheat) are worth 12 of salt. The different rates clearly reflect carrying charges; beneficial rates are earned at the expense of hauling the goods.

THE CYCLE: GRAIN, SALT, AND RICE

The Tarangpurians use a portion of this salt to satisfy their own subsistence needs (as described in chap. 3), and those whose grain production is just at the subsistence level can acquire only enough for themselves. But some families acquire more salt than they can consume, and the surplus is transported even farther south to the middle hills, where it is exchanged for rice. Tichurong people most commonly trade buckwheat and chinu millet for salt, but other varieties of grain or a different crop, such as beans, may also be exchanged. The exchange ratios vary because they are influenced by the seasonal and political pressures already indicated, but within these limits the ratios tend to be relatively constant, traditional, and undebatable. Hence women often carry out these transactions in Tarangpur, when bargaining is not necessary or the traditional price parameters are so well known that it is impossible for either party to negotiate to any advantage. But when the salt is carried south, out of Tichurong, it is entirely in the hands of men.

Both the southbound salt and the northbound rice are carried up and down the river (or sometimes over the passes) in very small, woven, wool saddlebags on the backs of sheep and goats (Srivastava 1958).[1] Each half of the saddlebag holds about 15 manas (pints), so each animal carries a total of 30 manas (pints), which is less than half a bushel. Since the amount a single sheep or goat can carry is quite small, the herds have to be rather large to be economical, at least forty or fifty animals.

The rice for which the salt is traded is brought back north to Tarangpur, not because it is needed for everyday use but because it is served on festive and ritual occasions when large numbers of people must be feasted. Thus this most elemental of barter transactions must be assigned to the category of luxury goods. At none of the occasions when rice is served is it culturally compulsory— that is, not serving rice does not negate the marriage or vitiate the purity of a ritual. Rice is served simply because it is prestigious to do so.

Given the dietary preferences and ethnochemistry of Tichurong, the demand for salt is a basic, inelastic one which must be met from outside for life to go on as it does. Rice, by contrast, is an easily replaceable item in the context of an indigenous grain surplus; it is simply the most attractive commodity that can be acquired for surplus salt, which has been acquired for surplus grain. Unlike salt, rice could be eaten in smaller quantities, or even eliminated from the diet entirely if it became too expensive. Thus in this transactional sphere, local grain is traded for two different items: salt, which is vital, and rice, which is defined locally as a luxury good. Tibetan salt is the critical item, without which the

Bhotia economy would completely collapse and the Tarangpurians would be unable to barter for salt of any kind, since millet and buckwheat cannot be exchanged against salt in the rice-growing areas of southern Nepal or north India.

SALT AND SOCIAL RELATIONS

This exchange cycle involves more than just the shuttling of grain, salt, and rice over a wide expanse of western Nepal. Important social relationships sustain these exchanges and have important cultural consequences for those persons involved in them. Virtually all adult male Tarangpurians have special friendships with Bhotias to the north and Hindus to the south.[2] These relationships are of two kinds: the *mit* (Nepali, pronounced "meat"; Kaike, *gyampā;* Tibetan, *robo*) relationship, which is a formal, lifelong, blood-brother bond (see Okada 1957); and the *ishta* (Nepali, "friend") relationship, which is initiated more casually, maintained more ephemerally, and more readily broken off than the mit.[3] The mit relationship is sometimes formalized by the slaughter of a goat or sheep, or by the exchange of coins. A mit brother would in theory perform all the traditional obligations that a consanguineal brother would, and mit brothers observe the same kinds of marriage restrictions toward the women of one another's families that pertain between ritual or fictive brothers in India. Similarly, a mit brother would become mit father to one's children, and so on, so the relationship is extended to others in one's family. The ishta relationship is not ritualized in this way and can be characterized as stronger than casual friendship but weaker than the mit relationship.

To be one's mit or ishta implies a willingness to extend aid and comfort in times of need. In more down-to-earth terms this means that when traveling, one feels free (even obliged) to call in at the house of an ishta or mit for a meal or two and a night's lodging. More specifically, in an economic context these ritual and special friends become preferential trading partners. Given the great distances which separate both Bhot and the Hindu hills from Tichurong, it is frequently only in an economic context that these "friends" interact. From this perspective these ritual and special friendships are primarily economic relationships. The rhetoric of such relationships is couched in terms of kinship and morality, but the basic ingredients that sustain the relationships are essentially economic.

Generally speaking, the mit or ishta is a preferential trading partner, which gives him first refusal rights. If the two partners have mutually dependent needs and agree to exchange at the prevailing rate, they generally exchange with each other, but it is not compulsory that they do so. Since trading between such partners is optional, haggling is either nonexistent or low key. If neither wants to settle for the prevailing rate, he pursues the incremental advantage elsewhere, with no hard feelings. These relationships may endure over several generations. Even if trade does not take place between two such parties, one gives shelter and assistance in lining up other potential customers to buy the goods. Thus a series of distinctive social relationships is built up on the salt and rice that is regularly transported into Tichurong.

CULTURE: NORTH AND SOUTH

These social links connect Tarangpur to two different cultural systems in two different directions of the compass. Some of the relationships are with Buddhists to the north and some are with Hindus to the south. Historically the important population movements in western Nepal have been along the west-east axis: migrations of Aryan peoples into what is now Nepal from the west lasted for centuries. But now that the land has been largely settled, the flow of people is seasonal, from north to south and north again.

The quality of the social relationships in which Tarangpurians engage in both directions is the same: their form and meaning, the way they are initiated and sustained, is similar. But despite the apparent identity of these north-south relationships in social and economic terms, it is the vital cultural differences that are important for understanding the hinge function of the Tarangpur traders.

With the salt comes contact with the distinctive life-style, pervasive over the northern border areas of Nepal, of Tibetan Buddhism: most obviously, the form of Mahayana Buddhism (sometimes called Lamaism) as it exists in several of its sects, but also the dress—ankle-length dresses worn by women, the full, knee-length coats worn by men, and the rope-sole boots with wool tops extending to the knee worn by men and women; the music—both monastic, with its long, deep trumpets, gongs, and drums; and folk, with the Tibetan banjo; the spoken and written Tibetan language; and the relatively egalitarian social life. Contact with Tibetan or "Bhotia"[4] (as those citizens of Nepal with Tibetan cultural roots are called) life-styles is reinforced by the demographic shift in winter, which almost turns Tarangpur into a Tibetan village. The Bhotia influence has been strong particularly in the religious sphere: lamas of great learning and supernatural powers are known to have lived in Bhot, and many of them have visited Tichurong. Tibetan Buddhism was such an attractive model that Tarangpurians have long since engaged the services of lamas for performing life-cycle rituals, rites purging houses of malevolent forces, and medical curing of disease.

The combination of these social and economic contacts has resulted in a strong Buddhist influence, brought about because the power believed to be possessed by great lamas and the good fortune which accrues to those who follow their teachings are regarded as worth transacting for. Tarangpurians now deem Buddhist beliefs and practices as important as the cult of their own indigenous mountain gods. This influence is strong among men and women, but women identify more readily with some of the peripheral symbols of the Tibetan Buddhist tradition, partly perhaps because women stay in the village during the winter months when more Bhotias and lamas live in the village and partly because, unlike the men, they must rely on more locally available means of controlling impersonal forces. By their dress and social system all Tarangpurians clearly demarcate themselves from Bhotias, but women wear Tibetan boots all winter, which no Tarangpur male would ever do under any circumstances. This custom is related to the pollution concept involved in the division of labor: Tarangpurians rank Bhotias as somewhat lower than themselves, and hence more polluting, and whereas women often engage in polluting activities, men should remain pure.

With the rice comes contact with Hindu and Hinduized life-styles, association with different caste groups, acquaintances with ideas of caste ranking, more elaborate concepts of purity and pollution, and so on. The practice of Hinduism requires at some point the ritual expertise and ecclesiastical competence possessed by Brahmins. But it is a distinctive peculiarity of Tichurong, and generally of isolated areas in the high Himalayas inhabited by other non-Hindu minority groups (the Sherpas in the Mount Everest region, for example), that the penetration of Hinduism there has been exclusively by low-caste, so-called untouchable groups, not by Brahmins or other high castes. Thus Magar interaction with Hindus within Tichurong is limited to members of the Blacksmith and Tailor castes (whose rank is about as low as any group's rank in the hills of Nepal), with whom they have extensive economic and social dealings.[5]

The Tarangpurians thus are engaged in almost constant movement in and out of Tichurong, but the total demographic flow northward is very different from the southward flow. The Tarangpur traders travel north to the Tibetan-speaking areas, but just as often, the Bhotias come to Tarangpur. Lamas and other Bhotias come south in winter to live, even if they have nothing to trade but their labor. But although the Tarangpur traders go south with salt, the Hindus with whom they trade never come north to Tarangpur; the movement is entirely unidirectional. Men of Tarangpur are relatively well traveled and have seen much of western Nepal and India, but apart from Bhotias, few outsiders ever come to Tichurong. The valley is in this sense much more isolated than are many of the people who live there.

Two different roles can be isolated which link distant places and persons: the trader and the lama. The Tarangpur lamas have weak, tenuous, and uninstitutionalized relationships with other lamas to the north, but no relationships at all to the south. Local lamas acknowledge the authority and superior learning of some of the lamas to the north, and they unhesitatingly defer to those whose reputations are well established. But there is no regularized or formal connection with lamas or monasteries to the north, and no links at all with the Hindus to the south and west. The traders, in contrast, mediate goods in both directions and maintain active social relationships in both places. Because of the strikingly different cultural settings in which they operate, they must select from an inventory of multiple statuses one which is appropriate to different times, places, and persons.

IMPRESSION MANAGEMENT

To conduct business and simply to present an acceptable social
face in such diverse settings requires astute impression management.[6] The Bhotia and Hindu models are too distinct, opposed,
and mutually alien for a single consistent status to be consonant
with both. The Tarangpur trader must endeavor to be all things
to all men. He must use the Tibetan language in his transactions
to acquire salt, and he must use the Nepali language in his transactions to get rid of it. To the Bhotia he wants to appear a worthy
Buddhist—and indeed, he is one of sorts, though not of the unalloyed kind of Bhot and Tibet. To the Hindus he wants to appear
sophisticated about ideas of caste ranking, concepts of purity and
pollution, clothing styles, "correct" Nepali, and the other ac-
coutrements by which Hindu sophistication is measured in the
hills of west Nepal.

And yet the pull is not equal: from the north he can acquire
religious ideology, sacred objects, and ritual expertise, all of which
help provide a matrix of meaning and tools to overcome some of
the individual crises of life, such as those caused by birth, disease,
and death. But the scope of both meaning and pragmatism is
limited to the religious domain at the individual level.

The south represents not just another culture, but a local version
of the social and cultural system which constitutes most of the rest
of Nepal. These two life-styles are not only contrastive, they are
clearly ranked: from the point of view of the dominant, national
Hindu segment, Tibetan culture is definitely inferior. One measure
of the degree to which it is regarded as inferior is the fact that the
Nepali word "Bhotia" is not just ethnic nomenclature; it is frequently a term of abuse. The fact that Hindus consider Bhotias
inferior is not a matter of great concern to the Bhotias. Their own
system has been so far removed from the mainstream of Nepal
that the Hindu ranking system could only be regarded as amusing
or irrelevant. But to the Tarangpurians, whose relations with
Hindus are a built-in part of their lives, the Hindu rank order is
of the utmost importance. What is ranked is not so much a caste
as a culture. Since Bhotias and Hindus interact so infrequently
with each other, there is little point in considering them castes
ranked vis-à-vis each other. Rather, it is the Bhotias' generally

polluting attributes, such as beef-eating—not their interaction with Hindus—which consign them to a low rank in the hierarchy.

Because the Tibetan influence has been so strong in such readily identifiable ways—in personal names, for example, which are Tibetan, since lamas give them at birth—the Tarangpur trader must suppress certain status indicators; that is, he must be careful to disguise any behavior that would "give him away" and must substitute others: in other words, he must practice impression management. So when he is in Hindu areas, he not only speaks a different language but also takes an entirely different name and identity. He does not use his lama-given Tibetan name (such as Tsering, or Namgyal, or Pasang), which sounds alien and crude to a Hindu; instead, he takes a Hindu-sounding name (like Krishna Bahadur, or Chandra Lal, or Raji Man). This is not merely a convenience for Hindus who would have difficulty pronouncing Tibetan names; it is conscious repression of a status that is a positive liability to him as long as he lives and operates in Hindu areas. Nor is this name-changing without historical precedent. Names on the tax records of 1846 (which would have been taken by Hindu, Nepalese officials) show that 40 percent of the men's names are Tibetan, 39 percent Nepalese, and the rest are indeterminant. In 1968, 67 percent of the men's names given to me (a Nepali speaker) on my first-round census were Nepali; 23 percent were Tibetan, and the rest were indeterminant.

GOODS AND SYMBOLS: BROKERS AND BLOCKERS

Thus the grain-salt-rice trade involves not only goods and a particular set of social relationships but also familiarity with two entirely different sets of linguistic, religious, sartorial, culinary, and hierarchical symbols. These two symbol sets struggle for the collective mind of Tarangpur, which perennially looks in two mutually exclusive directions. Both models are influential in their own spheres, and as long as they do not confront each other, and those in the middle confront them in different places at different times, each can continue to exert its influence. The Tarangpurians clearly represent a cultural buffer between two opposing cultural poles, and while salt and rice pass between the cultural frontiers, all ideas stop in the middle, where they are absorbed in a variety of different ways.

As in the division of labor, the impact is felt differently among men and women. Women, like lamas, may not sin. Neither women nor lamas ever kill animals or, ideally, even hurt them. Just as lamas and women are equivalents in the labor force, so they both observe the same Buddhist strictures against certain activities, such as animal sacrifice. The Tarangpur lamas look and dress just like other Tarangpur men, except that they wear Tibetan boots, as the women (but no other men) do. Men openly kill animals, wear the tuft-of-hair Hindu topknot, and generally resemble Hindus anywhere else.

The two poles—represented by Hindus and Buddhists—remain unaffected by each other. Buddhists see and learn little of Hindus, and Hindus see and learn little of Buddhists. As commercial middlemen, Tarangpur traders are brokers of goods; but as ideological hinges, they are blockers of ideas, since from each side they must hide the parts of themselves which display evidence of the other. Instead of being cultural brokers between two alien groups, the men are in effect cultural brokers (or idea men) for their women. This blockage of ideas between the two contrasting ecological and ideological zones to the north and south results in a kind of integration between the three symbiotic regions that is distinctively economic.

A TRIBE PURSUED BY TWO GREAT TRADITIONS

The Magars of Tarangpur are not a tribe in search of a great tradition (Orans 1965) but a tribe torn between two great traditions. Unlike Orans's Santal, they have not conceded rank (not yet, at least) because their interactions with Hindus to the south and with Buddhists to the north are too problematic, both in and of themselves and vis-à-vis each other. What Tarangpurians concede to the Hindu world in which they increasingly trade (see chap. 5) is not rank, but power (Orans 1965:125). They see their larger social and political interests served by the south and proceed, as Barth predicts, to repress some behaviors and enhance others (by speaking the right language, having the right name, wearing the right clothes, eating the right food, and so on), so that their status is appropriate and commensurate with that of their counterparts in the transactional relationship.

Yet there is always the simultaneous, countervailing tug from the north. In addition to the omnipresent (if rather ineffectual) village lamas, on whom they must rely for power of a different sort, there is the occasional evangelical lama from the north who demands a hearing and exhorts backsliders in no uncertain terms to keep the faith. In the mid-1950s an apparently charismatic old lama, the Lama of Shang (see Snellgrove 1961), stormed into Tarangpur, berating the people for their lackadaisical Buddhism and such practices as animal sacrifice. He confronted the dhami at his shrine (where the animals are sacrificed) and said that his power was much greater than the dhami's—and that if it were not, let the dhami's god strike him dead. When he survived the villagers were much impressed, but by 1968 massive backsliding had wiped out whatever gains the Lama of Shang had produced. Villagers shrug off their errant ways, saying that it is one thing for a powerful lama to keep to the letter of the law in these matters, but that as poor, impotent villagers, they must come to terms with whatever spiritual forces are present in their environment as best they can. It is this cultural juxtaposition and balancing and impression management which is at the heart of the changing Tarangpur scene.

DECLINE OF THE SALT CIRCUIT

For the resolution of this cultural confrontation, and as an additional complication to it, we must now look at a second series of transactions that have evolved over the last forty or fifty years. Old men say that as recently as forty years ago, most families in the village had sizable herds of sheep and goats to carry the salt and grain—a large herd containing as many as 160 animals. Over the years the size and number of herds have declined so drastically that only six families now have sheep and goats in sufficient numbers to be called a herd, and even these herds are small by former standards.

The decline in the grain-salt-rice circuit can be explained partly by the disadvantages of animals and foodstuffs as a form of capital, and by the inherently precarious nature of animal husbandry: the loss of animals through disease, exhaustion, or bad weather can reduce a man from riches to ruin in a few years. Examples of such disasters are well known and are frequently the subject of conversations around the fire during and after supper. During our stay there was a heavy snowfall out of season in Bhot which caused a wealthy yak owner (who had a herd of 80, "so many there were a black forest of them") to lose all but 10 of his animals. Animals and grain can both degenerate quickly and must be looked after and preserved carefully.

Another factor in the decline of this trading cycle is the slow but steady incursion into the hills of Indian salt, which has become increasingly available and economical. Moreover, Tibetan salt became more expensive during World War I, perhaps due to restrictions instituted from Kathmandu (Field 1959:463), and the price of Tibetan salt increased again after the Chinese occupation and control of Tibet in the late 1950s. Indian salt has been quick to capitalize on the opportunity to fill the gap by moving further and further up into the hills, where it nibbles at the retreating border that marks the southern limit of the Tibetan salt trade. In other words, a point of diminishing returns is reached at which the attractiveness of peddling salt is greatly reduced. As that point is reached, Tarangpur salt traders must consider alternative allocations of time and resources.

At the time of the research some 25 households still owned sheep and goats used for transporting grain and salt, but most had only a few animals. Of the more than 400 beasts of burden owned by villagers, more than half—280—were distributed among only six families in herds of from 30 to 60 animals. The others were kept by families in numbers from two to 30. The number of sheep/goats per family is summarized in table 11 (figures for the animal population in Tarangpur are detailed in appendix B).

Those with herds of much less than 30 animals must either combine forces for carrying on the salt trade or must put their animals in the care of someone with many more, who will look after the smaller herd with his own for a fee of Rs.3/- (30¢) per animal per trading expedition. People from different villages in Tichurong also combine their herds and travel together, and

TABLE 11
DISTRIBUTION OF SHEEP AND GOATS

Sheep and goats in herd	Families
30–60	6
20–29	1
10–19	4
5–9	7
2–4	7
Total	25

such combined herds of several hundred sheep and goats are not uncommon.

Thus less than one-third of the families of Tarangpur now own any salt/grain-carrying sheep and goats, and of these only six have herds large enough to be economically viable on their own. That is, all but six families either have to arrange to send their animals with someone else or have to take someone else's animals with them so that there will be enough animals for a viable herd. In either case, for most households dropping out of this exchange cycle generates considerable surplus time and resources for other pursuits. All this is in contrast to times within the ethnographic present when "nearly everyone" had herds of sheep and goats. Whatever the exact dimensions of animal ownership in the past, it is clear that the grain-salt-rice exchange circuit has shrunk drastically to its present truncated level, thus liberating time and resources for alternative allocations, which are discussed in chapter 5.

5

Transactions:
The Commodities Circuit

bolne ko pitho bikchha   A glib tongue can sell cornmeal;
nabolne ko chāmal bikdaina   a dumb man cannot sell even rice.
     —Nepali proverb

ELIMINATION OF THE MIDDLEMEN

As the grain-salt-rice exchange circuit began to contract, a second,
separate series of transactions, involving livestock, cloth, and manufactured goods, evolved and assumed increasing importance.
Until about forty years ago men wore all-woolen clothes, while
women wore cotton skirts and blouses which they bought from
merchants in Jumla, to the west. Then for reasons which are not
clear, but which may be related to the problems of impression
management already mentioned, men began wearing what they
wear now: cotton pants and tunics. At about the same time it
became apparent to the Tarangpurians that if they themselves
went to the Terai to purchase cloth, they would effect substantial
savings by eliminating the middlemen from Jumla (who also acquired their cloth there). By going directly to the Terai, the
Tarangpur men are able to save both the extra transportation
charges and the expense of supporting a middleman.

Going to the Terai involved complications in impression management for Tarangpurians: to go there and to be accepted as
anything other than hill-people, they had to wear cotton clothes
if they did not do so already, and this necessitated a considerable
increase in the amount of cotton bought. Today as then, going all
the way to the Terai also exposes the traders to the goods available

in a Terai market town—cigarettes, velveteen, flashlights, and the like. To finance these purchases in this second transaction circuit, sheep and goats are driven south over the Jangla passes in the fall, before they are closed for the winter, and are sold to Hindu villagers along the way to the Terai.

THE LIVESTOCK TRADE

To buy a herd of sheep and goats each year obviously requires considerable purchasing power, and it is therefore necessary to understand how cash was introduced into what was essentially a barter economy. At present, profits from the previous year's enterprises finance purchases of sheep and goats. Few families acquire sheep and goats (apart from those they will eat themselves) with grain, and those who do barter in this way generally buy only two or three. But over the years grain has been exchanged for products of these animals such as wool, blankets, sweaters, mufflers, and other woolen goods, which can be sold in Hindu areas for cash. As the volume of money from the sale of these items increases over the years, the accumulated profits can buy more and more sheep and goats. Alternatively, and probably of even greater historical importance, the very sheep and goats used for transporting salt and rice can be sold for cash, so that a herd of pack animals can be converted instantly (by fiat so to speak) into salable livestock. Thus in a single year a trader could switch entirely from using animals as beasts of burden to transport grain and salt for barter, as described in chapter 4, to selling the same herd of animals for cash.

The greatest Hindu festival of the year *Durga Pujā* or *Dasaiṅ* (Hindi, *Dasera*) takes place in late September or early October, and if a Hindu in this part of Nepal wants to ritually slaughter an animal, this is the preeminent sacrificial time. Naturally, then, during the fall sheep and goats are in great demand, and a man with a herd from outside the area will usually find a good price for his animals. The animals are often sold on short- or medium-term credit, but when payment is eventually made, it is made in cash.

Traffic in sheep and goats can be quite lucrative. A profit of Rs.

40 ($3.96) per animal is quite common, and if a herd of, say, 50 animals is disposed of in this way, a gain of Rs. 2,000 ($198.00) can be made. The figures in table 12 are buying and selling records in 1968–1969, and give some indication of the amounts of money that can be made in the sale of sheep and goats.

Of the examples in table 12, the greatest profit per animal is Rs. 60 ($5.94), and a profit of Rs. 30 ($2.97) or 40 ($3.96) is about average. In only one case did a trader take a loss on sheep and goats. In addition to the 10 households and 160 animals listed in table 12, another 15 households sold 268 animals. Thus a total of 25 households engaged in this sheep and goat trade, which involved a total of 428 animals, bought in Bhot (or, in three cases, in Jumla) and later sold in the Hindu or Hinduized areas to the south.

Assuming an average profit of Rs. 40 ($3.96) per animal, the total profit on these 428 animals for this one trading season in Tarangpur is Rs. 17,120 ($1,695.05). By shearing before selling, Rs. 10–15 ($.99–1.49) worth of wool or goat hair per animal (Rs. 5,350, or $529.70 for all the animals at Rs. 12.50/animal) is gained and thus added to the profit from sales, for total profits of $2,224.75 (Rs. 22,470).

By coincidence, the number of sheep and goats used for transporting grain and salt and those sold are approximately the same, but the two alternative uses of these animals are radically different. Using them as beasts of burden results in accumulation of prestigious grain; selling them results in tidy cash profits, which can then be used to buy more sheep, which generate still more profits. As will become clear, the total implications, economic and otherwise, of disposing of these animals by selling them rather than by using them for transport are vast and wide-ranging.

Sheep and goats are sold in the south, mostly in the areas around Baglung, Pokhara, and in villages that lie along the Kali Gandaki River. There are several ways of marketing the animals. Ideally, each trader sells a live sheep or goat to an individual for cash to be paid when the animal is delivered. But this cannot usually be so neatly arranged, so the trader is forced to sell the animals on credit. There is a great deal of bargaining both about the price and the date the credit is due. Prices vary according to the size of the animal and also the amount of fat on it,[1] regardless of size. If

TABLE 12

SAMPLE PROFIT MARGINS IN THE SALE OF SHEEP AND GOATS IN 10 TARANGPUR HOUSEHOLDS, 1968–69

Household	Buying price (Rs.)	Selling price (Rs.)	Profit/ animal (Rs.)	Animals/ household	Total profit household Rs.		Total profit household $	
1	120	165	45	16	720		71.29	
2	70	65	–5	5	–25		–2.48	
3	120	145	25	11	275		27.23	
4	110	140	30	7	210	250	20.80	24.76
	91	101	10	4	40		3.96	
5	127	155	28	4	112		11.09	
6	92	145	53	22	1166		115.45	
7	80	95	15	12	180		17.82	
8	110	150	40	23	920		91.09	
9	80	140	60	23	1380		136.63	
10	110	150	40	33	1320		130.70	

money is offered immediately, a slight reduction in price may be made, and if credit is arranged, the price is marginally higher. If the sale is on credit, the collection date may be set for a month or two or three months later, but sometimes it is as much as six months or a year until the money can be collected. Conditions for granting credit are not strict, and credit will be given to a total stranger provided he can be identified, for future reference, as belonging to a specific house or village. The extension of credit is widespread but is viewed increasingly with suspicion, since it often requires the patience, persistence, and finesse of a professional bill collector to collect debts, which in many cases cannot be collected at all.

If sheep and goats cannot be sold in this way, a trader will set up shop in a single place where he can slaughter his animals, divide the meat into portions of equal size and quality, and sell the portions to anyone who wants to buy them. There is always a ready market for meat in this form because many people are too poor to buy an entire animal but can and want to buy a more modest amount of meat. In these circumstances also, meat can be sold on credit. The trader either distributes the meat from a central place or takes the portions house to house to sell wherever he can.

The process of taking the animals south and of selling them one by one and then collecting the money that has not been paid at the time of the sale requires several months, but when debts have been collected, the Tarangpur traders then possess something they could never acquire while pursuing the grain-salt-rice transactional chain—namely, cash.

Even larger profits can be made on the sale of horses (the average profit per horse is Rs. 235, versus only about Rs. 35 per sheep or goat), but since they are also more costly to buy, relatively few people can afford to traffic in them. In the trading season of my residence only eight households sold horses, as opposed to twenty-five households selling sheep and goats. These horses, like the sheep and goats, are generally bought in one place (usually Bhot and occasionally Khasan or as far away as Jumla, where they are in ready supply), and are then moved to a place of greater demand for sale. But in a few cases a horse may be born and raised in Tarangpur, and the profits from the sale of such a horse are of course even larger. The figures in table 13 indicate the total number

TABLE 13
PROFIT MARGINS IN THE SALE OF HORSES

Household[a]	Buying price Rs.	Buying price $	Selling price Rs.	Selling price $	Profit/horse[b] Rs.	Profit/horse[b] $	No. of horses[c]	Total profit household Rs.	Total profit household $
1	350	34.65	650	64.36	300	29.70	3	900	89.11
2	500	49.51	600	59.41	100	9.90	2	200	19.80
3[d]	400	39.60 (small)	500	49.51	100	9.90	4 }		
	1,100	108.91 (medium)	1,400	138.61	300	29.70	4 }	2,400	237.62
	2,000	198.02 (large)	2,200	217.82	200	19.80	4 }		
4[d]	1,200	118.81	1,620	160.40	420	41.58	1 }		
	600	59.41	825	81.68	225	22.28	1 }	>645	>63.86
	(Raised in Tarangpur)		1,100	108.91	—	—	1 }		
	(Raised in Tarangpur)		2,430	240.60	—	—	1 }		
5[d]	—		1,000	99.01	—	—	1 }		
	—		720	71.29	—	—	1 }	—	
	—		725	7.78	—	—	1 }		
6	—		Traded with Rs. 250 for another horse		—	—	1	—	
7	—		Traded with Rs. 250 for another horse		—	—	1	—	
8	—		Traded with Rs. 200 for another horse		—	—	1	—	

aTotal number of households = 8. bAverage profit per horse = 235 Rs. ($23.27).
cTotal number of horses = 26. dA single household.

of horses sold during one season, and the prices paid and sold for most of them.

Horses are sold in areas generally to the west of those areas where sheep and goats are sold; the primary horse markets are found around Gulmi and as far west as Piuthan and Dang. Because they cost more, horses are harder to sell, and only a few rich people are able to buy them. Another consequence of the high prices which horses command is that they are more frequently sold on credit, and the credit tends to be longer term than that extended for sheep and goats. Debts for horses that are sold are often not due until the next season.

THE WOOLEN TRADE

Sheep, goats, and horses are the most lucrative items Tarangpurians can buy and sell, and when large profits are made they are made by trafficking in these animals. But while a not inconsiderable number of households deal in livestock, many more buy, make, and sell woolen goods either instead of or in addition to the sale of animals. Fortunes cannot be made in wool, but the woolen trade affects a greater number of Tarangpurians than does the livestock trade, since the entry costs are extremely low for the former and considerably higher for the latter. Like livestock transactions, the petty woolen trade involves the transfer between symbiotic regions of resources which are surplus in one and scarce in another.

Wool, like salt, must come from the north. Some sheep are brought from Jumla and sheared, some wool still crosses over the Tibetan border, and of course some wool can be sheared from the sheep that are kept permanently in Tarangpur to transport grain, salt, and rice. But when Tarangpurians acquire wool to manufacture knitted and woven goods, they usually get it from Bhot.

Unlike grain or salt, which is measured by volume, wool is measured by weight. A *dharni* of wool weighs between five and six pounds and costs a Tarangpurian Rs. 30 ($2.97). One dharni of wool can be used in a variety of different ways. To make one woolen blanket would completely consume one dharni of unspun wool. Alternatively, one dharni is enough wool to make four scarves, or one and a half waist sashes, or four sleeveless sweaters. But to calculate the cost of these goods, a factor must be taken into account which is not applicable to the cost of buying animals—namely, the cost of human labor. Of the four types of manufactured woolen products—blankets, scarves, sweaters, and waist sashes—all but the sweaters must be woven. Sweaters are knitted by Tarangpur men, never by women (for no reason relating to sin or pollution that I could ascertain). This work can be done during idle hours of gossiping and visiting, whether before winter trading trips, when there is nothing else to do, or during summer weeding periods, when men tend to sit around the village during the day.

When the wool is bought it is in the form of unprocessed wads just as it comes from the animal's back. First it is cleaned of the larger extraneous objects, such as burrs, and then it must be spun. Men, women, and children of all ages spin wool when they have free time. Like knitting, spinning wool involves the skillful but almost unconscious use of the hands, so it can be done during any other activity that does not require use of the hands. There is enough surplus time in relation to the amount of wool available (which is, like salt, not as readily obtainable now as it was before the advent of Chinese rule in Tibet) that Tarangpurians manage to spin all their wool themselves, without having to hire others to do it.

Producing the woven articles is a different and more complex matter. There is a technical speciality, involving the use of looms, which most Tarangpurians do not understand. The art is really a Tibetan one, and many of the Bhotia women who spend the winter in Tarangpur earn their living by weaving blankets, waist sashes, and scarves for Tarangpurians, who will then sell them in the middle hills during the next trading expedition. The number of days required to weave these goods and the cost of employing someone to do the work are indicated by the figures in table 14.

These figures are of course approximate and variable according to the quality of the work, closeness of weaving, and so on. Similarly, the prices that will be commanded depend on size, general quality, and the like. The figures in table 15 represent one

TABLE 14
USUAL COST OF WEAVING WOOLEN PRODUCTS

Woolen product	Weaving time required	Daily pay rate	Other expenses	Total cost	
				Rs.	$
Blanket	5 days	4 manas (pints) grain (= Rs. 4) plus prepared meals on working days (= Rs. 5)	Rs. 7.50 for Indian dyes[a]	52.50	5.20
Scarf	1½ days	as above	none	13.50	1.34
Waist sash (15 *hāt* in length; 1 hat = 1 cubit)	6 days	as above	Rs. 5 for Indian dyes, dyeing labor costs of 4 manas (pints) grain (= Rs. 4) plus Rs. 1	64	6.34

[a]The spun wool used to weave blankets is dyed before weaving, hence no additional labor is needed to dye the blankets, as is the case with waist sashes.

TABLE 15
One Trader's Profit Margins on Sales of Woolen Products

Article	Price paid		Price received		Profit/ article		No. of articles	Total profit	
	Rs.	$	Rs.	$	Rs.	$		Rs.	$
Good scarf	10	.99	15	1.49	5	.50	5	25	2.48
Poorer scarf	7	.69	12	1.19	5	.50	4	20	1.98
Good blanket	40	3.96	45	4.46	5	.50	7	45	4.46
Better blanket	60	5.94	90	8.91	30	2.97	15	450	44.55
Full-sleeve sweater	15	1.49	60	5.94	45	4.46	4	180	17.82
Sleeveless sweater	10	.99	30	2.97	20	1.98	6	120	11.88
Total	142	14.06	252	24.96	110	10.91	41	840	83.17

trader's sales for items of the same genre but of different quality. In this case the products were bought by the trader as already finished products.

Transactions in woolen goods are so variable and dependent on a variety of factors of workmanship, individual variation, and stylistic preferences that it is misleading to present one set of figures as representing typical prices. Moreover, it is important to remember that traders do not always make profits; especially with items such as woolen goods, considerable negotiation and patience is required in order to realize a worthwhile profit. It is by no means impossible for an unwary trader to take a loss on several items, as table 16 illustrates. This was the only case I discovered in which such large losses were incurred, and in this instance profits in sheep and goat sales put him back in the black.

The total volume of woolen goods and the extent of household participation in it is shown in table 17. These figures make it clear that the trading strategies pursued are extremely varied and not at all stereotyped. Some traders sell only sashes, others only blankets, and still others sell a more or less evenly distributed mix of the four kinds of woolen goods. Since the amount of capital needed to peddle a few homemade woolen goods is much smaller than that needed to enter the livestock trade, more families deal in wool than in livestock, and they can choose from a variety of product alternatives according to the time and resources they have to invest.

TRADERS AND NON-TRADERS

Many households diversify their activities and put their resources into several—or even all—of these kinds of exchanges. This is easily done because the trading area for all these items is in the same direction and often in the same locality. Excluding those people who followed the grain-salt-rice exchange circuit, there were fifty households involved in selling some combination of woolen goods, sheep and goats, and horses. Table 18 shows the number of households that employed each strategy. These figures summarize the number of households that moved trade goods (excluding grain, salt, and rice) from one economic zone to

TABLE 16

ONE TRADER'S LOSSES ON SALES OF WOOLEN PRODUCTS

Article	Cost		Selling price		Selling price − cost		No. of articles	Total loss or gain	
	Rs.	$	Rs.	$	Rs.	$		Rs.	$
Blanket	55	5.45	40	3.96	−15	−1.49	3	−45	−4.46
Scarf	12.60	1.25	9	.90	−3.60	−.36	5	−18	−1.78
Sleeveless sweaters	15	1.49	20	1.98	+5	+.50	2	+10	+.99
Waist sashes	64	6.34	65	.64	+1	+.10	3	+3	+.30
Total	146	14.53	134	7.48				−40	−4.95

TABLE 17
VOLUME AND VARIETY OF WOOLEN GOODS SALES
(by households)

Household	Blankets No.	Blankets %	Scarves No.	Scarves %	Sleeveless sweaters No.	Sleeveless sweaters %	Full-sleeve sweaters No.	Full-sleeve sweaters %	Waist sashes No.	Waist sashes %	Total articles per household[a]
1	3	23	5	39	2	15	0	0	3	23	3
2	0	0	0	0	0	0	0	0	3	100	3
3	22	46	9	19	6	13	4	8	7	15	48
4	0	0	0	0	0	0	0	0	2	100	2
5	6	30	4	20	3	15	0	0	7	35	20
6	10	36	5	18	10	36	0	0	3	11	28
7	6	100	0	0	0	0	0	0	0	0	6
8	0	0	12	44	5	19	0	0	10	37	27
9	6	43	0	0	8	57	0	0	0	0	14
10	17	65	7	27	7	27	0	0	0	0	26
11	25	56	10	22	10	22	0	0	0	0	45
12	0	0	0	0	0	0	0	0	4	100	4
13	5	39	3	23	5	29	0	0	0	0	13
14	0	0	0	0	0	0	0	0	7	100	7
15	0	0	0	0	0	0	0	0	25	100	25
16	12	100	0	0	0	0	0	0	0	0	12
17	21	50	21	50	0	0	0	0	0	0	42
18	0	0	0	0	0	0	0	0	8	100	8
19	0	0	0	0	0	0	0	0	15	100	15

20	0	0	0	0	0	0	0	0	15	100	15
21	0	0	4	8	0	0	0	0	46	92	50
22	12	100	0	0	0	0	0	0	0	0	12
23	0	0	0	0	0	0	0	0	40	100	40
24	0	0	2	25	3	0	0	0	15	100	15
25	0	0	0	0	0	38	0	0	3	38	8
26	0	0	0	0	4	0	0	0	5	100	5
27	0	0	0	0	1	100	2	0	0	0	4
28	4	57	0	0	4	14	0	29	0	0	7
29	0	0	0	0	0	29	0	0	10	71	14
30	7	47	6	21	15	0	0	0	8	53	15
31	5	18	4	25	5	54	0	0	2	7	28
32	5	31	0	0	0	31	0	0	2	13	16
33	6	100	0	0	0	0	0	0	0	0	6
34	12	100	0	0	6	0	0	0	0	0	12
35	0	0	0	0	0	100	0	0	0	0	6
36	0	0	4	100	0	0	0	0	0	0	4
Total (mean percentage)	179	35	96	19	94	18	6	1	240	47	615

[a]Data are incomplete for four other houses which sold woolen goods. The mean number of articles per household = 17.

TABLE 18
TRADING STRATEGIES BY TARANGPUR HOUSEHOLDS

	Households	
Strategy	*%*	*No.*
Only wool	38	19
Only sheep/goats	12	6
Only horses	6	3
Wool and horses	4	2
Wool and sheep/goats	34	17
Horses and sheep/goats	2	1
All three	4	2
Total	100	50

another, not the total number of households represented in the annual movement south to obtain their annual allotment of clothing with cash raised in some other way, such as by selling beer or distilled liquor or even by poaching musk deer.

Of the thirty-three households not engaged in the woolen and livestock circuit, only sixteen sent no one south during the winter. Of the seventeen who did, four households sent representatives who worked for more prosperous traders by carrying loads or helping manage a herd of salt-carrying sheep and goats; three worked for other households but also sold woolen goods on their own (which are included in table 17); five households contain only women, who went south with cash only; four households sent men with cash only; and one old couple went south on religious pilgrimage and engaged in commercial transactions only nominally (pilgrimages are discussed in more detail in chap. 6). Thus from the entire village, sixty-seven households sent one or more members south on some kind of errand, all of them economic except for the couple who went primarily to visit religious shrines; and sixteen households sent no one south during the winter trading season.

Of the sixteen houses in which everyone stayed home, a majority were kept at home only in that year and tended to resume southbound activities the following year. There were a variety of reasons

Tibetan ponies heading north along Jangla Pass toward Tichurong.

Tarangpur village on the hillside below the Jangla passes.

Tarangpurian houses built one on top of another against the hillside. The girl standing on a rooftop with her baby brother on her back is about to throw a snowball.

A *chortan* (cenotaph) at the entrance of Tarangpur.

A single bullock plow followed by women breaking soil clods and sowing seeds. Note rock and clay walls in the background.

Salt-filled saddlebags made of coarsely spun goathair are loaded on sheep for a trading expedition.

Harvesting millet with locally made, hand-held serrated sickle. Marijuana and amaranth are planted in the millet fields.

Threshing grain on the rooftops, where much Tarangpur social life takes place.

A Tibetan nomad refugee who lives in Tarangpur in the winter. She is the *mitini* of the daughter of the wealthiest man in Tarangpur.

A Tarangpurian woman and child.

A mother and daughter posing to display the changes in dress fashions over the past forty years. Note cloth patterns, size of waistband, and size of earrings.

A *patum* (part priest, part shaman) beating a drum during the annual, month-long winter ritual.

A *dhāmi* (animal-sacrificing shaman) dancing himself into a trancelike state.

An informal gathering of local men discussing village affairs. From left to right: assistant schoolteacher (standing on far left); householder; *pradhān* (chairman) of Tarangpur panchayat (standing); local panchayat secretary; government schoolteacher from Pokhara; district panchayat representative; untouchable (blacksmith caste) from Riwa village; constable from border checkpost.

Heavily laden traders returning from a winter's trading expedition being led into the village by a Damāi (Tailor caste) drummer.

A boy being dressed in new clothes after his first haircut.

Painting inside a *chortan* showing King Mahendra among Buddhist deities.

An elaborate design incorporated into the typical pattern of whitewash dots that decorates both the inside and outside of Tarangpurian houses.

A carved wooden figure outside of a house, believed to protect against ghosts.

for staying at home: some were too old or too poor to afford the trip on their own (five households each), and some had to stay behind to sort out a temporary political problem (three families). The three remaining cases were anomalous, being due to a need to perform annual rites for the indigenous cult of mountain gods, desire to rebuild an old house, and a single woman with small children to care for.

Thus for a variety of reasons—almost always economic—and in a variety of ways, most households temporarily lose at least one member to southern ports of call during the winter months. They may pursue either of two different exchange circuits, but rarely both. The historically important grain-salt-rice circuit has rapidly contracted, and in its place, the livestock and woolen circuit is occupying the time and resources of villagers. Thus far we have seen how Tarangpurians are able to shuttle resources south, and we have noted the complex cultural and linguistic adaptations they have made which enable them to perform this middleman role; we have yet to investigate how this mediating role begins to feed back into their own system. But first we must examine the other half of this second transactional circuit to see what it is that Tarangpurians choose to bring back with them from the south and how they dispose of it.

THE OTHER SIDE OF THE MOUNTAINS

By the time they have disposed of their livestock or woolen goods in the middle hills, Tarangpurians have completed only half of the transactions they must consummate in order to proceed the next year with the same round of activities. The middle hills can give them money for what they bring with them from Dolpo, but this cash must be converted back into something which will be in demand in Dolpo. Of course cash itself is in short supply in Dolpo, and it can be and is used to buy more sheep and goats or horses or wool. But by converting the cash into scarce goods, a profit can be made in both directions rather than just in one, and trade in each direction then becomes worthwhile in itself. This diversification provides a more solid base for the maintenance of the whole trading system, since if half of the circuit becomes uneconomical, the other half may still make the round-trip profitable.

Economic anthropology has documented in rich detail the roles and relevance of the markets of the world, and it is striking that all the Tarangpurian transactions thus far described are marketless ones—that is, they take place outside a central marketplace where the interaction of buyers and sellers sets prices. It is only when traders reach the Terai that marketplaces become part of the system; all the other transactions in both exchange circuits are conducted in relatively isolated, man-to-man circumstances. The Tarangpurians are essentially long-distance, slow-moving traveling salesmen.

Taking the cash that they have received for their animals and woolen goods, traders from Tarangpur move on from the villages of the middle hills and descend to the Terai, the flat extension of the Indian Gangetic plain. The change from the hills to the plains is geographically dramatic, and culturally and economically too, the Terai is a different world. Here there are roads, cars, buses, large bazaars, industrial towns, railroads that give access to all parts of India—in short, the Terai offers all the mixed blessings of the modern world. When the Tarangpurian enters the Terai, he is on the edge of that modern world, and his confrontation with it is essentially economic. Indeed, his whole rationale for going as far as the Terai is economic, for he wants the cotton cloth, velveteen material, cigarettes, and other assorted manufactured commodities that are made in the Terai or in parts of India sufficiently close to the Terai to be economically transported there.

The most accessible Terai market is the boomtown of Butwal, just at the edge of the hills. Most Tarangpurians go there as a matter of course, but occasionally trips are made to other bazaars—when the mountain passes are closed, for example, and the roundabout river route leads to other towns, such as Nepalganj. With the cheap and readily available railroad network of India at hand, Tarangpurians now frequently go beyond the Nepalese Terai to the source of the commodities in India itself. Relatively nearby is the north Indian industrial city of Kanpur, where cloth and dyes are somewhat cheaper than they are in Nepal. Some traders go farther, to the Darjeeling–Kalimpong area of West Bengal, where many goods are made for use by the large Tibetan population there. Tarangpur traders who bring back supplies to sell in Bhot go to Kalimpong to buy bricks of Tibetan tea, Tibetan coats, and Tibetan boots. A few go as far as Calcutta, sometimes to buy manufactured goods but especially to buy gold and jewelry, particularly coral and turquoise. The gold and jewelry are hoarded, not traded, and this is one of the principal ways of storing accumulated wealth deriving from the profits that accrue over the years.

THE COMMODITIES TRADE

Once these manufactured commodities have been purchased they are carried north again, through the hills and back over the high passes after the snows have melted in the spring (or should have melted—the year before the research period, a large number of Tarangpurians were trapped between the passes for three days by a blizzard). Relatively few goods are sold in Tarangpur and the neighboring villages of Tichurong, since most people there have their needs satisfied by a household member or relative who goes to the Terai to buy goods himself. During the summer months, after the plowing has been done, the traders have spare time (since weeding and general looking after the crops is done mostly by women) to transport their goods from the entrepôt of Tarangpur to potential buyers either in the Tibetan-speaking areas to the north or, to a lesser extent, to the Nepali-speaking areas (Khasan) down the Bheri River. Of the total amount of commodities brought back for sale from the Terai, approximately two-thirds are disposed of in Bhot and about one-third in Khasan.

Most households send someone to the Terai each year, but most of these purchasing expeditions are to acquire only what is needed at home, whether it be brass plates, clothes for the family, or iron to be forged into tools. These people participate in the seasonal round of movements and are exposed to all the influences that these trips entail. But they lack sufficient funds to bring back more than their domestic requirements, so they pack as much as they can afford into large, heavy wicker baskets, heft it on their backs, and carry it home.

Those with capital to invest in commodities for resale in Bhot and Khasan can choose from a variety of items for sale in the Terai and India. But the number of different kinds of goods and the quantity of goods carried back to Tichurong have increased over the years. Table 19 shows the approximate number of years each item has been brought back from the Terai.

This chronological measure of increasing involvement in the market system of southern Nepal and India is also a gauge of changing fashions—that is, of what a well-dressed Tarangpurian will wear. Although Indian, Western, Nepalese, and Tibetan clothing is imported from Indian and Nepalese markets, the Western, Nepalese, and Indian clothes are bought for some use and occasional sale, while the Tibetan clothes are bought exclusively for sale. Even those goods that are bought for home use are "essential" only in a cultural sense: there is nothing made in the Terai for which there is no traditional Tarangpur equivalent. Cotton clothing was traditionally all wool; locally grown tobacco and clay pipes and hookas were and still are used in place of cigarettes; flint and steel were used (and still are used by Bhotias) instead of matches; an ingenious wooden mousetrap built on the principle of the crossbow was and is used instead of steel traps or poison; sap-filled tapers were and are used instead of flashlights; the root of a local plant was and is used for soap; rope-soled shoes are made by cobblers in Khasan; and bees were and are kept to supply honey, which is used to make snacks. A daily schedule in which the measurement of minutes and hours is irrelevant makes watches of no practical value, and even now they are worn as a sign of wealth, like jewelry, rather than as a timepiece. Gold is the only item brought from the Terai and India for domestic consumption which seems to predate the beginning of this second transaction circuit, and perhaps gold was acquired in the past from the gold mines of western Tibet (see Srivastava 1958).

Thus none of the products that are so laboriously transported each year to Tarangpur are, like salt, necessary for survival; they are imported to pad out cultural images. Tibetan clothes are carried over the passes and transported through Tarangpur for economic reasons, but they cannot stay in Tarangpur households for cultural reasons: there is no place in the Tarangpur repertoire of statuses for Tibetan clothes.[2] In addition to these cultural considerations are the cold economic calculations which make it worthwhile for Tarangpur traders to bring back the bulk of commodities

TABLE 19

HISTORICAL DEPTH OF THE COMMODITIES TRADE

Article	Approx. no. of years brought from Terai
1. Cotton cloth	40
2. Velveteen	40
3. Topis (Nepali caps)	40
4. Dyes	40
5. Scissors	40
6. Cigarettes	40
7. Matches	40
8. Gold and other jewelry[a]	40
9. Cotton thread (for weaving wool blankets)	26
10. Mechanical rat traps[a]	22
11. Flashlights	20
12. Batteries	20
13. Tibetan coats	20
14. Tibetan boots	20
15. Tibetan tea	20
16. Shirts	20
17. Western-style sport coats[a]	16
18. Shoes	16
19. Soap (bar)	16
20. Watches[a]	13
21. Cotton quilt blankets	12
22. Sugar[a]	9
23. Rat poison[a]	9
24. Western-style pants (for boys)[a]	8
25. Kerosene	7
26. Thongs (sandals)	7
27. Colored cotton waist sashes[a]	6
28. Biscuits	5
29. Socks	5
30. Candy	5
31. Radios[a]	3
32. Toothbrushes and toothpaste	1

[a]For personal use only; not for resale.

that they do. Table 20 illustrates the lucrative nature of the commodities trade.

There is some variation in the amount of markup, depending on whether an item is sold in small quantities or in bulk, but as a very general approximation—and Tarangpurians tend to generalize in the same way about this—goods can be sold toward the northern border for about twice what they cost near the southern border. A 100 percent markup of course does not mean that there is a profit of equal magnitude. Between buying and selling runs a long and costly road, and this accounts for a large portion of the markup. The various expenses can be divided into four categories: living expenses on the trail and in market towns; porter fees or horsemen fees for extra loads; rail or plane fares for travel beyond the Terai to India and Kathmandu; and taxes. The living expenses must of course be met by anyone who travels to the Terai, whereas the porter fees and train tickets represent cash outlays only to

TABLE 20

PRICES OF PRINCIPAL COMMODITIES
(in Nepali rupees: $1.00 = Rs. 10.1)

Item	Bulk buying price in Terai (Rs.)	Selling price in Khasan (Rs.)	Selling price in Bhot (Rs.)
Cotton cloth	3–4/yard	6/yard	6/yard
Cotton thread	58/bundle	100/bundle	100/bundle
Cigarettes	13.55/bundle	25/bundle 23/bundle in bulk	25/bundle 23/bundle in bulk
Batteries	2.50/pair (Indian) 2.25/pair (Chinese)	5–6/pair 5–6/pair	5–6/pair 5–6/pair
Tibetan coat	16.20	—	26–30
Tibetan boots	21.60	—	45–48
Tibetan tea	250–260/package	—	800–1,000
Sugar[a]	2/mana (pint)	4–5/mana (pint)	—
Kerosene[a]	0.50/mana (pint)	4–5/mana (pint)	—
Thongs (sandals)	11/pair	16/pair	—
Toothbrush	2–3	5–6	—
Toothpaste	2–3	5–6	—

[a]Used mainly at home; not often sold.

those who buy more than they need for their own homes, or whose total purchases, meant for resale or not, are more than they can carry on their own backs. Taxes mainly affect goods taken out of Tichurong.

PARTICIPATION IN THE COMMODITIES TRADE

Of the sixty-seven households that sent one or more representatives south during the winter, thirty brought back commodities for themselves and for resale, while thirty-seven purchased only enough to satisfy their families' domestic needs. Thus these thirty-seven families were not involved in trading manufactured commodities, but simply sold enough animals or woolen goods to enable them to buy enough cloth, iron, plates, or whatever other amenities of life they needed at home. They are traders in only one direction—southward.

In the thirty other families that bring back more than they need at home from the Terai, the men are traders in the fullest sense, for they maintain in motion the circular flow of goods from the northern border to the southern and back again. But among this group also there is great diversity both in trading strategies and in the total volume of goods transported and sold. Of the thirty, sixteen traders bought only what they could carry on their own backs, while the other fourteen households needed more than their own backs to transport all their purchases. Quantities of goods varied enormously: at one extreme, a girl bought a "bundle" (roughly equivalent to a carton: 25 ten-cigarette packs) of cigarettes to sell by the pack (note that a purchase this small and straightforward is handled by a woman); at the other extreme were two traders who each brought back about thirty loads by a combination of horses, mules, and porters.

Table 21 shows the distribution of loads among those who transported commodities for resale. It makes clear the petty nature of most of the commercial activity of Tarangpur. Of the thirty families which bought more than they required, sixteen carried their extra goods themselves, twelve managed with between two and six loads, and only two traders needed more than six loads. These two needed thirty loads each, so that the two biggest traders

TABLE 21
DIFFERENTIAL PARTICIPATION IN THE COMMODITIES TRADE

No. of porter loads	No. of households
1	16
2	8
3	1
4	1
5	1
6	1
30	2

between them transported more loads to Tarangpur than all the other twenty-eight commodities traders combined.

PROFITS IN THE COMMODITIES TRADE

All fourteen traders who had extra loads (see table 21) had to meet the expenses of porters. The rate of Rs. 120 ($11.88) per porter per round trip (carrying a load only one way), plus food on the trail, is a fairly fixed one. Food on the trail and in the market towns is about Rs. 2.50 ($0.25) per day per porter. Since it takes about two weeks to carry a load to Tarangpur from the Terai (versus one week without a load to the Terai), a porter would consume food worth Rs. 52.50 ($5.20), giving a total cost per porter (food plus carrying fee) of roughly Rs. 173 ($17.13). To this must be added approximately Rs. 200 ($19.80) to cover one's own expenses on the trail and in the Terai. This figure does not include the several days' supply of grain carried from Tarangpur, but even so, it is larger than the sum calculated for porters because traders inevitably spend more on themselves. They spend a week or two in a bazaar town, and they must feed themselves while selling in the middle hills; moreover, they eat better than porters, buy whiskey from time to time, and generally spend money to enjoy themselves as much as possible. Many spend much more than Rs. 200 ($19.80), but such an amount would accurately characterize the expense accounts of most of the petty traders and travelers to the Terai each winter. The 37 traders who went south to buy only their own requirements needed Rs. 200 ($19.80) beyond the purchase price of their goods.

A local tax of 1 percent of the selling price is levied on all goods exported for sale south of Tichurong. At the time of the research a tax was contemplated on goods imported from the Terai, but no rate had yet been set. Cost of travel in India depends on the distance traveled. The price of the longest distance, from Butwal to Calcutta (close to 1,500 miles), is Rs. 120 ($11.88) for a third-class train ticket.

Now that the cost of traveling the high road to the Terai and back is known, it is possible to make a rough estimate of the profit margins that are possible in the commodities business. As an example, one way of making up a full load is to carry three packages (20 bundles per package) of cigarettes. If bought by the package, the cost per bundle is Rs. 13.55 ($1.34); therefore one package (20 bundles) costs Rs. 271 ($26.83), and three packages cost Rs. 813 ($80.50). If the cigarettes are sold by the ten-cigarette pack at Rs. 0.50 ($.05) per pack, the entire load (three packages = 60 bundles = 3,000 packs) can be sold for Rs. 1,500 ($148.55). Subtracting the original purchase price of Rs. 813 ($80.50) and transportation costs of Rs. 173 ($17.13) leaves Rs. 514 ($50.89) for each such load.

From this figure must be subtracted the costs of moving the goods from Tarangpur to their ultimate destinations in Khasan or Bhot. The exact cost varies according to the distance to the particular village, and the villages of Bhot are generally farther than those of Khasan. But if we take one of the first villages of Bhot as a hypothetical destination, the cost is Rs. 25 ($2.48) for about three days' walk, plus food at Rs. 2.50 ($.25) per day, for a total of about Rs. 33 ($3.27). To go farther into Bhot would usually involve transfer to yaks, but if we assume that the load of cigarettes is sold at this point, the total profit would be Rs. 514 ($50.89) minus Rs. 33 ($3.27), or Rs. 481 ($47.62) per manload. A man with 30 such similarly profitable loads could clear Rs. 14,430 ($1,428.71) in the commodities business alone.

The amount of money that can be saved if porters are replaced with horses can also be calculated. Only in the last four years have horses been used to carry loads, but the number of people who elect to utilize their horses in this way will probably increase, since the savings are considerable. A horseman's fee for the trip from the Terai to Tarangpur is Rs. 160 ($15.84) plus food, Rs. 40 ($3.96)—more than a porter's wages, but a trader needs only one or two horsemen (i.e., someone employed to help load, unload, feed, and generally look after horses) to manage a herd of ten or twenty horses. Horses are able to forage on the grass along the way and at grazing areas where they spend the night; even after allowing for the six manas (pints) of grain a loaded horse must be fed per day, the savings are considerable, so a trader with a number of loads to move can dramatically cut costs by using horses. One of the traders with thirty loads brought back twelve loads by horses, twelve by porters, and six by mules. He estimates that in that year alone he saved about Rs. 2,000 ($198.02) by using horses. Using rented mules saved him some more, since although the charge per mule was the same as the charge per porter (Rs. 120, or $11.88), the mule's food is included, unlike the porter's, and each mule carries more than a man does.

NORTH FROM TARANGPUR

When the goods have been transported to Tarangpur by mid- or late spring they remain there until the plowing has been done. Plowing is begun in March, but since barley and sweet buckwheat are double-cropped on the same field, more plowing has to be done as late as July. By late July and August there is nothing to be done in the fields but weeding, so those traders with goods to sell leave on the second leg of their annual northward march from the Terai: from Tarangpur to Khasan or Bhot, or both.

In the research period, thirteen traders made trips to Bhot to market the commodities they had bought. For the most part, the items designed for sale in Bhot were bought in Kalimpong. This is true of Tibetan clothes and Tibetan tea, but a few commodities not specifically Tibetan, such as cigarettes and snuff, were bought in the Terai. To move goods on up to the villages of Bhot becomes expensive as porter and yak fees add up, so only those with several loads go to the most remote villages.

It is much closer to the villages of Khasan. To reach villages a day and a half away costs Rs. 8–10 ($0.79–$0.99) per load, plus food. The number of government personnel in Dolpo is increasing, especially in the offices of the district capital one day's walk down river, and even in Tarangpur itself, where a police border checkpost with a complement of officers and constables totaling 21 men (about half of whom are on duty at any given time) was established a few months prior to the research year. Therefore many of the Tarangpur traders buy goods—such as biscuits, sugar, and cigarettes and matches—with this emergent clientele in mind.

The goods that are sold in Bhot are often bartered against the sheep, goats, or wool which the Tarangpurian wants to take south again in the next season. Otherwise transactions are made in cash, but even when they are bartered, the prices are determined first in rupees and then converted to the goods which the Bhotia wants to barter. In Khasan, however, goods are usually sold directly for cash. Their cash comes from purchases of horses, sheep and goats, and particularly barley seed, which Tarangpurians buy annually since they do not grow enough barley to be able to use it to brew beer and still save enough seed for the next crop. Barley is much more common in Khasan, so it can be bought cheaply there. The Khasan people then spend the cash to buy cloth and other goods from the south.

COMMODITIES AND CHOICE

Most traders must decide whether to opt for Bhot or Khasan as a major selling area (those households with sufficient personnel may choose both), and this choice partially determines the range of goods they buy in the Terai or India. But even after this decision is made there are many different combinations of goods possible and several different strategies open. Table 22 shows the variety of manufactured goods that Tarangpur traders bought and sold during one trading season.

The most popular items are cigarettes (eighteen traders), cloth (fourteen traders), and Tibetan tea (nine traders). These are all traditional items, and someone just beginning to trade, or someone

TABLE 22
COMMODITY STRATEGIES AMONG TRADERS

Commodities	No. of Traders
Cigarettes only	7
Cigarettes and cloth	5
Cigarettes and dye	1
Cigarettes, dye, and Tibetan tea	1
Cloth and Tibetan tea	2
Cloth	2
Cloth and shoes	1
Cloth, biscuits, and sugar	1
Tibetan tea	4
Tibetan coats	1
Cigarettes, cloth, sugar, soap, batteries, candy, and biscuits	1
Cigarettes, sugar, batteries, candy, Tibetan boots, and Tibetan coats	1
Cigarettes, cloth, soap, Tibetan tea, Tibetan boots, and *bidi* (small cigarettes)	1
Cigarettes, sugar, batteries, candy, biscuits, soap, tennis shoes, *bidi*, cloth, and Tibetan tea	1
Cigarettes and sugar	1
Total	30

with little capital or expertise, will tend to buy these relatively safe articles. Generally, those with the largest volume of total goods tend to have the most diversified inventories. Not only differential profit margins but also different degrees of durability influence the choice of which goods to trade. Cigarettes are always popular and in demand, but they are also highly perishable, subject to ruin from dampness and to being crushed if not properly packed. None of these potential disadvantages occurs with cloth, but since people can use cloth left over from last year if necessary, the demand for it is not quite as dependable over the short run. Everyone can prolong the life of the clothing on their backs for a little while, but there is no substitute for consumed cigarettes (apart from local pipes, which are considered less elegant) except for new cigarettes, and the cancer scare has yet to reach this corner of the Himalayas.

COMPARISONS WITH THAKALIS AND OTHERS

Detailing all the multifarious transactions that these Tarangpur traders engage in each year should not make us forget how atypical they are for most of this part of Nepal, including several of the other villages of Tichurong. There are traders—a few of them very wealthy—in the nearby villages, but there are proportionally more in Tarangpur than elsewhere in Tichurong. Although Tarangpur is undoubtedly an out-of-the-way spot from our point of view, its inhabitants regard it as the center of all that is sophisticated and modern, as far as these things go in Tichurong, and consider villages three hours' walk away as isolated, hopelessly rustic, and very nearly without redeeming social value. The reasons for Tarangpur's commercial dominance lie partly in its physical location, astride the shortest route, just below the Jangla passes, from Bhot to the Terai. Tarangpurians are able to capitalize on their geographic opportunity because of their linguistic ability, but beyond that, it is their ability to operate as cultural chameleons that allows them to dominate the north–south trade of both exchange circuits.

Beyond these linguistic and cultural factors is the shrewdness and nerve required to engage in as risk-laden and uncertain an activity as transhumant trading. It is said, perhaps patronizingly, that one reason the Khasanis do not trade much is that they just do not know how to go about it. Tarangpurians often trade adult horses for poorer ones—that is, for younger horses plus some cash to make up the difference. Then they are able to sell that horse, when it matures, for a larger profit. But about sixteen years ago some Khasanis traded young horses for older ones in the south and were stuck with old horses, which progressively decreased in value. Since that experience, most Khasanis have not tried their luck much at trading, or so the story goes. Tarangpurians are also at an advantage as buyers, in that they can rely on competition between Jumla and Tichurong traders to keep prices reasonable.

While the Tarangpurians are quite exceptional in their area, there are other groups in other parts of Nepal who perform similar goods-shuttling functions, sometimes in more economically sophisticated ways than the Tarangpurians. The Sherpas in northeast Nepal are one example; another is the Thakalis just to the east of Dhaulagiri, in the Kali Gandaki Valley, who engage in similar transaction circuits, and do it more prosperously (or at least did so prior to Chinese curtailment of border trade). The Thakalis appear to have been involved in long-distance trade for a longer time than the Tarangpurians, and this is undoubtedly a factor underlying other reasons which Tarangpurians give to account for the different success the two groups enjoy.

One of these reasons is tied directly to ecological constraints: because of the high passes which must be traversed, Tarangpurians can go south only once a year. The Thakalis can go up and down the Kali Gandaki valley as often as they wish to or find necessary. Second, the Thakali women organize and manage *bhaṭṭis* (cheap "hotels" where travelers can stay and buy prepared meals), which bring in supplementary income most of the year, while their husbands may be trading elsewhere. Tarangpur women engage in almost no commercial pursuits and have developed no business skills, and Tarangpur men worry that their women would be regarded as prostitutes if they ran bhattis as the Thakali women do. Third, Thakalis maintain a businesslike attitude toward everyone, including relatives, whereas Tarangpurians would feel obligated to provide their relatives with free food in a bhatti. One Tarangpurian opened a "hotel" in the district capital one day's walk down river, but he gave away so much food to friends and relatives that he had to close it. A fourth reason lies in the fact that the Thakalis must live by their wits if they are to live at all. There is virtually no agricultural base undergirding the Thakali trade system, as there is in Tarangpur, so trading has been elevated to a high art—the only one available.

Finally, Tarangpurians regard the widespread practice of giving credit as a brake on their economic activity. As presently constituted, credit seems to be essential to the system, but when debts are collected with difficulty—or not collected at all—realizing the full profits of sales becomes an impossibility. According to Tarangpurians, this extensive use of credit apparently does not characterize Thakali transactions. An adventuresome Thakali woman came to the district capital recently to open a "hotel" but felt obliged in the area to extend credit by accepting IOUs, most of which were never honored. In the end, she left with nothing. Thus the reasons for the flourishing trade opportunities that Tarangpurians have availed themselves of must be set against the ecological and cultural constraints which have kept their trading activity at levels lower than those achieved in other parts of Nepal.

THE TWO CIRCUITS COMPARED

Choice is involved not only in the selection of which items to take south and which manufactured goods to bring north but also in the determination of which major exchange circuit to pursue, and the consequences of this decision are considerably different. The second commodities cycle of exchange has gradually evolved over the last forty years in such a way that it is essentially independent of the first. The grain-salt-rice exchange continues in attenuated form but parallel with, rather than overlapping, the burgeoning new cycle. In fact, for any given management unit (i.e., the nuclear household), these two transaction circuits represent mutually exclusive choices. They involve different kinds of goods, transported to different directions by different means, but at the same time. In each case an adult male must be in charge of the expedition (given the male/female division of labor), and in a nuclear family there is usually only one such male. Occasionally there are more than one, as when two grown brothers have not married, but this is generally a temporary situation, and long-range trading strategies cannot assume it to be stable. So diversification is impossible between the two circuits; they must be selected, not straddled. A choice has to be made: one or the other. The first cycle—a well-known, reliable exchange between a very limited number of goods—offers reasonable security and avoids entanglement in unreliable credit risks. It is not a cycle without pitfalls, but they are so well known that they can be anticipated and discounted.

Unlike the first cycle, the second cycle involves nothing that is necessary to sustain life: the commodities are simply items which contribute to a life-style (cotton clothes instead of traditional woolen, for example) which Tarangpurians want to emulate. The most economical way to acquire those commodities is to avoid a middleman and buy the goods at or close to their source in the Terai or in India. To do this successfully, given the requirements of impression management discussed in chapter 4, presupposes having (or at least pretending to have) the life-style they are trying so hard to emulate.

All this seasonal movement means that a good part of the year is spent outside the village, regardless of which circuit is pursued. In the case of several traders, well over half the year is spent outside the valley of Tichurong. This means that over half the year is spent practising impression management of the kind described earlier. All this time attempting to pass as someone else is not without its effects on the individual actors involved, nor, ultimately, on the society and culture of Tarangpur.

The most obvious effect is the psychological uncertainty characteristic of any "passing" behavior. One can never be sure that the façade will hold; the mask might slip, and then all will be found out. This psychological uncertainty manifests itself as cultural uncertainty in the clearly unflattering perceptions Tarangpurians have of their own culture. A conspicuous case in point concerns language. Kaike-speakers generally hold their language in low regard because it is felt to be unsophisticated and unexpressive. No songs with Kaike words exist (one villager had even made a concerted effort to compose Kaike songs, but to no avail), although singing Tibetan and Nepali songs is a most popular form of entertainment. Kaike numbers go up to 20 only, and villagers were convinced Kaike has no proverbs, although I ultimately recorded about fifteen that were spontaneously uttered in the course of conversations.

This cultural uncertainty is also reflected in the villagers' reluctance to talk about their way of life in conversation with outsiders. For example, Jest (1971) was told, and apparently believed, that marriage by capture is a relic of the past and that since 1950 the bride arrives at her husband's house in a palequin, in classic Hindu style. But every marriage that I observed or even heard about was by capture. In the same vein, toward the end of my stay in the village I asked how many days of mourning were observed at the death of a close relative. The answer was "thirteen days," but then my informant added, "Well, we should mourn for thirteen days, but we don't really; that's just what we normally tell people because that's what proper Hindus do. But you've been here so long now I guess there's no point in trying to keep on fooling you."

While the impression management demands for the two circuits are similar, there are also differences between them. First, the second circuit takes the Tarangpur trader not just to the world of Hinduism but to modern competitive markets. Salt and rice are exchanged within the traditional, interregional symbiotic area, in which exchanges are made at well-established rates that change only glacially. But in the entrepôts of the Terai and of India, exchanges are clearly part and parcel of the competitive market matrix. Goods are sold at as high a price as possible and remuneration is immediate, and always in hard cash. What differentiates the second circuit from the first, then, is the social stage of the urbanized, market world of lowland South Asia. It is here, at the southern extreme of the circuit, that reciprocity of an entirely different character exists; the villagers are brought into the impersonal, instrumental matrices that characterize the modern world.

Second, the salt circuit does offer reasonable security and a well-known, reliable exchange among a very limited number of goods, but the exchanges are not cumulative. They may continue and endure indefinitely, but the annual payoff is always the same: a pile of rice, which ultimately can only rot or be consumed, whether by rodents, Tarangpurians, or the occasional wealthy Bhotia to whom rice is sometimes sold.

The commodities circuit starts with the same basic material and temporal resources but uses them differently and applies them to different ends—namely, the accumulation of wealth that can be stored or utilized in different ways. The fact that most Tarangpurians opt for this second cycle is significant: the kinds of transactions they choose to engage in indicate value preferences. As the animals/wool-cash-commodities circuit increasingly dominates the commercial sector of the economy, and as wealth accumulates, it becomes possible to show how different economic choices result in different kinds of wants. Thus economic decisions are double-barreled: they both satisfy wants and help formulate them. It is not rice or sheep or cloth per se that is valued. Nor, despite the investment of time, is it trading itself which is the prime value; rather, it is what can be done with the rewards of trading. The rewards are both financial and cultural, and the uses to which these rewards are put are intelligible only within the context of the inner workings of the local Tarangpur system, which is the subject of the next two chapters.

6

Control and Uses of Wealth:
The Traditional Context

ista nahune mānche kāno
dhan nahune mānche sāno
    —Nepali proverb

A man without friends is blind in one eye;
a man without wealth is small.

THE LUST FOR WEALTH

For a variety of mutually compatible reasons, Tarangpurians do seek to raise their economic level as far above what they define as subsistence as possible, and the attempt to increase one's wealth is a very high-priority activity. This lust for wealth is not immediately apparent, because most of the observable manifestations which differences in wealth might reflect do not vary from person to person or from house to house. House exteriors and interiors, for example, are uniform. The cementless, mud-stuccoed, thick stone walls and beam-supported earth roofs do deteriorate and have to be rebuilt every sixty or eighty years; hence at any given time some houses are brand new and some are in a state of collapse, but they do not necessarily belong to wealthy and poor families, respectively. Similarly, the interiors, partitioned into separate rooms by wattle and daub walls, need repair from time to time, but the basic design, with an open-on-all-sides cooking fire in the main room, opposite rough wooden shelves built into the wall, is the same in all houses.

Clothing too is fairly uniform; women wear long, barrel-width cotton skirts drawn tight around the waist under a wide cotton sash wound several times around the midriff; a long-sleeved tunic-style velveteen blouse is worn on top. Men wear a long-skirted

cotton tunic-blouse over cotton pants voluminous in the seat
(drawn tight with a drawstring around the waist) and almost
skintight over the calves. There is some variation in color and
pattern, but the same range of variation applies to everyone, rich
or poor. Since even the wealthy families must work their fields,
clothes for normal daily wear are frequently in a tattered state,
and this applies across the board to everyone, regardless of
economic levels.

The same kind of uniformity applies also to food; wealthy
people eat basically the same diet as poor people. They can afford
better food, and may eat more meat, but villagers have a saying
that rich people always eat food made from coarse flour (i.e., with
some chaff) while poor people eat bread made from finer-textured
flour. In other words, the rich are willing to economize on food
while the poor carefully separate out all the chaff, even if the
volume of flour is thereby reduced. Thus it is clear that conspicuous
consumption does not motivate Tarangpurians to strive for ever
greater amounts of wealth. Tarangpurians do not use wealth to
transform life-styles in ways which economists or development
planners would describe as "raising the standard of living."

Despite all this uniformity of life-style, Tarangpurians do try to
amass wealth whenever they can, and some do so much more
successfully than others; as chapter 7 will demonstrate, considerable differences in wealth do exist. Although these differences are
not visible in daily expenditure patterns in a vivid way, they do
result in different kinds of spending on special occasions, such as
life-cycle rituals. For example, a rich man will spend more for the
celebration of his first son's first haircut than will a poor man. He
will serve rice instead of chinu millet, and his supply of distilled
liquor will outlast the capacity of his guests to absorb it. Such an
occasion will be a burden for a poor man, even if he substitutes
chinu millet for rice, beer for liquor, and so on. He may have to
borrow to get through such responsibilities at all (although monetary gifts to the son usually balance expenditures for the feast).
Thus wealth is desired not to provide a better standard of living
for oneself but for others. Wealth is sought not so that a man can
eat better, but so that he may feed others better. This desire to
provide high-grade hospitality, which is not peculiar to the Magars
of Tarangpur but which also characterizes many other com-

munities in the Himalayas, is one reason for converting so much time and so many resources into forms that can be stored more or less indefinitely and then dispensed. It is not the only reason, however.

Trading is very closely associated with masculinity. To be a good trader is a mark and verification of manhood; it is a sign of male prowess to end up on the long end of a transaction. Thus most men are constantly on the lookout for a profitable trade, a sale that will bring in some rupees which can then be used to finance further deals. A poor man will accompany a richer friend on a trading trip, ostensibly for companionship, but always with the hope of using his wages to turn a profitable series of transactions himself. Most men would like to be successful traders, not only because it is a sign of male prowess but also because it is a mark of intelligence. Understanding the world well enough to manipulate it is one way intelligence is gauged, and successful trading is one way this ability can be demonstrated. Thus one's transactions in the trading cycles do take on some of the aura of a competitive game. The competition is too traditional and too deeply embedded in social relations to be cutthroat, but one still wants to make a comfortable profit. To make a profit consistently establishes one as shrewd, and shrewdness is one component— neither necessary nor sufficient, but still important—of what is most highly treasured: respect.

DEVICES FOR STORING WEALTH

For the most part wealth differences are not obvious, but there are indicators that mark plateaus. Tarangpur women are famous far beyond the domains of Tichurong for the size of the gold earrings they wear on special occasions. Many hill women throughout Nepal store wealth in the form of thin but solid gold earring disks two or three inches in diameter, but the women of Tarangpur and neighboring villages wear earrings about five inches in diameter—large enough to touch their shoulders. Forty years ago Tarangpur women wore three-inch earrings, but as the commodities trading cycle became established, the increased earnings were invested in part in larger earrings. Over the generations the size has increased to its present state. Limitations imposed by human anatomy make still larger earrings an impossibility, but until recently this was an item of jewelry with "planned obsolescence" built into it. As the size increased, it became socially impossible to wear any size smaller than the largest size made. At present a woman would be too embarrassed to wear an old pair of smaller earrings, but would wait until more gold could be purchased so that the small earrings could be melted into a larger size. In the meantime, she would not wear any at all.

Thirty-seven households, almost half the village, are wealthy enough to own the large-size earrings. Many of the remaining families own smaller earrings, which are kept in storage until enough additional gold can be bought to convert them to the present fashionable size. At current gold prices even a small pair of solid gold earrings represents considerable wealth. In Calcutta gold costs Rs. 285 ($28.22) per *tolā*, which is about half an ounce. A big earring of the kind Tarangpurians wear weighs about 10 tola, which represents an investment of Rs. 2,850 ($282.18), a not inconsiderable sum in Tichurong. At least two households own three pairs each. Men complain that their wives demand big earrings and insist that extra money be spent on gold before investment in any other kind of enterprise.

Wealth is stored in other kinds of jewelry as well. Most women own necklaces strung with turquoise and coral. Depending on the size, quality, and number of stones, such necklaces are worth from Rs. 400 ($39.60) to Rs. 1,800 ($178.22). An average necklace is worth about Rs. 1,000 ($99.09). A few of the wealthiest women own square gold lockets worth Rs. 1,000 ($99.09) each, and a few own another kind of gold piece worn on a necklace and valued at Rs. 2,800 ($277.23). All women own a pair of silver bracelets worth about Rs. 300 ($29.70) per pair, and most women own silver earlobe plugs, which are worn daily in some cases; these are worth about Rs. 100 ($9.90). Finally, most households own a single large piece of turquoise worth from Rs. 1,000 ($99.09) to Rs. 3,000 ($297.03).

Although a family will first of all hoard savings in the form of jewelry that can be displayed publicly on certain occasions, a family which has acquired as much jewelry as it can reasonably display at one time must find other ways of storing wealth. One method is to buy copper jugs, brass plates, and other such kitchen vessels. These are then hidden away in back rooms of houses where they cannot be seen. A rich man cannot expect to keep the existence of his wealth a secret, but the particular details are not a matter of public knowledge. Fear of thieves or government taxes make silence the most prudent policy. Another way of storing wealth is to keep silver rupee coins, minted many years ago, in the metal vessels. Each silver rupee is worth Rs. 6 in today's paper currency, and it is estimated that at least five houses hold more than Rs. 1,000 in such coin, equivalent to Rs. 6,000 ($594.06) if converted into modern paper money. It is illegal to hoard these old coins, and this adds to the normal reticence about discussing such matters.

CONTROL OF WEALTH AND INHERITANCE

The Tarangpur/Thakali comparison in chapter 5 makes it clear that Tarangpur traders are considerably less cutthroat than other northern border traders, and the intense emphasis on village solidarity and the equality of its citizens (described in chap. 7) helps explain why. But agonistic striving after wealth nevertheless does characterize much Tarangpur economic activity, particularly outside the village, where it is a sign of savvy to come out at the high end of a transaction. Even within the village population, some traders strain to get the upper hand over fellow villagers when they compete in the same markets outside of Tarangpur. For example, the two wealthiest traders, who were on good terms and had even betrothed their children to each other, competed for some of the same customers in Bhot; each tried to gain an advantage by starting his trading trip earlier than the other one.

The existence of these two wealthy men, with their many horse and porter loads of goods each year (see chap. 7, table 30), demonstrates that some strive for wealth with considerably more success than others. Economic strategies differ from house to house, and those with more resources at their disposal deploy them differently from those who barely manage to scrape together a living without receiving charity. Those at the top of the financial pile have more to lose, but it is also easier for them to gain, and wide wealth differences endure. According to my calculations the wealthiest family is worth more than Rs. 100,000 ($9,900.99) in total assets, and the poorest (excluding those immigrants utterly without land or houses) is worth only Rs. 2,000 ($198.02). Thus a factor of 50 separates rags from riches—about the same gap that divides the largest landholder from the smallest (see chap. 3, figs. 3 and 4).

No one's financial position is frozen, and in an economy as diversified as Tarangpur's, the fortunes of particular families do rise and fall over time. For example, three families of moderate means are descendants of a man who was very wealthy, but simply through division of property by inheritance the present descendants have fallen to their present state—still well-to-do, but no longer at the top of the financial pyramid. This illustrates the more general point that wealth assessments are not so much measurements of individuals as of estates. Wealth is owned by families, and although senior family members make decisions regarding the deployment of resources, all family members are regarded as having certain inalienable rights to the family property. Thus family membership determines wealth levels for individuals; a man is as wealthy as the entire estate in which he has a claim. If the estate is divided, his net worth declines proportionately, and often drastically.

Thus the nuclear family is the basic group in control of economic assets. It makes day-to-day decisions concerning the allocation of time and resources and controls the wealth it owns. Within the family the most senior member generally has final say over big decisions; the senior member is the custodian of the property, and no sale of land, for instance, could take place without his or her consent.

Most property is passed from older to younger generations through the male line. Sons inherit the bulk of the land, and if sons marry they establish separate homes and divide the property evenly among themselves. The youngest son generally receives the family house as his own, but if an older son must then build a new house for himself, the younger son must contribute an equal share of the building expenses.

Land is divided piece by piece; that is, each field is split into two equal sections (or as many sections as there are brothers). A mutual friend then takes two stones or pieces of wood, each contributed by one of the brothers but without the friend knowing which is which, and throws one stick or stone on one half of the field and the other on the other half. Whichever brother chose the stone or piece of wood that lands in a given half is then the owner of that half. If there is no natural object already dividing the fields, a large stone is planted between them as a permanent boundary marker.

Daughters do not inherit land in this way unless there are no sons, in which case all the land passes to them. Daughters do own land, but they receive it as dowry rather than through inheritance at the division of an estate. At marriage a bride is given a small amount of land—perhaps half a hul or one hul (14 to 28 percent of an acre)—as dowry. The poorer her family, the less land she gets, but she must get a token amount. This land is hers, and if a marriage is dissolved, she retains ownership of the land when she leaves her husband's house.

Normally, a newly married couple will live in the husband's house and farm his fields. If there are no sons to inherit the house and fields, a daughter may inherit them and continue to live in her house with her husband and children. When the son-in-law comes to live in his wife's house, her family property passes to her, and although he may be regarded as the head of the house, he could not sell the fields she inherits without her express consent. A son-in-law who lives with his wife's family loses inheritance rights in the estate of his own natal family. For inheritance purposes he is treated like a daughter and receives only a nominal amount of land. He does not share equally with his other brothers.

For most practical purposes the daily life of a family in which the son-in-law lives with his wife's family is not very different from the normal patrilocal family. But aside from the limitations on rights to alienate land, there are other ways in which such a husband is not quite master of his own house, as he would be living in his own home and farming fields inherited in his own right. Such a man cannot bring a second wife to his house, even if his first wife has died and he has children to care for. If he wants to remarry he must leave and return to his own home, if possible, or establish a new house. A man in this position has little choice but to stay in his wife's house or marry another woman with her own house and fields.

A woman who leaves her husband's home has a similar problem, but her choices are more attractive. She can live with one of her brothers, in which case she need not worry about owning her own property, or she can marry another man with property of his own. If her husband dies she must leave his house to remarry, but in a patrilocal, patrilineal society, she has more places to go than would her husband surviving her in her own house.

These rules governing the flow of property apply to legitimate children—that is, to children born of a man and woman openly living together, whether they have celebrated a marriage feast or not. Usually informal obligations exist toward illegitimate children too. If the paternity of illegitimate children is unquestioned, some property will be left to them, although not necessarily a share equivalent to that received by legitimate children.

In addition to rules governing the flow of property over time in usually patrilineal channels, other aspects of the control of wealth concern the gradations of rights in property.

OWNERSHIP

Ownership of property, particularly of land, is of course not absolute. Ownership of land consists only of certain rights in land, and these rights differ according to the way the land was acquired. Land that has been inherited from one's parents or bought from someone is owned in the fullest and most exclusive sense. It must pass to a man's heirs when he dies, but while he lives he may use it as he pleases and may sell it to anyone for any price. His rights to agricultural products and to disposal of the land do not include exclusive rights over nuts from walnut trees (if any), nor do they include rights against trespass. A network of trails laces the hillside so that each field can be reached by whoever needs to cultivate it. If a much-used trail cuts across a man's fields there is not much he can do about it. He cannot order others off his land if an established trail leads across it.

Most agricultural land is owned in this way, but occasionally a household will cultivate land it may not sell. In one such Tarangpur case, a man married a woman without brothers. She then eloped with another man. The divorce settlement was hotly contested, but the final verdict was that the first husband be awarded half the lands of his former wife. These lands are his to cultivate but not to alienate. If he has heirs, the land becomes theirs entirely, in the same way that land is usually owned. But he may not sell the land to someone else, and should he die without heirs the land would revert to his ex-wife or her heirs, to be theirs to the same extent that it was originally.

Agricultural land is owned by households, and most economically valuable land is of this type. But some land is communally owned, and it is available to all villagers. Such land includes forests and grazing pastures. Tarangpur's forests and wasteland pastures extend from a stream separating a neighboring village's lands from Tarangpur's domain on one side, to a shrine at the top of a hill separating the lands of another adjacent village on the other. Above the village usable land fades into the Jangla pass itself. Below the village the Bheri River marks the boundary between lands that belong to villages on the left bank from those that belong to villages on the right bank. To graze sheep or goats across the river, except while in transit, would require a payment to the villages there.

Occasionally land that can be used by anyone is divided up among whatever households exist at the time of division. Thus three years before my period of residence a series of terraced fields which had obviously once been cultivated but which are now barren were divided for private use. They had lain fallow for so long that no one could remember to whom they belonged. The fields were divided into three large sections, each under the charge of one man. Then the villagers allied themselves with one of the three, according to their preference (the three groups were roughly the same size) and subdivided each section into a plot for each household. At the time I left the village, all these fields remained fallow; no one had yet broken ground in his new plot.

Within the village there are areas, such as paths and land areas between and next to houses, which are not privately owned, and these are considered open to use by the entire community or by people passing through. These areas include the large pounding stones, shaped somewhat like an oversized mortar, in which villagers beat the chaff from the chinu millet by means of a long wooden pole with smooth, rounded ends.

Although most agriculturally productive land is owned by discrete households, sometimes fields or gardens are owned collectively. Gardens are located among the odd bits and pieces of land between and next to houses, so they are often quite small. When such a garden plot is divided through inheritance, the parcel of land per household becomes even smaller. If such a garden has been inherited but not subdivided, the rights to equal shares are usually waived because of the small crop involved and the close kinship bonds which tie the parties together. In such cases, if one person needs the crop more than the others equally entitled to it, they just let him have it. But all these arrangements depend on the generosity and disposition of the parties involved. One such example is diagrammed in figure 5.

In this case, a garden plot behind the house of family E has been subdivided into two sections: one is owned by families A and B, and the second is owned by families A, B, C, and D. The section

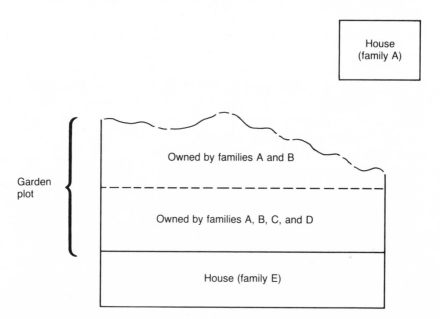

Figure 5. Diagram of Jointly Owned Land

owned jointly by four families has not been subdivided into four discrete sections; instead, family B cultivates the entire section and receives the entire crop. Similarly, family B cultivates the entire section owned by families A and B (but not subdivided) and again is allowed to keep the entire crop, thus farming the entire garden plot even though three other families own shares of it. All the families are very distantly related and are on good terms. None of the families is wealthy, but family B is poorer than the others and hence is given everything produced on the plot.

Generally, if a man cultivates someone else's field they split the crop evenly. This form of sharecropping rarely exists on regular village fields, but it is sometimes practiced if a family has fields in another village—acquired, for example, as dowry when a girl leaves her natal village. In such cases the amount of land is too small to justify the time and trouble to travel back and forth cultivating it—hence the sharecropping arrangement, which works to the convenience and benefit of both parties.

FUNDS OF RENT

We have seen that the basic economic unit—both of ownership and of decision making—is the domestic nuclear household, and that each household follows a strategy (trading and agricultural) based on the number of people and resources available to it. These strategies account for and perpetuate wealth differences. But in addition to expenditures for subsistence and trade, there is an additional series of expenditures, required to maintain membership in good standing in the social system, which cuts into household budgets at irregular or infrequent intervals. These expenditures also maintain wealth differences in some cases, but to the extent that they take a greater percentage of the wealth of the more well-to-do families, they also act as leveling mechanisms. Following Wolf (1966), I include these expenditures under the general rubrics of ceremonial fund and funds of rent.

What Wolf calls "funds of rent" are virtually nonexistent in Tarangpur. The land taxes average about $0.07 per person annually (the exact amounts differ from household to household according to what land has been inherited from a land settlement

which somehow assessed land values in the distant past).[1] Occasionally a field will be cultivated by someone other than the owner,
who then receives half the crop, but this variety of usufruct is
exercised only in the odd piece of land far removed from the
village (as in the dowry of a wife from another village), and the
rationale is one of convenience only. Large-scale absentee land
ownership is not a characteristic of Tichurong agriculture.

Wolf (1966) takes the fund of rent to be the critical distinguishing mark of the peasant, as opposed to the primitive cultivator.
For Tarangpurians, the extensive economic relations with towns
and markets seem much more significant for the changes taking
place within Tarangpur than the minuscule funds of rent would
suggest. So although Tarangpurians may not be strong candidates
for peasants in Wolf's sense, they are in Redfield's (1953), and it
is these peasant-town relations which make social and cultural
change in Tarangpur intelligible.

THE CEREMONIAL FUND

The first substantial drain on the ceremonial fund begins at birth.
At the birth of a first child, the maternal grandmother gives her
daughter a large amount of food. If the grandmother is no longer
living, some other female relative—such as a mother's brother's
wife—must give it. The mother's conjugal household is obliged to
give the mother several chickens—usually about fifteen—to help
her regain her strength and vigor. On the other side of the ledger,
after the birth of her first child, the new mother gives her own
mother a set of new clothes. These birth-related expenditures and
their monetary equivalents are summarized in table 23.

All these expenditures except the last apply to the firstborn only.
For subsequent children, only the chickens from her own house
are required. Since most families do not own so many chickens at
one time, the family of a woman who has just given birth must
buy or, much more commonly, borrow the necessary chickens.

Finally, the household of the newborn must engage the services
of a lama to read from classical Tibetan texts and perform a rite
in which the infant receives a name. The expenses for such services
include a meal and a few manas (pints) of grain, plus nominal

TABLE 23
TYPICAL BIRTH-RELATED EXPENDITURES

Female relations and expenditures	Rs.	$
From the maternal grandmother to the mother		
5 chickens	40	3.96
20 manas (pints) chinu millet	10	.99
20 manas (pints) beer	10	.99
20 manas (pints) wheat flour	40	3.96
1 dharni (ca. 5 lbs) oil	15	1.49
Total	115	11.39
From the mother to the grandmother		
1 blouse	10.00	.99
1 skirt	5.50	.55
1 cotton shawl	15.00	1.49
Total	30.50	3.02
From mother's conjugal house-hold to mother		
15 chickens	120	11.88

amounts of beer and flour, from which the dough figures for the rite are made. In sum, the costs to a family incurred by a birth are largely canceled out in the case of a first birth by gifts of food from the maternal grandmother.

The next life-cycle stage at which large amounts of money change hands is the first haircut, at the age of seven, of the first male child born to a woman. The haircut ceremony must be performed for the first male child of any woman, so if a man marries more than once, the ceremony must be performed for the first male child of each of his wives. The haircut always takes place before the full moon in the Nepalese calendar month of Baisakh (mid-April to mid-May); the exact date is determined by consulting a lama or shaman or some high-caste Hindu from Khasan. Such consultations are only necessary because Tarangpurians schedule this event by the Hindu (*Bikram Sambat*) calendar and have no way of their own to determine when a full moon will appear. The high-caste Hindus do not attend the ceremony or influence it in any other way.

On such occasions the Tailor family in Tarangpur provides drumming and is given a meal plus grain and, optionally, a few rupees. The main expense is the feast that must be provided for the villagers, relatives who attend from other villages, and anyone else invited to the ceremony. The amount and quality of food and drink varies with the wealth of the family, but an average feast would require the expenses listed in table 24.

The haircut ritual entails large expenditures for feasting, but most of this expense comes from reserves in kind, not from cash. If grain reserves are not sufficient, grain can be borrowed from relatives, so a large cash outflow is not required. On the contrary, the ceremony requires cash gifts to the boy by all who attend, so a family hosting a first-haircut ceremony hopes for as large an attendance as possible. Any family acquires a considerable net cash gain, since the cash gifts amount to more than the cost of the meal. The amounts given vary according to how close a relative is or how friendly a neighbor or villager may be. Table 25 illustrates the size of cash gifts to one family at a haircut ceremony in Tarangpur from friends and relatives in four nearby villages.

The contributions from the four other villages totaled Rs. 422 ($41.78). The bigger gifts were given by close relatives, and the largest gift—Rs. 80 ($7.92)—was given by the boy's mother's brother. The residents of Tarangpur who attended contributed another Rs. 832 ($82.38), bringing the funds collected to a total of Rs. 1,254 ($124.16). In this particular case, the feast was larger

TABLE 24
TYPICAL FEAST EXPENSES FOR FIRST HAIRCUT

Item	Rs.	$
1 goat or sheep	120	11.88
220 manas (pints) beer	110	10.89
105 manas (pints) rice	190	18.81
10 manas (pints) dal (lentils)	5	.50
Total	425	42.08

TABLE 25
SUM OF GIFTS TO A FAMILY FROM FOUR VILLAGES
AT HAIRCUT CEREMONY

Village	No. of households attending	Donation per household	
		Rs.	$
A	5	10	.99
		10	.99
		10	.99
		10	.99
		20	1.98
Total		60	5.94
B	6	10	.99
		20	1.98
		20	1.98
		20	1.98
		22	2.18
		35	3.47
Total		127	12.57
C	3	10	.99
		20	1.98
		50	4.95
Total		80	7.92
D	3	25	2.48
		50	4.95
		80	7.92
Total		155	13.35
Total 4	17	1,254	124.16

than normal, but comparing the cost of the feast (Rs. 425 or $42.08; see table 24) with the value of the presents received (Rs. 1,254 or $124.16; see table 25) reveals that income is almost three times greater than expenditure. These "unsolicited" gifts are all recorded, so that if invitations are reciprocated there will be no doubt about what constitutes a matching return amount.

Another category of contributions comes from those families who were "returning" contributions which the father of the boy had previously made at the haircut ceremonies of other firstborn sons. This type of gift accounted for more than Rs. 900 ($89.11), so the grand total of all gifts received at the first haircut was about Rs. 2,200 ($217.82) in this case. Those gifts which are in response to a prior gift are not recorded, unless the amount given is greater than that originally received, in which case only the amount above and beyond the original gift is written down. If the ledger is balanced on both sides there is no need for written records as reference, since no repayment is in order: the debts are canceled, and future gifts would be given on the basis of a clean slate.

After the haircut ceremony, the next big rite of passage is marriage. Marriage is exclusively by capture (whether authentic or, as is much more common, as arranged in advance by the two conniving parties). The captured spouse's family is required to object vociferously, even if they have planned the capture themselves. When they finally consent to let the capturing party hold a feast, the marriage is socially recognized as legitimate, and the feast itself is the event which, more than anything else, pronounces a couple man and wife.

Since marriage guests do not make cash donations, there is no effort to invite as many people as possible, and the feast is therefore not quite as large as that for a first haircut. Nevertheless, representatives of many of the village households do attend, as do relatives from other villages. Initially, each household (except any with whom there is a serious quarrel) is invited. This first invitation is regarded as a formality, and no one accepts it. Then second and third invitations are extended to close relatives, friends, and neighbors—all those whom one really wants to attend—and they then accept. Except for unusually close relatives or friends, only one member of each invited household attends. Food for a typical marriage feast would consist of the items appearing in table 26.

In addition to the cost of the feast, the groom must bear two other expenses: presentation of a set of new clothes (worth about Rs. 100 or $9.90) to his bride at the time of the marriage, and preparation of fried rice cakes and beer for the bride's family a

TABLE 26
TYPICAL EXPENSES FOR MARRIAGE FEAST

Item	Rs.	$
1 goat	120	11.88
200 manas (pints) beer	100	9.90
95 manas (pints) rice	172	17.03
7.5 manas (pints) dal	4	.40
Total	396	39.21

few days after the wedding. The bride's family then distributes the cakes to close friends and to those households from whom bread has been received in the past. The number of pieces varies according to the number of people to receive them and the rice stores (or sometimes chinu millet reserves, for those without rice) of the groom. The number of pieces ranges between 250 and 500, which would require between 40 and 80 manas (pints) of rice. Costs associated with the rice cakes are tabulated in table 27. Thus this post-marriage food preparation costs more than half as much as the original feast, and the total of both is Rs. 641 (about $63).

The fourth and last life-cycle occurs at death. When a person dies, the bereaved family distributes fried bread made from sweet buckwheat to all the village houses, even those of any enemies. The entire crop of sweet buckwheat for a single year is required

TABLE 27
TYPICAL COST OF FRIED RICE CAKES

Item	Rs.	$
60 manas (pints) rice (average)	108	10.69
2 dharni (10–12 lbs) honey	30	2.97
3 dharni (15–18 lbs) oil	35	3.47
30 manas (pints) beer	60	5.94
roasted barley	12	1.19
Total	245	24.26

for the funeral of one person. The amount of buckwheat needed depends on the size of bread: three muris (7.2 bushels) for small bread, five or six muris (12 or 14.4 bushels) for average size bread, and eight or nine muris (19.2 or 21.6 bushels) for large pieces of bread. Calculating on the basis of average-sized pieces, the cost of this funeral bread would be about Rs. 480 (or $47.52, at Rs. 80 per muri). If no one dies during the year, some of the sweet buckwheat will be eaten and some saved. In such circumstances, from a sweet buckwheat crop of five muris (12 bushels), two muris (4.8 bushels) would be eaten and three (7.2 bushels) would be saved.

A much larger ritual expense, although it must be borne by a given household only once every thirty or forty years, is involved with the annual celebrations for the pantheon of local mountain gods. The bulk of these rituals takes place in the middle of winter and in the spring. Each year two households are selected, by rotation, to be host for the year. Their duties are to see that the *patum,* the ritual specialist for this indigenous cult, and his assistants are fed during periods of celebration. The longest such period lasts for about twenty-five consecutive days. The entire village must also be feasted, and this too is a huge burden. This annual ritual period is by far the largest financial cross Tarangpurians have to bear, and since it comes in orderly rotation, any particular household will probably have to face it only once in a given person's lifetime, and certainly not more than twice. Table 28 details the amount of food needed by each host to feast the entire village.

For the duration of the main ritual period, which continues for about twenty-five days, the patum and his assistants must be fed the finest food—that is, not chinu millet but rice, and not the usual buckwheat but the sweet buckwheat. The amount of food needed for this period is shown in table 29. All these ritual expenses together, in this hypothetical average case, amount to Rs. 1,249 ($123.66); the range is between Rs. 1,000 ($99.01) and Rs. 1,500 ($148.51), depending on the lavishness or poverty of the host. The host has a few minor additional expenses for other brief rituals during the course of the year, and during the major winter rite each household contributes a few rupees worth of beer and negligible amounts of flour as ritual ingredients.

TABLE 28

AMOUNT OF FOOD NEEDED TO FEAST THE VILLAGE

Item	Rs.	$
Feast I		
1 goat or sheep	120.00	11.88
9 chickens	72.00	7.13
330 manas (pints) buckwheat	82.50	8.17
120 manas (pints) rice	180.00	17.82
flour	18.00	1.78
0.5 mana (pints) honey	3.00	.30
ghee (clarified butter)	1.00	.10
2 manas (pints) oil	4.00	.40
4 manas (pints) wheat flour	8.00	.79
2 manas (pints) chinu and one mana (pint) rice	2.50	.25
16 manas (pints) beans	8.00	.79
4 manas (pints) salt	3.00	.30
fat	2.00	.20
Total	505.50	50.05
Feast II		
0.5 dharni (ca. 2½ lbs) ghee	25.00	2.48
1 goat	120.00	11.88
4 chickens	32.00	3.17
800 manas (pints) buckwheat	200.00	19.80
Total	377.00	37.33

Many host households would be forced to borrow some part of this large amount of food from relatives; repayment in such a case is without interest and is deferred until whenever the borrowing household can afford it.

There are a few additional religious expenditures involving occasional animal sacrifice. When anyone returns from a trading expedition, a chicken is slaughtered at the door of the animal shed. Similarly, a chicken is killed during the annual celebration of

TABLE 29
TYPICAL FOOD EXPENDITURES FOR RITUAL SPECIALIST
(PATUM) AND ASSISTANTS

Item	Rs.	$
40 manas (pints) rice	72.00	7.13
20 manas (pints) Tibetan dried cheese	40.00	3.96
40 manas (pints) barley	20.00	1.98
20 manas (pints) rice (for beer)	36.00	3.56
1 dharni (5 lbs) cooking oil	15.00	1.49
1 dharni (5 lbs) ghee	16.00	1.58
80 manas (pints) sweet buckwheat flour	120.00	11.88
20 manas (pints) wheat flour	22.50	2.23
10 manas (pints) salt	7.50	.74
30 manas (pints) chili peppers	10.00	.99
fat	8.00	.79
Total	367.00	36.34

Sāune Sankrānti and also when a new roof is being put on a house. A goat is sacrificed every year or two by those households that can afford it. All these animal sacrifices are for the purpose of purging a house (or, in the case of the returning trader, a person) of whatever malignant forces, including disease, may have accumulated. These isolated and small expenditures conclude the list of expenses incurred in the category of ceremonial funds.

These social and religious expenses are all traditional, or predictable, and hence they can be planned for by any Tarangpur family. There is always a range that characterizes these financial drains: wealthier families can spend more on large quantities of food or food of better quality, while a poor family has to scrape together just enough modest fare, borrowing from relatives to meet its obligations. Expenses for some rituals are balanced by return gifts, and in the long run of reciprocal invitations, accounts are even; no one would hesitate to get married, for example, because of the expense of a feast.

Tarangpur Magars have little sense of choice about expending wealth for these social and ceremonial purposes. To be a citizen of Tarangpur is to support and participate in these communal and life-cycle rituals, and it is in one's pragmatic self-interest to secure the protection afforded by the sacrifices. There is no way in which a villager could opt out of the ceremonial cycles and still be a member of the moral community. Participation in ritual life is a way of affirming membership in the social order. In this elemental sense, these expenses are unavoidable. They are culturally constituted ways of disposing of wealth. For all the choices Tarangpurians have in their economic life, being a member in good standing of the village is not one of them. In the most fundamental sense, just as one can never choose to be born, one cannot realistically choose to reside in the village and not pay one's social dues. All these obligations just come with the territory.

INVESTING IN MERIT

Another genre of religious expenditures includes charitable donations and the expenses of pilgrimage. Unlike the expenditures for communal and household rites just mentioned, these capital outlays do not validate one's place in the social system. Their sole purpose is to add to the store of merit of the individual who makes the expenditure. Increased merit redounds to the benefit of the person who holds it in the form of a more auspicious rebirth. Examples of charitable disbursements include donations to visiting lamas collecting funds for some purpose, such as construction of a new monastery, and donations for some public works project that will benefit the village or area as a whole, such as a new bridge. These gifts are large only in the case of wealthy families; less affluent households make only nominal contributions.

A religious pilgrimage is a relatively major undertaking. As in the case of donations to lamas or for public works, pilgrimages are made to acquire religious merit. There is normally no economic gain associated with a pilgrimage, since the main pilgrimage destination, the Buddhist temples and shrines of the Kathmandu Valley, does not lie at the end of the usual trade routes to the Terai. Consequently, a decision to go on pilgrimage is usually a decision to abandon trading for the year. In any given year there are some Tarangpurians on pilgrimage, but each individual goes rarely, in many cases only once in a lifetime, and some people, particularly poor women, never go on pilgrimage to a place as far away as Kathmandu. A round trip from Tarangpur to Kathmandu, plus a stay in Kathmandu of a week or two, costs about Rs. 400 ($39.60). This is too large a cash outlay for most families to manage frequently, especially since there is no economic return on the expenditure.

Certain years are more auspicious than others for pilgrimage, so the number of people who go to Kathmandu varies widely from year to year. Normally, persons from about four or five households become pilgrims during the winter, but during 1969–70, thirty-seven people from twenty-four Tarangpur households visited Kathmandu for religious purposes (three other households went for political reasons and one went on business). Tarangpurians follow both the official Nepalese, Hindu calendar (Bikram Sambat) and the Tibetan calendrical cycle, depending on the purpose for which time is being measured. In the Tibetan calendar, 1969–70 was the Year of the Bird, which is regarded as a particularly auspicious year for pilgrimage. Many of these thirty-seven pilgrims had never been to Kathmandu before and most will probably not return again.

There are superficial similarities between trading trips and religious pilgrimages, but they are not as important as the differences. Pilgrimages are long-distance, long-term, interregional excursions, but unlike trading trips, they are infrequent and involve no commercial or cultural transactions. Pilgrims in Kathmandu lodge near the shrines and move almost entirely in Buddhist social circles. They have very few, if any, direct dealings with Hindus; they do not even frequent modern shops. Like Americans in luxury hotels abroad, it is almost as if they had never left home; at best, it is as if they were visiting shrines in Bhot instead of the capital city of the only Hindu kingdom in the world. Thus the crucial transactional contacts that characterize the trading cycles are missing on the pilgrimage routes. Even if they were present, trading trips occur almost every year, while pilgrimages take place, for any individual, only once or twice in a lifetime, if that often. The key to the changing world of Tarangpur and its relations with the rest of the planet lies in the economic transformations it is undergoing, not in occasional religious pilgrimages.

To fully assess the impact of the commodities circuit on Tarangpur, it is necessary to discover what sets of symbols are emphasized locally which influence the ways in which Tarangpurians put their new-found wealth to work for them. We must uncover not only basic economic facts about the distribution of wealth but also how Tarangpurians view wealth differences. Only then will it be possible to understand the significance of wealth and why the wealth compounded in the commodities cycle is expended as it is. In other words, if transactions with the outside world are so critical to an understanding of the gradual transformation of Tarangpur, then transactions that take place within the village context must also be examined to see how they compare and contrast with the transaction circuits described thus far.

7

Transactions: The Village Context

nām pā   The village is the father
nām mā   the village is the mother.
    —Kaike proverb

On the one hand, Tarangpur is changing in response to the
economic opportunities that have presented themselves to this
village, which is so well situated ecologically and culturally to
capitalize on them. On the other hand, Tarangpur remains distinctive—it has not dissolved its own cultural heritage and substituted
a merely attenuated Hindu-Buddhist synthesis. Our task is thus to
sort out the distinctive symbols and structures that are relevant to
an understanding of how and why Tarangpurians invest their
increased resources and time the way they do, and then to determine what consequences for their way of life follow from these
investments. Tarangpurians' preference curves are shifting, but we
cannot look exclusively to external Hindu and Buddhist models
(as we have tended to do thus far) to discover the direction of their
movement: we must also look directly at indigenous evidence—
namely, the statements and behavior revealed in transactions that
Tarangpurians make among themselves. A close empirical look at
such evidence is required to gain insight into the dynamics of the
local system.

HIERARCHY

Marriage Classes versus Wealth

The conundrum of ethnic identity is partly linguistic, in that the
answer to questions about it depends on the language in which

they are asked. To an outsider's query about what group membership they claim, all Tarangpur residents (with the clear and obvious
exceptions of the Tailors and the odd recent Tibetan refugee)
answer that they are members of the Magar jat—at least that is
what they say if they are asked the question in Nepali. The question
makes no sense in Kaike (since most Kaike-speakers know one
another, the question would sound contrived), and not much more
in Tibetan.

But that Tarangpurians consider themselves all the same strain
of people (whether or not the term Magar is used) seems beyond
doubt. Even the handful of families descended from high-caste
Thakuri immigrants, who regularly intermarry with the other
families of Tarangpur, regard themselves as Magars. (These
Thakuris have long since given up wearing the sacred thread and,
as a further indicator of their Magarization, modify their clan
name to "Thakula," which simultaneously suggests their high-
caste origins and their present fallen status).[1] But in an essentially
single-caste village, this gross category differentiates nothing. Nor
does clan membership: clan names (e.g., Rokaya, Budha, Gharti,
Jhankri) are not status signals because anyone can claim one of
these major clan names (loosely, at least) without argument. The
Lama families, for instance, refer to themselves as Budhas[2] even
though, having arrived in the village only a few generations ago,
they could not possibly belong to the aboriginal clan of that name
said to be descended from a goddess. Clan names are tossed
around fairly casually, since everyone knows, for example, that
the Lamas are not "real" Budhas like the others. Adopting a clan
name is the first step in breaking into the local social system, and
it has been going on for a long time (see chap. 2 n. 27).

What counts in determining individual status within the village
is the location of one's position in a peculiar social hierarchy based
on two sets of independent criteria: one concerns purity and pollution;[3] the other involves the amount of power an individual
wields, measured by wealth and the degree of respect felt by and
allegiance commanded from others (see the following sections).

Crosscutting the system of exogamous clans is a series of otherwise unnamed categories of persons which I call marriage classes.
There are three marriage classes in Tarangpur, plus a fourth collection of individuals who do not constitute an intermarrying group

in the sense of a marriage class per se, but who do share the quality of exclusion from the other three classes. Unlike clan membership, marriage-class membership is not publicly admitted; in fact, Tarangpurians do whatever they can to conceal the very existence of marriage classes from those outside the system. Marriage-class membership is not a subject of open conversation among the villagers (at least not among villagers of different marriage classes). This is because the classes, unlike the clans, are ranked. The distinctions are therefore invidious in this society, whose people are so relentlessly egalitarian among themselves that any hint of inequality is immediately taken as an affront.

Giving everyone a clan name is, in effect, a way of masking membership in unequal marriage classes. To an outsider, clan name is no guide to marriage class, as someone with a given clan name might be a member of any marriage class. Since the marriage classes are such unnamed and unspoken-of entities, their very existence is difficult to detect. It was several months before I was able to discover their presence. The first hint occurred when someone told me that the reason he could not marry someone else was because their "mouths don't match."[4] This does capture the essence of the matter, since the two things members of the same marriage class can do that are proscribed to others are (1) intermarry, and (2) eat food or drink liquid that has come into contact, directly or indirectly, with one another's mouths.

Commensality, in the Indian intercaste sense, is totally irrelevant: all villagers of all marriage classes (excluding of course the low-caste Tailor family, which falls outside the Magar social system altogether) sit down to meals together from a common pot, and there are no restrictions against entering kitchen areas. Anyone may serve any kind of food to anyone else. But once food has been eaten from an individual's plate, the food remaining on that plate may not be eaten by another person unless he or she is a member of the same marriage class. He or she may marry these same people unless they are fellow clan members, in which case marriage is proscribed by the rule of clan exogamy. But he or she should not marry outside his/her marriage class.

To the extent that they are endogamous, hereditary, ranked groups, marriage classes are somewhat like castes, although it seems counterintuitive to think of such small, like-minded, unnamed groups in this way. Unlike traditional South Asian caste behavior, neither the "marriage" nor "eating" components of marriage-class behavior can be readily observed. Marriage lists do not reveal the existence of marriage classes, although in theory they might be statistically detectable if genealogies of far greater time depth existed. Eating and feasting together are common among people of different marriage classes, but since everyone eats from individual plates, the second criterion that defines marriage classes also cannot be directly observed.

The only way to find out about the composition of these groups, or to discover which group a given individual is in, is to ask about individual cases. On such a hush-hush topic, I was not able to go house-to-house asking about marriage-class membership, but instead relied on three or four informants from the top two classes. It was my strong impression that assigning families to marriage classes was not a controversial issue, nor was the question of their rank order. But it is true that my view tends to be derived from the top of the system. While I doubt that class IV members, for example, would contest their rank as I have given it, they might also be contemptuous of the entire system. This would certainly be true of the Bhotias and Tibetans, who are probably more amused than anything else by the Magar-oriented hierarchy. This general problem characterizes all discussion of rank in Nepal: the high-caste assignment of lower ranks to distant Tibeto-Burman groups like the Sherpas is for these groups a matter of amusement or scorn more than anything else.

Marriage class and marriage choice are conceptually different matters. While marriage partners should come from the same marriage class, within that class the most desirable mate is determined by the operation of other criteria. These include wealth, physical attractiveness, compatibility of personality, freedom from witchcraft accusation, age (the difference should not be more than ten years), and location. Women generally prefer to stay in their own villages, although in some "remote" places like Kola or Tachen, some would welcome a match in relatively cosmopolitan Tarangpur, and some Tarangpur girls say they would prefer the poorest local village boy to the richest one in a place like Kani.

The highest class, class I, contains forty-five households in Tarangpur—that is, more than half the village. Class II contains only eight households; class IV, the class composed of Lamas, includes twelve households; and sixteen households are not a group as such but a de facto collection of people excluded from the other classes, and are ranked between classes II and IV. The Tailor household, a few indentured servants from outside the village, and an immigrant Bhotia household fall outside the system altogether. Of the total village population of 365, then, 340 (or 93 percent) are Magars in one of the four marriage classes. The remaining twenty-five persons are immigrants or indentured servants who have come from outside the village: ten are Tibetan refugees or Bhotias, six are Magars from elsewhere in Tichurong, two are Magars from Khasan, one is from Thakkhola, and six constitute the Tailor family.

The other Tichurong villages where Tarangpurians frequently find their mates have their own distribution of persons in marriage classes, as well as persons who are outside the system. A complete description of the marriage rules in all of Tichurong would no doubt result in a more complex system than the one I partially account for here.

It is difficult to determine criteria by which families are included in class I or excluded from it. The only obvious standard is descent: a child born of class I parents belongs to class I. Yet genealogies show that immigrants have been able to break into the system—the present-day "Thakula" families, mostly members of class I, are but one instance of this. Thus class I contains members of all the exogamous clans (Gharti, Rokaya, Budha, Jankri, and Thakuri), but Class II and IV consist entirely of descendants of relatively recently arrived groups who have all taken the clan name of Budha. Historically, what seems to have happened is that what I call class I was once a unitary tribal group, consisting of several clans (Gharti, Rokaya, and Budha, if the origin legend is any guide). This group has gradually incorporated some of the later arrivals, such as the Thakuris. Classes II and IV are made up of more recent arrivals who have been either unable, uninterested, or unwilling to join the first, higher class, and who now constitute marriage classes themselves. Class II consists of descendants—or of families linked financially to descendants—of the Palpa soldier who came to Tarangpur about a century ago en route to a war with Tibet.[5] These families are called Palpali Budhas.[6] Similarly, class IV is composed of those families who are descended from Lamas. Finally, class III consists of families who were originally in one of the top two marriage classes and who have now "fallen," or of families descended from ancestors who "fell" from one of the upper two marriage classes. As in class I, all clans are represented among class III members.

To fall from a marriage class involves violating one of the two restrictions placed on membership in it: (1) eating symbolically contaminated food (i.e., food that someone outside the marriage class has shared); or (2) marrying someone outside the marriage class, since cohabitation would eventually compromise the purity of one's food. Once these restrictions have been violated, there is no immediate way the damage can be undone. The rules of restriction are firm and the consequences of violation—disbarment from the marriage class—are irrevocable, at least over the short run of two or three generations. Violations against dietary or commensal restrictions for certain other castes in India and Nepal—for instance, eating improperly prepared food in Gurkha regiments overseas—can be rectified by Brahmin priests, who can erase such transgressions by manipulating symbols in a purifactory rite for the errant individual. But there are no such ritual specialists in the Tarangpur system: once purity is sacrificed, the consequences are final.

Thus the sense of pollution is even stricter and more powerful—and prohibition against it even stronger—than in traditional Hindu culture. This view takes exception to and is offered in refutation of the conventional view (see Berreman 1963) that restrictions against polluting behavior are not as strict in the hills as in the purportedly more orthodox plains.

The lines between marriage classes are firmly drawn, but they are not immutable. As genealogies show, it is possible for someone not born into class I to become a member of that class. This transformation is not accomplished readily, but it has been achieved in some cases. Provided there is no egregious indiscretion in one's life, the descendant of an outsider or an individual in the fallen category (especially one descended from someone who fell from class I) can gain bona fide class I status. To become a new class I member one must pay a large sum of money (several hundred rupees) and secure the acceptance of all other class I members, symbolized by drinking from a common cup.

Thus the social system of Tarangpur village is rigidly stratified in a way that differs in important respects from the ranked castes of traditional South Asian villages (Marriott 1965). But as the previous chapters have emphasized, Tarangpur is not an island unto itself, and a number of other groups must be accommodated somewhere on a hierarchical scale. Representatives of those groups who live in Tichurong, or who visit it regularly, include other Magars in Tichurong, other Magars elsewhere in Nepal, Bhotias, Tibetans, Carpenter/Blacksmiths, and Tailors. Grouped with the marriage classes, the list takes the following form, from the point of view of those at the top:

1. Class I Tichurong Magars
2. Class II Tichurong Magars
3. Class III Tichurong Magars
4. Class IV Tichurong Magars (Lamas) and other Tichurong Magars
5. Magars elsewhere in Nepal
6. Bhotias
7. Tibetans

- -

8. Carpenter/Blacksmiths (Kami)
9. Tailors (Damai)

From the perspective of Tarangpur Magars, groups 1 through 7 constitute a continuum along which interdining and entrance to houses and kitchens is permitted. Food may not be eaten with groups 8 or 9, nor may any members of these classes enter the homes of Tarangpurian members of groups 1 to 7. Marriage normally takes place within the group, since it is the criterion which establishes them, but exceptions to the rules, which account for most of class III, do take place among the Magar groups up to and including group 5. Marriage has occurred between groups 1 and 2, 1 and 3, 1 and 4, 2 and 3, 2 and 4, 2 and 5, and 4 and 5. The last two categories of intermarriages are represented by only one instance each; both marriages, which took place during the research period, united Tarangpur women with police and army personnel stationed in Tichurong. Marriage could occur between group 5 and any of the higher groups, but historically, the circumstances under which such a union might take place have been virtually nonexistent. Marriage between a Tarangpur Magar and someone from group 6 or below would be unthinkable. Yet the commensal line is drawn above group 8; only groups 8 and 9 are not permitted to enter the houses of or interdine with Tarang-purian members of the first seven categories.

Tarangpurians are acutely aware of all these distinctions and have to think in hierarchical terms in the course of daily life. The concept of hierarchy is deeply embedded in the social structure and is not simply an idea imported from Hinduism, though of course the ranking systems of high-caste Hindus, who are met in excursions to the middle hills and the Terai, reinforce indigenous concerns with purity and pollution. Tichurong Magars acknowledge the superior rank of high-caste Hindus such as Brahmins, Chhetris, and Thakuris, but the nature of their relations with these groups is of an entirely different order, in that there are no regular contacts between Magars and these groups within Tichurong. Class I Magars would not pretend to higher status than these high castes, but neither would they admit them to class I status. Thus a member of class I cannot marry or accept *juṭho* (ritually contaminated food) from a high-caste Hindu. To do so would topple one from class I to class III (as happened recently, when a Tarangpur girl ran off with a Thakuri from near Jumla) as surely as would marriage to a Bhotia. In terms of marriage, class I is at the top of the social heap; all social climbing from there can lead in only one direction—down.

Nevertheless, some people do marry down. Those who willfully marry someone out of their marriage class have decided to place other considerations above membership in their marriage class, which is then forfeited. Sometimes the application of various exclusions restricts the pool of eligible partners so drastically that there is little choice but to look outside the marriage class. If such people's descendants have higher social aspirations, wealth becomes essential to attaining them. For those already in class I, wealth is not required to maintain membership; class I families range from extremely poor to wealthy. But considerable resources are required to elevate a family to class I, and it would be virtually impossible for a pauper to rise out of his marriage class. A low marriage-class family with high social aspirations thus has an ever-ready allocation for whatever wealth it has or can acquire.

Wealth has nothing to do with rank determined by purity of descent and avoidance of pollution, but it is important as an indicator of status more generally and as a possible counterweight to low marriage-class membership. At the grossest classificatory level Tarangpurians recognize two economic levels: rich and poor. There is a fairly clear consensus as to who falls into which class, but villagers also know that many families are almost rich or almost poor. Asked to break down wealth differences into either rich or not rich, one informant listed twenty-two households as rich and the rest as not rich. Another informant differentiated more carefully among all Tarangpurians and suggested a typology of eight different economic levels, and this typology also represents conventional village wisdom. Figure 6 shows the distribution of Tarangpur families into these eight levels (excluding two sets of parents who have already given most of their property to their

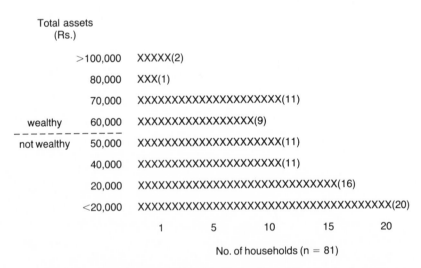

Figure 6. Distribution of Households by Size of Economic Assets*

*Note that the number of the distinguishing different asset categories is not the same, therefore this is not a traditional wealth histogram.

children, so that they no longer form property-owning units in the normal sense).

Collapsing the eight distinctions into a binary rich/poor opposition places the cutoff point between groups 4 and 5, so that the four upper groups are generally considered wealthy and the four lower groups are considered not wealthy. It is difficult to state what is meant by these eight categories in explicitly quantifiable terms, since Tarangpurians rarely add up all their assets and still more rarely state the sum in terms of a number of rupees. It is easier to calculate the total assets of those at the top and bottom of the pyramid, since their unusual wealth or poverty is so clearly and inescapably recognized. Table 30 presents a calculation, based partly on observation of and information supplied by the household in question and partly on the estimates of knowledgeable informants, of the total assets of the less wealthy of the two wealthiest households.[7]

Thus the total wealth of the two richest families amounts to

TABLE 30
TOTAL ASSETS OF THE SECOND WEALTHIEST FAMILY
IN TARANGPUR

Item	Rs.	$
Gold jewelry	13,000	1,287.13
Turquoise	3,000	297.03
Coral	4,000	396.04
Old coins	6,000	594.06
Copper water jugs	5,000	495.05
Brass plates	1,000	99.01
Horses	22,000	2,178.22
Bullocks	800	79.21
Land	20,000[a]	1,980.20
House	3,000	297.03
Second house	1,100	108.91
Paper money, clothes	30,000	2,970.30
Total	108,900	10,782.18

[a]At Rs. 400 per hul.

well over Rs. 100,000 (about $10,000) each. The one household in the second group is worth roughly Rs. 80,000 ($7,920.92), and each of the next four groups is worth about Rs. 10,000 ($990.00) less than the one above it, so that the households in group 6 are each worth approximately Rs. 40,000 ($3,960.40). There is a more precipitous drop below that—group 7 members are worth only about Rs. 20,000 ($1,980.20). There is more internal variation in the lowest group (group 8). The landless, houseless Tailor family has virtually nothing, while others own their own houses, a few fields, a little jewelry, and the like.

There is no inherent, logical connection between marriage-class rank and position in the financial ranks, but immigrants and descendants of immigrants (such as Lamas) do share the twin disadvantages of little property and low marriage-class rank: these families tend to cluster in the poorer strata. Table 31 shows the relation of marriage-class membership to wealth.

Leadership

The uses of wealth gauge the strength of values held. The financial obligations toward the ceremonial, rent, and merit funds are all traditional and static. Their meaning and amount does not seem to have changed in the last forty years, so these measures do not give any indication of what Tarangpurians do with the wealth that has been accumulating since the onset and firm entrenchment of the commodities circuit.

An entirely different major class of expenditures arises from the pursuit of political power. In addition to the hierarchy of marriage classes, another measure of differential status is the amount of power an individual or family holds. This power is measured partly by the ability to badger or threaten opponents in disputes with enough strength and determination to defeat them or to overpower them with litigation, which is costly in both time and money. But power is also measured by the authority of commanded allegiance—by the attention and, above all, the respect paid to the spoken word of a village leader. Thus there is this congruence between trading and politics: both are motivated by the intensely felt need to command respect.

TABLE 31

RELATION OF MARRIAGE-CLASS MEMBERSHIP TO WEALTH GROUP MEMBERSHIP

No. and % of households in

Wealth group	Class I No.	%	Class II No.	%	Class III No.	%	Class IV No.	%	Outside the system No.	%
1	2	2.4	—		—		—		—	
2	1	1.2	—		—		—		—	
3	9	10.8	—		1	1.2	1	1.2	—	
4	8	9.6	1	1.2	—		—		—	
5	9	10.8	2	2.4	—		—		—	
6	8	9.6	1	1.2	2	2.4	—		—	
7	6	7.2	3	3.6	6	7.2	3	3.6	—	
8	3	3.6	1	1.2	7	8.4	7	8.4	2	2.4

No. and % of households in

Marriage group	Group 1 No.	%	Group 2 No.	%	Group 3 No.	%	Group 4 No.	%	Group 5 No.	%	Group 6 No.	%	Group 7 No.	%	Group 8 No.	%
I	2	2.4	1	1.2	9	10.8	8	9.6	9	10.8	8	9.6	6	7.2	3	3.6
II	—		—		—		1	1.2	2	2.4	1	1.2	3	3.6	1	1.2
III	—		—		1	1.2	—		—		2	2.4	6	7.2	7	8.4
IV	—		—		1	1.2	—		—		—		3	3.6	7	8.4
Outside the system	—		—		—		—		—		—		—		2	2.4

Leadership is a social expression of power. To be a leader means to be successful in village politics, and to be successful in village politics increasingly demands the investment of considerable financial resources. Matching the dramatic economic changes of the last forty years are equally dramatic changes in village politics over the last six years. To understand the social consequences of economic change, we must understand how the Tarangpur political system has operated and how it is responding to the accumulation and concentration of wealth.

POLITICS

Village, District, and Nation

Until very recently, relations between Tarangpur and the national political machinery were restricted to annual tax payments and occasional governmental mediation of disputes too fractious to be successfully sorted out locally. To facilitate payment of the taxes to the government, four adult male Tarangpurians held the hereditary position of *mukhiyā*. Originally there were four mukhiya, representing the three original clans plus the Palpali Budhas. Government agents from Jumla came to Tarangpur once a year to collect land taxes, once to collect beer and liquor taxes, and irregularly to investigate and settle disputes and to trade. When government officials came to Tarangpur, they expected free room and board. Government officials from Jumla are universally remembered for being high-handed, arbitrary, and even cruel. Stories of beatings are common.

About thirty-five years ago, the number of mukhiya was enlarged to thirteen: nine more mukhiyas were added by officials in Jumla because they were rich or influential. This number proved to be unwieldy, however, and about sixteen years ago the nine new appointees were removed, leaving only the original four. In 1965, His Majesty's Government decided the system would be even more efficient with only one mukhiya. The villagers decided to select their one mukhiya by a throw of the dice, so the four clan mukhiyas played a Tibetan gambling game, and the winner became the sole official tax collector. Similarly, each village of

Tichurong now has a single tax collector responsible for turning over to the government all taxes collected from his village. Prior to the 1960s the mukhiyas not only collected taxes but also served as general liaisons between the national government and the village.

Alongside the hereditary position of mukhiya, a parallel but separate, unofficial system of village leadership emerged. Men who displayed leadership ability and commanded respect from villagers when community decisions had to be made were called *thalus*.[8] A thalu had no formal sanctions at his disposal and no connection at all with the official government hierarchy, but the role of thalu was clearly an honored one, and thalus are remembered with affection and respect by their descendants. "Thalu" referred not so much to a structural position as to a personal quality. Thalus' ability to resolve disputes and speak well is reflected in the Kaike proverb, *dhant thutu tānan/loa rowrow tānan* (roughly, "dishes are cleaned by washing, problems are solved by discussion"). Tarangpur men with political ambitions have always aspired to being a thalu simply for the prestige (which is of course a form of respect) accorded to one whom others choose to follow.

Recent years have brought dramatic political change throughout Nepal, not only at the highest levels. The palace revolt in 1950 ended over 100 years of hereditary rule by the Rana family, restored power to the king, and ushered in a decade of active political participation by several political parties. The popularly elected government of the Congress Party was deposed by King Mahendra in 1960.[9] In its place he instituted a reorganization of government that has come to be called the *panchayat* system (traditionally in Hindu South Asia, panchayats were bodies of caste or village elders endowed with various jural powers). The panchayat system consists of councils of elected representatives, beginning at the village level and forming a pyramid that ascends through the district level to the national level.

With the introduction of the panchayat system of government throughout Nepal, those who had exhibited the leadership qualities of a thalu in Tichurong gained recourse to external resources for proving leadership and to external rewards for demonstrating it. The panchayat system is a multitiered series of representative bodies, at the apex of which is the National Panchayat (analogous

to a national parliament), which meets in Kathmandu. Each panchayat body is elected from the one immediately below it, and at
the bottom of the pyramid is the village panchayat. The village
panchayat is elected by all village residents who are at least twenty-
one years old and who care to vote. A village panchayat typically
consists of representatives of a cluster of several villages, since each
village panchayat should represent some 2,000 people, and few
single villages in Nepal are this big. In the case of Tarangpur, all
the Tichurong villages on the left bank of the Bheri River (see map
4) belong to the Tarangpur Village Panchayat, while those on the
right bank belong to the Lawan Village Panchayat. All Tichurong
villages belong to one or the other of these two village panchayats.
A village panchayat contains eleven members by statute: nine
representatives plus the chairman (*pradhān*) and an assistant
pradhan, both elected at large. Each of the seven villages which
comprise the Tarangpur Village Panchayat is entitled to a representative, and the two largest villages, one of which is Tarangpur,
each have two.

In the early 1960s, when the system was initiated, few people
in Tarangpur wanted to contest the posts because of disagreeable
memories associated with former liaison duty between government
and village. But when it became apparent not only that the post
generated considerable local prestige and power but also that
considerable financial rewards could be obtained by those who
successfully achieved higher ranks in the system, genuine political
competition began to develop. Within five years electoral competition for these posts had become so intense that men who had
any chance at all for success at the polls poured as much time and
as many resources into political activity as they could.

This intensification of political activity is more characteristic of
Tarangpur than of other Tichurong villages, partly because of
Tarangpur's longer and more penetrating association with Hindu
areas and Tarangpurians' ability to deal with those areas, and
partly because of the greater amount of wealth (derived from
trading) available to Tarangpurians for investment in politics. As
a result of the local election of 1968, for instance, Tarangpur
residents accounted for four of the eleven members of the
Tarangpur Village Panchayat: the two representatives to which it
is entitled, plus the pradhan and the assistant pradhan as well.

Other villages in the Tarangpur Panchayat have their politicians too, but Tarangpur is generally considered politically preeminent, just as it is considered economically and culturally pacesetting. Of the four Tarangpurians serving in the village panchayat, one went on to be elected to the next level, the district panchayat, and a fifth Tarangpurian now represents all of Dolpo District in the National Panchayat in Kathmandu.

Yet it would be wrong to portray Tichurong as an aroused and mobilized citizenry. The political information gap across generations is enormous. Youngsters who have attended classes in the village primary school[10] all know some elementary facts about the state of their nation, including some details about the composition of the royal family. But the older generation is scarcely aware that they live in a nation at all. Once when I was taking a census of a village across the river, an old man shrugged and said he guessed America would be their raja now. This seemed to be a matter of indifference to him, as the central government had always been so remote from his experience. And in Tarangpur an old man, seeing the button I was wearing with King Mahendra's picture on it, wanted to know if he were America's raja.

The Costs

The men who have entered the political arena have gone to great lengths to reach the positions they have obtained. To make a political beginning, support must first be drummed up for election to a village post. This is done initially by rallying as many friends and relatives as possible and securing their support. To do this at all requires a prior reputation for leadership. In Tarangpur, leadership is demonstrated, in day-to-day terms, by one's ability to resolve disputes. The number of petty quarrels, misunderstandings, and insults—imagined and real—is very high in Tarangpur, and most individuals have a running feud with someone at any given time. Some people are more cantankerous than others and quarrel with more people than they are on friendly terms with. Others are quiet and mild-mannered and rarely engage in the public verbal battles—waged between rooftops at maximum decibel level—that are such a common feature of daily life in Tarangpur.

Much of this feuding blows over almost as soon as it has started, but either the contested issue or rash and hasty remarks made during debate frequently result in estrangement, which can only be repaired by a third party. Such an intermediary must be a person known for sound judgment and good character, and he must be on friendly terms with both the aggrieved parties. Thalus have these qualities and are influential in settling disputes. If such a man wants to acquire even more influence, the logical way to increase his influence and prestige is to convert his reputation in the informal hierarchy of village leaders into the formally recognized role of representative in the village panchayat. As a village panchayat member he not only carries the mandate of support from the village, which is an explicit statement of the high regard in which villagers hold him, but also is a link between the village and the governmental world beyond it. This world, which was formerly something to be avoided whenever and wherever possible, has now become something to be exploited both for financial and social gain.

With universal franchise at the local level, it is difficult to rig elections; if a seat is contested, the most competent and highly regarded candidate will usually win. But this is not invariably the case; in a village panchayat in Khasan, two candidates for pradhan campaigned by feasting the village. One candidate slaughtered one goat and the other slaughtered two goats, and the candidate who served the most meat won. But generally the pattern at the local level has been that the man with the most support at the grassroots level wins. Beyond the level of the village panchayat, it is a different matter.

Each village panchayat elects one member to serve on the district assembly, and the district assembly elects eleven of these delegates to serve on the district panchayat. The number of village panchayat representatives in the district assembly depends on the size of the district; in Dolpo, there are twenty village panchayats and therefore twenty members in the district assembly. Of the twenty, eleven are elected to the district panchayat and nine are not. Thus of the twenty village panchayats in Dolpo, eleven are represented in the district panchayat and nine have no representation at that level at all. A member of the village panchayat who wants to be elected to the district assembly has only a few opponents at most and only a plurality of the ten other electors whose support must be obtained. Similarly, a member of the district assembly who aspires to serve in the district panchayat has only a few opposing candidates to worry about and only a plurality of the nineteen other electors who must be persuaded to support him.

Thus it is not surprising that considerable funds are invested in these elections. One of the Tarangpur representatives, who has worked his way up to the district panchayat, spent Rs. 1,100 ($109.00) on his election to that body. As of 1969, the local member of the National Panchayat was reliably reported to have spent Rs. 24,000 ($2,376) on his election. His unsuccessful opponent is commonly believed to have spent, ruefully no doubt, Rs. 26,000 ($2,574.00) on his own unsuccessful campaign. In these contexts, campaign expenses refer to cash outlays to other electors in return for a promise of their vote. These enormous sums really are without rival in any other sphere of Tarangpur life. We have already seen that people frequently make donations to esteemed lamas or to projects conducive to the public good for the sake of acquiring merit. But these donations rarely amount to more than Rs. 100 ($9.90), even from a wealthy family. Some of the village chortens, located mostly around the entrances to the village, are in a state of disrepair. Refurbishing these chortens would be an ideal merit-producing project, yet no one volunteers to commission the job. For today's Tarangpurians, politics is the arena in which to pour excess capital—or, increasingly, even scarce capital.

The combination of the vast sums required and vaulting political ambition has produced an intolerable strain on the finances of some individuals, who have had to resort to illegal activities— poaching musk deer and stealing religious idols—to continue the pursuit of political activities. Minute quantities of musk bring enormous sums (Rs. 500 per tola or 0.5 oz.) in Kathmandu, and hunting musk has long been a traditional—though illegal— source of extra cash. Stealing religious images is an entirely new development.

The Rewards

The pursuit of higher politics demands strenuous efforts and a huge commitment of time and money, but it promises even greater rewards—both social and financial—to those who succeed. Depending on how high in the system a politician can rise, there are not inconsiderable financial rewards to be won as part of the political prize. Village panchayat, district panchayat, and district assembly members receive no regular remuneration at all, except for the chairman of the district panchayat, who receives Rs. 200 ($19.80) per month. But both the pradhan and assistant pradhan are eligible for per diem and travel allowances during any special training program. A member of the district assembly receives an allowance of Rs. 4 ($0.40) for every two miles of the distance between his village and district headquarters when on official business; in the case of Tarangpur, this amounts to Rs. 32 ($3.17) per round-trip, plus a per diem of Rs. 10 ($0.99) while at the district office. A member of the district panchayat receives Rs. 400 ($39.60) per round-trip to the zonal capital at Baglung, plus Rs. 1,500 ($148.52) in allowances for training programs. These programs are not held frequently, but when they are held they provide income which more than adequately covers expenses.

Finally, at the top of the political heap, a member of the National Panchayat receives a salary of Rs. 500 ($49.51) per month when the panchayat is not in session, and Rs. 700 ($69.31) per month when it is. He receives in addition Rs. 25 ($2.48) per diem while the panchayat is in session, and a travel allowance from his home to the capital of Rs. 4 ($0.40) each two miles. For the National Panchayat member from Tarangpur, this amounts to Rs. 800 ($79.21) per round-trip. Taking all these sources of money together, knowledgeable villagers calculate that the National Panchayat member from Dolpo receives some Rs. 10,000 ($990.10) in salary and allowance per year. Since his term of office is six years, he can count on an income from his political job alone of approximately Rs. 60,000 ($5,940.60), and this does not include whatever graft may accrue to the position, depending on the scruples of the incumbent.

An annual income of Rs. 10,000 ($990.10) is more than even the wealthiest Tarangpur trader makes in a year, so such high political office carries with it not only high honor but financial rewards beyond the reach of even the most successful trader. Yet there is only one such office available for all of Dolpo, and it would be highly unrealistic to stake one's financial future on securing it.

An illusory aura permeates much political planning, and the optimism of many would-be politicians is utterly unwarranted. The financial rewards that are available to politicians are important in motivating their political activity, but in view of the enormous expenses involved in scaling the political ladder, there must be another reason for the frenetic activity of Tarangpurian politicians—the social acclaim accorded to village leaders.

Aside from marriage-class rank, moral leadership is an index of social worth. Even a man in the top marriage class who wants prestige must pursue it in the political field, which now embraces nationally recognized roles. To speak for one's village in the higher councils of the nation attests to one's leadership, intelligence, power, and savoir faire. Success beyond the village is a way of securing and consolidating rank within the village.

POLITICS AND TRADE

To a certain extent, big business and politics simply do not mix, not for moral reasons, but for ecological ones. A man who is seriously involved in trading must be physically removed from the village for well over half the year, whereas the conduct of village politics and demands of the national government require that whoever represents the village or district be accessible most of the time. When representatives of the national government arrive in the village to initiate or pursue some political or developmental activity, the duly elected local officials should be there to receive them. For ecological reasons outlined earlier, trading involves long seasonal absences from the village, so an avid trader has to choose either politics or economics as the major arena in which to invest his time and resources.

Even if he chooses politics, wealth is not the ultimate key to political success. The three wealthiest families in Tarangpur are not involved in politics, because the men in those families would be unable to win local elections regardless of their wealth; they lack the basic leadership qualities necessary to win local elections in the first place. Once a local leader has successfully launched a political career, further success depends very much on his ability to mobilize enough capital to contest higher echelon (district, zonal) elections. But money alone will not guarantee a successful life in politics—or indeed, any political life at all.

Nevertheless, although wealth and political power are not isomorphic, wealth is the sine qua non of political success at higher levels, and the continuation and intensification of political pursuits are not comprehensible except as a consequence of the economic shifts of the last forty years. The capital formation made possible by the slow but sure switch from the grain-salt-rice exchange cycle to the commodities circuit has resulted in increased wealth for which multiple uses exist. Hoarding in forms such as jewelry is one way of handling this excess, just as excess grain is traditionally hoarded in huge underground pits. Gifts to religious persons and places, to acquire merit, is another possibility well within cultural bounds. But none of these has attracted the flow of capital and commitment of time and energy that has been invested in the pursuit of prestige through political power.

HIERARCHY AND RECIPROCITY

We have seen how a profound concern with social station—measured both by marriage-class membership based on maintenance of hereditarily pure status and by ability to earn respect by commanding the allegiance of others—is at the core of much Tarangpur behavior. One way of bolstering an otherwise shaky claim to social worth is through the acquisition of wealth, because financial success is a mark of intelligence, shrewdness, and power—and because it can be used, more recently, to further political ambitions. Despite similar living standards, large wealth differences exist between rich and poor, and a variety of different mechanisms exist in the course of social and ritual life to deplete savings and, occasionally, to add to them. The differences in wealth, in social status, and in political power are measurable and intensely real to those who want to increase one or more of them. Maximizing their control over persons and their command over resources keeps Tarangpurians busily engaged in the agonistic striving observed in the processes of daily life.

Despite the internal cleavages of wealth, status, and power, interpersonal relations in the village are pervaded by an aura of diffuse reciprocity. In this unbalanced or generalized (Sahlins

1965) reciprocity, the material side of a transaction is repressed by the social side, and the expectation of a direct return is at best implicit. By contrast, transactions with outsiders—whether on trading expeditions or in politics—are carried out in the spirit of two other kinds of reciprocity that Sahlins identifies: balanced and negative. Reciprocity is balanced when returns of commensurate worth are stipulated within a finite and narrow period—in other words, when books are kept, formally or informally, and ledgers must be brought into balance. Negative reciprocity is the unsociable extreme, the attempt to gain the unearned increment. Forms of negative reciprocity run the gamut from haggling in the spirit of "what the traffic will bear" through various degrees of cunning, stealth, and violence to the finesse of a well-conducted horse raid (Sahlins 1965).

There seems little point in calling a horse raid either transactional or reciprocal, however negative, but the contrast between relations with the outside world on the one hand, and relations with the village on the other, is a sharp one. It is this generalized reciprocity—perhaps better expressed as the ideology of equality—which characterizes intravillage relations more than anything else and which defines the boundary between the Magars of Tarangpur and the rest of the world. The key word here is ideology, for at the level of manifest behavior, there are obviously tremendous differences in wealth and status and power. Yet these differences are not referred to casually; in fact, many of them are explicitly forbidden subjects of conversation both among Tarangpurians and to outsiders (and this makes investigation of them difficult). Even the existence of marriage classes is more of an open secret than a freely acknowledged fact of social structure. A few men are so poor that they have to work for richer men from time to time, but both parties to such an arrangement are loath to admit publicly that this is the case.

EXCHANGE LABOR

The most obvious example of intravillage reciprocity is the phenomenon of cooperative labor. Most agricultural labor is performed by labor gangs, which are formed on an exchange basis with friends, neighbors, and relatives. These are transient, free-floating groups which change in composition daily, but the basis for recruitment is always reciprocity between parties, whether rich or poor, high marriage class or low, politically powerful or politically impotent. For each person (or bullock) who works for another family for a day, the second family will repay the first with a worker (or bullock) of its own for a day.

Agreements for exchange labor are based largely on convenience. Neighbors often exchange labor with each other, whether they are related or not or particularly friendly or not, because physical proximity facilitates the fixing of times and dates. Almost anyone can exchange labor with anyone else; the only categories of persons purposely avoided are former spouses and those with whom one has a serious dispute (not a temporary misunderstanding, which may flare up in the morning and be forgotten by the afternoon). Exchange is sought with particularly hard workers and is avoided with those considered to be lazy or inefficient (there are about ten households in each category), but since exchanges are reciprocal, degrees of industriousness tend to find their own level.

In labor exchanges, bullocks and humans are equivalent. The few families who do not own their own bullock have to exchange their own labor for that of a bullock, but even families with more than one bullock have to exchange their own labor, too; the demand for extra bullocks is not so great that a family with several can rely on loaning them out in exchange for human labor.

The sense of reciprocity is so strong in exchange labor that to opt out of the system altogether would be well beyond the bounds of propriety. Even if a family has enough human labor and animal traction to meet its own needs (and a few families are self-sufficient this way), it is morally bound to exchange with less well-endowed families who need help. Like taking one's turn hosting the entire village every thirty or forty years, such cooperation comes with moral citizenship. These are dues that have to be paid.

VILLAGE SOLIDARITY

What is true of the reciprocal obligations characteristic of the agricultural sector is also true of other forms of economic activity.

Any relationship not based on reciprocity is avoided or, if unavoidable, denied or disguised in reciprocal terms—that is to say, rendered culturally acceptable. The norm which dictates against employer-employee relationships among villagers is strong. Although a few of the poorest villagers do occasionally work for wealthier ones—by carrying loads, for example—it is considered demeaning to be in the employ of a fellow villager, and one puts himself in such a subordinate position only when necessary, and even then, the relationship is rationalized in such a way that the dyad is cast in some kind of egalitarian mode. One example of this economic masquerade was carried out by two friends, both young men in their early twenties, who went trading together during the winter of my residence. One is an avid trader whose total assets put him in the third wealth group; the other is in the eighth, or poorest group. The two spent the trading season together, and on the return trip from the Terai, the poorer of the two carried a regular load for the wealthy man, in exchange for his expenses for the entire trip, clothes, and a few cartons of cigarettes which he could then sell on his own. By these devices payment of a cash fee for services was avoided; instead he was "given" his expenses and some commodities, and what would normally have been an employer–employee relationship was papered over with transactions of egalitarian reciprocity.

Other examples of this feeling of village solidarity include "pure gifts" to those who have suffered some misfortune. One young man who had been away from the village for several years attending school returned to take up daily life. He had no bullock or fertilizer and his barren fields, which had lain fallow for so long, were difficult to bring under cultivation again. The rest of the village contributed fertilizer, bullocks, and even labor to help this man make a new start. A feeling of gratitude and indebtedness results, but no one who helped expected to be repaid. The same thing happens if someone's house should burn. Even without a calamity of such proportions, help is extended without thought of repayment to those who need it. For instance, a man with no livestock of his own will not have a source of fertilizer for his fields, so those who do own animals let them stay overnight for long periods of time in the barnyards of those without cattle. This kind of loan is never repaid.

Generalized reciprocity spills over into the commercial sector of the economy as well. One trader from a neighboring village had died the year before, and his family found itself in difficult straits. Some families from Tarangpur bought some of his tea, even if they did not need it at the time, just to help someone who had fallen on hard times.

Thus despite stratification along several lines, generalized or unbalanced reciprocity characterizes much of the interaction between Tarangpurians and their fellow villagers and relatives. "Unbalanced" is a more descriptive term than "generalized," because it emphasizes the moral quality of unscheduled give and unspecified take. Some hard-luck loans are not expected to be repaid, but the man with a problem today may extend a helping hand to someone else tomorrow. Even the case of the work gangs, where labor is exchanged on a more explicitly tit-for-tat basis, illustrates this point: there are counter-obligations, but they are not stipulated by time, quantity, or quality.

JAJMANI

There is one more set of distinctively reciprocal—but in this case asymmetrical—relations at the local level. I refer to the Tichurong variant of what is known in the literature of Indian village economics as the *jajmani* system. The words *jajman* (patron) and *kamin* (client) are unknown in the languages of Tichurong, but the concepts that these terms denote do exist.

In addition to the overwhelming majority of Buddhist, Mongoloid inhabitants, there is a minority of relatively latecomers, who are Indo-Aryan and low-caste Hindu, in Tichurong. Except for the one family of Tailors (*Damai*) in Tarangpur, all these low-caste households belong to the Blacksmith caste (*Kami*). Some Kami households do not specialize in blacksmithing but instead make baskets or work gold, and most families do crude carpentry as well. Of the thirty-six Kami families in Tichurong, eighteen are the sole inhabitants of the closest village to Tarangpur, barely three-quarters of an hour's walk away. Most of the others (fourteen) are concentrated in a Magar village across the river, and the rest are scattered in three other villages. The Kamis came up the river from Khasan over 125 years ago and have increased in numbers since then. The Damais came to Tarangpur about forty years ago and still are regarded by Magars and by themselves as visitors in Tarangpur.

There are adult males living in sixteen of the eighteen Kami families of the nearby Kami village, and ten of these families have regular, long-established patron-client relationships with the families of Tarangpur and other Tichurong villages. Three families have clients in villages other than Tarangpur, and the three families which make fiber baskets do so on a piecework basis and have no jajmans anywhere.

These relationships connect families rather than individuals, and they are therefore inherited. Application of inheritance rules sometimes skews the one-to-one pattern, so that some families have more than one Kami. For instance, if a Kami with two sons has seven clients, the two sons split the clients, three each, with the seventh served by both, each of whom receives a half share of grain. Or conversely, should a Tarangpur man inherit both his own lands and those of his wife, he must retain both Kamis and give them each a share. The distribution of patrons among clients is not even; the rise and fall of families, availability of patrons in other villages, a recently arrived Kami from Khasan—these are some of the factors which account for the fact that one Kami has nineteen and a half patrons in Tarangpur and another has only half a patron. The others range between three and ten.

The founders of Kami village in the first half of the nineteenth century worked whatever land above their village had not been claimed and cultivated by the Magars, who had arrived centuries before. Such land was limited, and Kamis today have a relatively small land base—some own none at all, and five huls (about 1.4 acres) is the most that any single family claims.

Kamis receive their income primarily in the form of annual grain payments from hereditary patrons for blacksmith services—that is, for any metal work, such as repairing cooking pots or other metal tools and utensils. Other kinds of work, such as carpentry, goldsmithing, and basket-making are compensated for on a piecework basis. The annual payment to a Kami consists of 20 to 30 manas (pints) of grain per year, the exact amount depending on the generosity of the patron. In addition, Kamis are regularly invited to any special occasion, such as a marriage feast, at the patron's house. At such times they are given food for the whole family, plus clothes (sometimes new and sometimes old). Kamis often do additional work—in the fields or carrying loads—for extra income.

The Kamis are clearly the employees of the Magars; they not only perform artisan services for the Magars but also work in their fields and carry loads for them. Ritually, too, there is no question about who is higher. Kamis may not go into Magar houses at all, and they must sit a respectable distance apart while eating. At one level it is absurd to refer to relations between two such asymmetrically powerful parties as reciprocal. Yet these relationships are not like those with outsiders, either. Despite the asymmetry, a strong paternalistic bias gives the relationship a reciprocal tone unlike any of the modes which Sahlins (1965) differentiates.

It is remarkable, in the South Asian context, that all Kamis are trying to expand their business by acquiring more patrons in other villages on a jajmani, annual payment-in-kind basis. The Tailor family—newcomers compared to the Kamis—has only ten patrons and works for others on a piecework, catch-as-catch-can basis, but the Tailors much prefer regular patrons and envy the Kamis their large clientele. Thus the Kamis and Damais are trying to expand rather than contract their traditional jajmani business, and they are able to extract from the transactions that tie them to their patrons what they regard as a satisfactory bargain. While jajmani relations are beating a retreat in most of India, dissolving in a growing cash economy, in Tichurong they are still flourishing and expanding.

8

Summary and Conclusions:
Ethnicity and Interaction

It is a complex notion that inspires the economic actions we have described, a notion neither of purely free and gratuitous prestations, nor of purely interested and utilitarian production and exchange; it is a kind of hybrid.

—Marcel Mauss, *The Gift*

All the first manned flights to the moon, including the initial landing on its surface, took place while I was in Tarangpur. My only source of information about them was a twice-daily English-language, ten-minute newscast heard (when reception was good) on the Japanese portable radio that belonged to a constable in the recently established border checkpost. Tarangpurians were immensely curious about all this for their own cosmological reasons,[1] but perhaps their most engrossing observation was their comparison of Dolpo with the moon. Judged by the standards of a one-week lunar round-trip and live lunar television transmission, Tarangpur is a far more remote and inaccessible place than the back side of the moon.

Difficulties of transportation and, for most purposes, communication, render Tarangpur as isolated today as it has been for all the centuries since Mongoloid tribesmen first settled there. Tarangpur is a largely self-sufficient community, but the ways in which it is interdependent with the outside world are more important and more analytically intriguing than the ways in which it is self-contained.

Important social relations are maintained across the boundaries that separate the mountain peasants of Tarangpur from other kinds of people, and these relations are based on and depend upon

183

dichotomized ethnic statuses. Ethnic distinctions thus do not depend on an absence of social interaction but are, on the contrary,
the very foundations on which embracing social systems are built.
In such a social system, interaction does not lead to the liquidation
of ethnic differences through acculturation; cultural differences
persist in spite of interethnic contact and interdependence (Barth
1969).

Virtually every biological and physical need could be satisfied
from the resources available in Tichurong. But at indigenous
technology levels, there is no local source of salt. Salt must be
imported, and the most accessible salt is that mined in western
Tibet. This salt is acquired from Bhotias to the north, who have
in turn crossed over into Tibet and obtained it from Tibetans, who
have brought it from its source. Thus salt is the crucial commodity
which has triggered a series of transactions described here as
circuits.

The trilingual setting of Tichurong has given the people there—
especially those whose regular social and economic contacts with
Nepali- and Tibetan-speakers render them most fluent—the linguistic tools to shuttle resources back and forth between the northern and southern borders of the country. The tricultural milieu
provides the arsenal of appropriate behaviors for transacting between drastically different cultural zones. The perspective of cultural ecology developed in the preceding chapters considers not
only the natural features of habitat but also—and especially—the
relations between cultures, the superorganic setting (see Sahlins
and Service 1960:49).

In an agrarian context, Tarangpur's ecological niche is a narrow
and delicate one. But because of favorable climate and land/man
ratios, the farmers of Tarangpur have been able to exploit their
environment successfully and produce a net food grain surplus
(consisting mostly of millet and buckwheat). Most families are
able to feed themselves from what they produce on their privately
owned land. Some surplus grain is exchanged for salt, which is
then transported in small saddlebags carried by sheep and goats
farther south to be exchanged for rice, which Tarangpurians serve
on festive occasions.

Like anyone anywhere else in the world (or on the moon, for
that matter), Tarangpurians have a limited number of resources

and a finite amount of time with which to utilize or ignore, destroy or develop those resources. At any point, the allocation of that time and those resources can be more or less accurately described; each such allocation is in part determined by choices made in the past and in part "canalizes" future choices. In Tarangpur, the allocation of time and resources has been changing over the last forty years, and the cultural implications of these changes, which have transformed the character of its links with the rest of the world, have been wide-ranging and dramatic. An examination of these changing time and resource allocations has provided insights into the direction in which Tarangpur is moving.

A declining salt market, brought about by a variety of local and international causes, resulted in a switch from the grain-salt-rice circuit to a second circuit involving both the movement of manufactured commodities against animals and the introduction of cash. Thus from a goods-goods-goods circuit, transactions were increasingly cast into a goods-cash-goods mode. The declining salt market (an economic consideration) and the increasing orientation toward Hindu areas, the source and inspiration of social and political power (cultural considerations) have combined to provide the constraints and incentives that have affected the ledger of value gained and lost, changed the strategic situation, and thereby canalized subsequent choices (Barth 1966:4).

Contact with burgeoning market towns of the Terai has brought in its wake traffic in manufactured goods for which there is a market both north of Tichurong and in Tichurong itself. Journeys to manufacturing cities of India, including the huge Asian entrepôt of Calcutta, have extended the economic frontier even farther, as trade has shifted from the first circuit to the second. The switch was gradual, but for any specific trader, it must be sudden. Since both commercial cycles take place primarily during the winter months, and since both follow routes that diverge from each other by and large, an unequivocal choice must be made between the two strategies. A man with adequate resources may pursue one or the other transaction circuit, but not both. Only a handful of traders still drive their grain- and salt-laden flocks north and south. The overwhelming majority sell their animals or woolen products in the middle hills, use the cash proceeds to finance the purchase of manufactured commodities in the Terai or India, carry them north again in the spring when the passes to Tichurong are no longer blocked with snow and ice, sell them in Khasan and Bhot, and use the profits to buy more animals and/or wool, thus beginning the sequence of the next season's trading all over again.

Adoption of this alternative resource allocation has had important repercussions on the society and culture of Tarangpur. Intravillage relations are cast in egalitarian terms, but agonistic striving after wealth is a way of proving personal worth in a context of explicit, measurable financial and social inequality. The tension between ideology and behavior is seen in the pursuit of wealth, power, and prestige as a way of asserting, or perhaps confirming, claims of equality. In brief, Tarangpurians attempt to increase their command over resources and/or their control over persons.

The key to success in these efforts lies to the south, in the kinds of interactions that take place with the people one encounters in the second exchange circuit. The introduction of cash into the economy, with its potential for capital formation, has laid the basis for important symbolic, political, and structural shifts. The penetration of the economic frontier can be thought of as a kind of parameter or gauge along which continuity between past and present can be measured. The facts of ecological variation between zones persist, but they are exploited in novel ways and with novel consequences for the rest of the sociocultural system. The direction and movement of goods and symbols can be stated in terms of trade routes, which allow us to map these changes in terms of their ecological components: salt and Buddhism flow down the river; rice and Hinduism move up the river; and modernism (or a Hindu variant of it) comes over the pass.

The trend toward the second circuit and away from the first seems well established. The reasons are essentially economic, but they reflect changing preference schedules and self-images. The more preferences change, the more they affect economic decisions. Put another way, once basic economic decisions are made, for whatever reasons, the impact is felt in other, noneconomic spheres. As resources accumulate, further choices have to be made as to how they should be utilized. What distinguishes the second circuit from the first is the possibility of increased resources accumulating and compounding in a way that can never happen in the first cycle.

This difference can be illustrated diagrammatically, as in figures 7 and 8.

Charting the flow of goods and services in terms of the transactions in which the flow is embedded profiles the relative strength of changing values. The flow and counterflow of prestations consists not only of goods and services but also of ideas, including those about how societies ought to operate. Tarangpurians try to bring their own society into line with what they perceive to be the Hindu or modern model (or, in a Hindu kingdom, modernist Hindu), because this is the model most relevant to increasing social status and acquiring political power. In the south one learns how

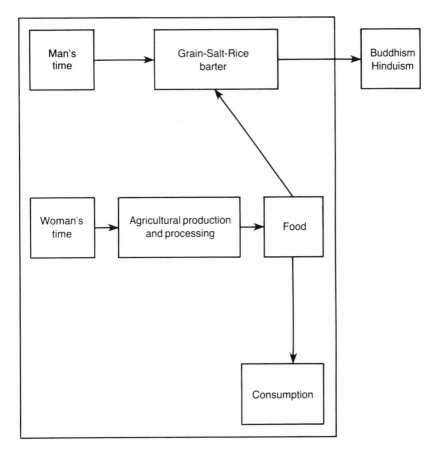

Figure 7. Diagram of the Grain-Salt-Rice Transaction Circuit

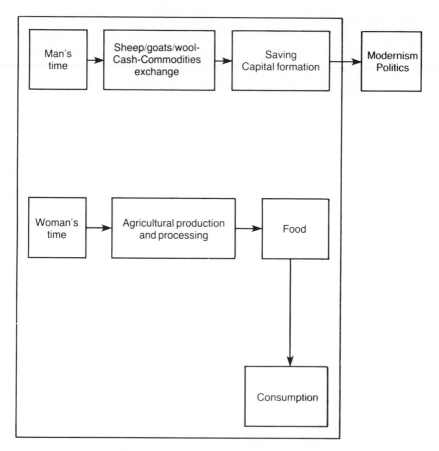

Figure 8. Diagram of the Livestock/Wool-Cash-Commodities
Transaction Circuit

to deal with Hindu society on a stronger, if not equal, footing.
Along with concepts of caste ranking come ideas of democracy
and equality, which are acquired partly through political contacts
in very recent years, but which have been absorbed through traditional economic contacts for a longer period of time.

These ideas directly affect the social structure. A few months
before I arrived in Tarangpur there was a large meeting, the result
of attempts to resolve a private quarrel. The dispute was resolved
and the meeting concluded when—publicly, formally, and symbolically—the members of the two highest marriage classes voted to
change their marriage rules and merge the two groups into a single

intermarrying group. Two of the compelling arguments leading to this decision were (1) that people in other, more progressive (i.e., Hindu) parts of Nepal do not have such cumbersome and backward marriage rules, and (2) that under the new laws, everyone is supposed to be equal anyway. Thus as a direct result of ideas that have been imported via the commodities circuit, Tarangpurians have consciously and deliberately altered a fundamental part of their social structure.

Like tribes elsewhere in South Asia, the Magars of Tarangpur live on the fringes of Hindu society, but unlike most of these other tribal peoples, they also live on the fringes of Buddhist society. The complex integration into the national society described for Tarangpur serves as a model to be tested against the general features of social and cultural change among other ethnic minorities along the salt-starved northern border of Nepal. The problem is not only the integration of an encysted ethnic minority into a complex society but also the mode of accommodation reached between two major systems. The symbol systems of two different great traditions compete for commitment, so that executing the transactional chain requires a double-edged, Janus-faced form of impression management—hence the present cultural heterogeneity of Tarangpur—of a society which is nominally Buddhist, strongly Hinduized, and still partly tribal.

Impression management blocks the flow of information at crucial junctures: hence the distinctive, almost exclusively economic links between the three regions. Since Hinduism and Buddhism are not undifferentiated entities but whole encyclopedias of meaning, the solution worked out between these two great traditions is syncretistic. (Having to juggle two great traditions simultaneously is a problem Indian tribals have not had to face.) This solution was stable as long as the requirements of ecological symbiosis remained the same, but economic shifts initiated changes in the social and cultural spheres which transformations in the national political system concluded. Forced to choose between Hinduism and Buddhism, Tarangpurians appear to choose Hinduism.

This does not mean that they import Brahmins and scuttle their lamas. Buddhism retains its important place because lamas retain their power to ease Tarangpurians through many of the crises with which they must deal, beginning with birth and ending with death.

But they no longer pour resources into religion by building or refurbishing prayer-walls or chortens, all of which are in a state of advanced disrepair. When I offered a sizable donation to help reconstruct the chortens at the entrances to the village (see map 5) if the villagers would come up with a similar level of support, I found no takers.

The preference is not one of one religion over another but a preference for politics over religion, because politics is inextricably bound up with the core of Tarangpur life—namely, the pursuit of power, status, and wealth. The key to securing these lies in the hands of the Hindu modernists—the national élite in Kathmandu and their functionaries in outlying areas, who are directly and explicitly attempting to integrate Tarangpur into modernist Hindu political and economic structures. There is no comparable pull from the north. Ironically, the mountaineers of Tarangpur look up to the lowlanders.

Rather than either "Sanskritization" or "Tibetanization," a process of religious triangulation is under way. For the descendants of the few high-caste Thakuri families who settled and intermarried and were hence "Magarized," the process is even more complex. The indigenous cult, centered on local mountain deities, has been overlaid with Tibetan Buddhism, and this in turn has been challenged by Hinduism. Formerly, villagers had two names: a Tibetan one given by a lama at birth, and a second Hindu name to use in interaction with Hindus. Now villagers often make a point of asking lamas to give their newborn infants a Hindu name in the first place, to avoid the bother and ambiguity of having to change names later. As in highland Burma, historically there have been three models to choose from,[2] but as national identity grows apace, the movement becomes less like a pendulum and more like that of an irreversible amalgamation—a process similar to what Bista (1982) has called Nepalization.

A frequently reiterated theme of this study has been that economic metamorphosis has been the entering wedge of cultural change. The transactional analysis has shown that in the past, as actors picked their way through a choice-laden system, the economy has been the leading sector in knocking a traditional society and culture off-center; in the future, that role will be assumed by the polity.

Such well-worn anthropological concepts as acculturation and assimilation do not deal adequately with situations as complex as this exchange network among culturally diverse segments in different social settings. This study has dealt with cultural contact and change but has emphasized the quality of interaction, the synapses of relationships that connect the local system to the larger ones which it links, not the billiard-ball movement and fact of contact itself. The problem has been to get at the distinctive kinds of interaction which characterize different cultural confrontations, the meanings these confrontations have for the actors in them, and the changes that ensue from such confrontations. To do all this, I have tried to trace out the material and ethnic transactions that connect Tarangpurians to one another and to the rest of the world. This process pinpoints the changes that are slowly but inexorably engulfing the people of Tarangpur, blurring and maintaining boundary mechanisms between them and the rest of the ever-approaching world beyond their valley.

Appendix A
Kinship Terms

The following chart lists Kaike kinship terms. Some terms are obviously of Nepali origin, some are of Tibetan origin, and some are different from either language. A peculiar feature is that the core terms of elder and younger brother and younger sister are Nepali terms, yet older sister is not. In Murdock's typology (1949), Kaike kinship in Tarangpur is Normal Dakota type character-ized by (1) patrilineal descent with exogamy in the patriline, (2) Iroquois type cousin terminology, with cross and parallel cousins differentiated and parallel cousins called by sibling terms, (3) patrilocal or neolocal residence, (4) patriclans with temples (gombas) and sections of fields associated with clans but no clan communities, (5) polygyny allowed but with incidence less than 20 percent, (6) bifurcate collateral aunt terms, and (7) niece terms.

Matrilateral and patrilateral cross-cousin marriage is preferred. Only 42 percent of the households are nuclear, although that is the ideal. Another 11 percent are nuclear but with one spouse deceased. In 42 percent of the households there are married per-sons belonging to two generations, but in only 15 percent of these are all four spouses living. Finally, one household has three mar-riages within it (a widow and two married sons), and 5 percent (four households) consist of people who have never married.

Gloss and Denotative Definitions of Tarangpur Kinship Lexemes

Kaike lexeme	English gloss	Denotata[a]
paki	paternal great-great grandfather	FaFaFaFa
maki	paternal great-great grandmother	FaFaFaMo

193

Kaike lexeme	English gloss	Denotata[a]
khyepul	paternal great grand-father	FaFaFa
mampul	paternal great grand-mother	FaFaMo
khe	paternal grandfather; father-in-law	FaFa; FaFaBr; FaMoBr; SpFa; SpFaBr; FaMoSiHu
mom	paternal grandmother; mother-in-law	FaMo; FaMoSi; SpMo; SpMoSi; FaFaBrWi
mubha	maternal grandfather	MoFa; MoMoBr; MoFaBr; MoFaFa; MoFaFaBr; MoMoBrDaHu; MoFaBrDaHu; MoFaFaBrSo
iu	maternal grandmother	MoMo; MoMoSi; MoFaBrWi; MoMoBrDa
payi	"great aunt"	FaFaSi; MoFaSi; MoFaFaBrDa
malyang	———	FaGyWi
palyang	———	FaGy
pya	"uncle"	FaSiHu
pa	father	Fa
ma	mother	Mo
paren	"uncle"	FaEBr; FaGyBr and FaFaBrSo, if elder; MoFaBrDaHu if older than Ego's parent
pang	"uncle"	FaYBr; FaGyBr, FaFaBrSo, MoFaBrDaHu if younger than Ego's parent
nyi	"aunt"	FaSi; FaFaBrDa
maren	"aunt"	MoESi; FaEBrWi; FaGyEBrWi; MoFaBrDa if elder to mother
mea	"aunt"	FaYBrWi; MoBrWi; FaGyYBrWi; MoFaSiSoWi
ku	"uncle"	MoBr; MoFaSiSo; MoPaBrSo; FaFaSiSo; MoBrSo if older than Ego
chyong	"aunt"	MoYSi; SpESi; MoFaSiDa; MoFaBrDa; younger ElBrWi; FaFaSiDa; MoFa-BrSoDa
daju	elder brother	EBr; FaBrSo, FaGySo, MoSiSo, if older than Ego

Kaike lexeme	*English gloss*	*Denotata*[a]
bhai	younger brother	YBr; FaBrSo, FaGySo, MoSiSo, MoFaBr-DaSo if younger than Ego
ti	elder sister	ESi, FaBrDa, FaGyDa, MoSiDa if older than Ego
bahini	younger sister	YSi; FaBrDa, FaGyDa, MoSiDa if younger than Ego
misa	wife	Wi
pasa	husband	Hu
kawn	"brother-in-law"	ESiHu; SpEBr
kuppoo	"brother-in-law"	WiYBr
nyimu	"sister-in-law"	SpYSi
mapa	"son-in-law"	DaHu; YSiHu
gyampa	"ritual friend"	Gy
koncha	nephew, grandson	ChSo; ChChSo, BrSo; SiSo; FaSiSo; FaFaSiChSo; BrSoSo, etc.; MoBrSo if younger than Ego
ojo	son	So
chame	daughter	Da
jhang	"daughter-in-law"	SoWi; ChSoWi
komme	niece, granddaughter	ChDa; ChChDa; BrDa; SiDa; FaSiDa; MoFaBrSoDa; FaFaSiChDa; MoBrDa if younger than Ego
sauta (Nepali)[b]	co-wife	HuWi
dharm-putra[b]	adopted son	———
samdhi[b]	———	ChSpFa
solti[b]	"sister-in-law"	BrWiSi; SiHuSi; WiBrWi
sardu daju[b]	"brother-in-law"	WiSiHu if older than Ego
sardu bhai[b]	"brother-in-law"	WiSiHu if younger than Ego

[a]Type notations used are those of Murdock (1949), with these additions: E = elder; Y = younger; Gy = gyampa; Pa = parent (either sex); Ch = child (either sex)

[b]Informants knew these terms, but they are Nepali terms not often used in the village.

Appendix B
Animal Population of Tarangpur

The following table lists all animals owned by Tarangpur households, the number of households that own each type, and the mean
for all households.

Animal species	Total animals	Animal-owning households	Mean/household (n = 83)
Oxen	83	53	1
Cows	82	23	.99
Calves	7	3	.08
Yak	17	3	.21
Sheep/goats	420	22	5.66
Horses	82	14	.99
Chickens	370	56	4.46
Dogs	40	36	.48

Appendix C

Principal Tarangpur Crops in English, Latin, Kaike, Tibetan, and Nepali

English	Latin	Kaike	Tibetan	Nepali
Sour buckwheat	Fagopyrum tataricum	bharo	bra-bu	titia popper
Millet	Panicum miliaceum	lā	chi-ji	chinu chāmal
Sweet buckwheat	Fagopyrum esculentum	rang bharo	kyav-re	mitia popper
Barley	Hordeum vulgare	na-jan	nas ("ney")	ua
Japanese millet	Echinochloa frumentaceum	kodo	kodo	kodo
Amaranth	Amaranthus caudatus	masherā palmā (white mashera)	masherā karbo (white mashera)	marshia
		masherā lomā (red mashera)	masherā modo (red mashera)	
Italian millet	Setarica italica	ran	the	kauna
Marijuana	Cannabis sativa	pachi	paji	bhāng
Mustard	Sinapis arvensis	chū	tsug	tori
French beans		shimi	shimi	shimi

Appendix D
Weights, Measures, and Equivalents

Monetary
    $1.00 = Rs. 10.1

Weight
    Tola = 11.66 grams; about ½ oz.
    Seer = .93 kilograms; 2.06 lbs.
    Dharni = 2.27 kilograms; almost 5 lbs.

Volume
    mana = 545 cc
    pint = 568 cc
    pathi = 8 mana; 4.36 liters
    20 pathi = 1 muri; 87.22 liters; ca. 2.4 bushels
    bushel = .42 muri

Area
    acre = 4047 sq m or 43,560 sq. ft.
    hul = .28 acre
    acre = 3.6 hul

Appendix E

Landholdings

The following shows the area (in square feet) of 41 rectangular fields owned by one typical landowner.

Field no.	Total ft^2	% uncultivatable	Cultivated ft^2
1	6,402	10	5,762
2	2,920	10	2,628
3	435	0	435
4	1,152	0	1,152
5	1,147	0	1,147
6	3,267	0	3,267
7	2,994	0	2,994
8	6,541	5	6,214
9	5,247	10	4,722
10	8,704	0	8,704
11	840	0	840
12	51,714	20	41,371
13	1,984	0	1,984
14	43,516	60	26,110
15	1,416	0	1,416
16	4,587	0	4,587
17	594	0	594
18	4,625	0	4,625
19	2,112	0	2,112
20	1,772	14	1,696
21	7,670	10	6,903
22	1,829	0	1,829
23	5,805	0	5,805
24	5,670	10	5,103
25	1,488	0	1,488
26	744	0	744
27	8,690	0	8,690

Field no.	Total ft²	% uncultivatable	Cultivated ft²
28	3,306	20	2,975
29	1,062	0	1,062
30	755	0	755
31	888	20	710
32	3,875	0	3,875
33	2,244	0	2,244
34	1,914	20	1,531
35	1,360	0	1,360
36	4,370	0	4,370
37	1,155	10	1,040
38	2,065	20	1,652
39	968	0	968
40	4,697	10	4,228
41	1,643	20	1,314
Total	214,167		181,006

Appendix F

Amount of Cultivated and Uncultivated Arable Land per Household

House no.	Adults	Children	Cultivated land		Uncultivated land	
			Huls	Acres	Huls	Acres
1	4	0	6	1.68	0	0
2	5	2	12	3.36	0	0
3	2	2	6	1.68	0	0
4	3	3	15	4.2	0	0
5	4	0	7	1.96	0	0
6	2	2	3	.84	0	0
7	3	2	10	2.8	0	0
8	2	0	8	2.24	0	0
9	5	0	10	2.8	0	0
10	2	0	3	.84	0	0
11	2	0	16	4.48	1	.28
12	2	0	16	4.48	1	.28
13	3	1	17	4.76	0	0
14	2	1	16	4.48	3	.84
15	4	1	22	6.16	3	.84
16	3	0	16	4.48	1	.28
17	4	1	11	3.08	1	.28
18	2	0	22	6.16	5	1.4
19	6	0	40	11.2	4	1.12
20	2	2	10	5.04	0	0
21	4	0	30	8.4	2	.56
22	5	0	8	2.24	0	0
23	3	0	8	2.24	0	0
24	2	3	8	2.24	0	0
25	3	0	30	8.4	3	.84

House no.	Adults	Children	Cultivated land		Uncultivated land	
			Huls	*Acres*	*Huls*	*Acres*
26	3	4	16	4.48	2	.56
27	3	1	16	4.48	0	0
28	3	0	20	5.6	0	0
29	3	0	13	3.64	2	.56
30	6	4	40	11.2	7	1.96
31	2	0	26	7.28	2	.56
32	4	0	23	6.44	1	.28
33	3	0	13	3.64	1	.28
34	4	2	15	4.2	5	1.4
35	2	1	12	3.36	0	0
36	1	0	0	0	0	0
37	1	0	8	2.24	1	.28
38	5	2	50	14	2	.56
39	2	1	12	3.36	1[a]	.28
40	2	0	10	2.8	1	.28
41	3	1	18	4.48	3	.84
42	3	0	21	5.88	13	3.64
43	3	1	20	5.6	3	.84
44	4	2	25	7	2	.56
45	3	2	20	5.6	0	0
46	5	1	25	7	3	.84
47	3	3	20	5.6	2	.56
48	3	1	20	5.6	5	1.4
49	2	3	14	3.92	0	0
50	3	3	10	2.8	3	.84
51	4	1	40	11.2	1	.28
52	4	2	0	0	0	0
53	2	1	12	3.36	0	0
54	3	1	40	11.2	26	7.28
55	3	1	25	7	3	.84
56	4	1	30	8.4	0	0
57	2	3	15	4.2	0	0
58	3	3	40	11.2	10	2.8
59	3	2	15	4.2	0.5	.14
60	4	0	14	3.92	4	1.12
61	3	2	26	7.28	12	3.36
62	3	1	13	3.64	0	0
63	3	2	15	4.2	0	0
64	5	2	22	6.16	2	.56

House no.	Adults	Children	Cultivated land		Uncultivated land	
			Huls	*Acres*	*Huls*	*Acres*
65	2	0	3	.84	0	0
66	1	0	15	4.2	0	0
67	3	0	12	3.36	1[b]	.28
68	3	3	17	4.76	3	.84
69	3	0	10	2.8	3	.84
70	5	0	16	4.48	3	.84
71	4	1	15	4.2	0	0
72	6	5	26	7.28	4	1.12
73	3	3	26	7.28	0	0
74	2	0	12	3.36	2	.56
75	4	1	20	5.6	2	.56
76	2	0	15	4.2	1	0.28
77	4	2	13	3.64	0	0
78	4	3	14	3.92	2	.56
79	5	1	24	6.72	3	.84
80	1	1	16	4.48	0	0
81	5	0	15	4.2	2	.56
82	5	4	25	7	1	.28
83	2	2	15	4.2	2	.56
Total	265	100	1,439	403	169.5	47.5

[a]Jointly with 67.
[b]Jointly with 39.

Notes

1. Introduction

1. A. R. Radcliffe-Brown, in noting that in a world without completely isolated communities the network of social relations spreads everywhere, gently scolded sociologists for not facing the "difficulty of defining what is meant by the term 'a society'" (1952:193). More recently the viability of the village as a self-contained isolate in as ancient and complex a civilization as India has been critically examined by Marriott (1955).

2. "Tarangpur," a pseudonym for the research site, is glossed differently in each of the three languages spoken by its citizens (see appendix A). Although it is the largest village in the area, none of the three names appears on any published map. Dolpo District was, at the time of the research, one of four districts in Dhaulagiri Zone, the other three being Mustang, Myagdi, and Baglung. The zonal name is from Mt. Dhaulagiri. A direct transliteration of the official Devanagri name for the district would be Dolpā. In this case the word is Tibetan, and since the spelling Dolpo is now widely known, I use it rather than the Devanagri-based spelling (cf. the spellings in Snellgrove 1967).

3. All present tense descriptions in this study refer exclusively to conditions as they were in 1968–69. Many changes have taken place since then—for example, the borders of Dolpo District have been redrawn, and it is now a part of Karnali Zone (see maps 1 and 2 for the different district and zonal boundaries as they were in 1969 and in 1979). Similarly, there is now, and has been for more than ten years, scheduled air service most of the year to Jumla. A road from Kathmandu to Pokhara has been in existence even longer; more roads north of Pokhara are planned, but I doubt that any road will ever be built within several days walk of Tichurong (see chap. 2 for more on this area).

4. Malinowski reports that because of "their central position half way between Dobu and the Trobriands, they [the Amphlett islanders] have succeeded in becoming in several respects the monopolists of this part of the world. They have also the main characteristics of monopolists: grasping and mean, inhospitable and greedy, keen on keeping the trade and exchange in their own hands, yet unprepared to make any sacrifice towards improving it; shy, yet arrogant to anyone who has any dealings with them; they contrast unfavorably with their southern and northern neighbors. And this is not only the white man's impression" (1922:46–47).

5. We thereby continued an honorable literary tradition initiated by Boas in the arctic; but whereas Boas read Kant's *Critique of Pure Reason,* we preferred blood-and-guts novels, such as James Michener's *Caravans* and James Clavell's *Tai-Pan.*

2. The Land and Its People

1. All the proverbs quoted in this book, whether in Nepali, Tibetan, or Kaike, were collected in Tarangpur village.

2. The Khas are a group of obscure origin but of considerable importance in the history of western Nepal (see Hitchcock 1978).

3. I use the Nepali term, *Bhot* and *Bhotia* to refer to those parts of Nepal (and its inhabitants, respectively) which are culturally Tibetan but politically Nepalese. "Tibet" and "Tibetan" then refer to the land and people comprising the Tibet Autonomous Region of the People's Republic of China. Where there is no difference between the two the adjective "Tibetan" is used.

4. Snellgrove, the first scholar to identify this area by its Tibetan name (1961:33), derives its meaning—"valley of fragrant water"—from the probable classical spelling *dri-chu-rong,* and Jest (1971) translates it as "valley of deep water." But neither of these meanings—nor, indeed, any other—was known to most of the local inhabitants. Those who offered an etymology translated Tichurong (perversely perhaps, but in all seriousness) as "valley of malodorous water."

5. Strictly speaking, both Buddhism and Bon, the pre-Buddhist religion of Tibet, are found in Tichurong and Bhot. But since lay villagers, at least in Tichurong, do not for most practical purposes distinguish between the two (villagers hire ritual specialists of either tradition indifferently), and since they are so similar in many ways, I use the term *Buddhist* loosely to refer to either. Almost all Tichurong "temples" (Tibetan, *gomba*) are Nyingmapa (see Jest 1971 for a partial listing of gombas with their affiliated sects), and villagers refer casually to all Buddhist lamas as *chos-pa* ("Buddhist monks"), as distinguished from *bon-po* ("Bon priests"). Bon is represented in Tichurong only by the lama at Pale, who is far more educated and sophisticated than any of the Buddhist lamas resident there. He spends his winters in India conferring with other bon-po clergy.

6. The population pyramid below shows the distribution of men and women at different ages. For 33 women (out of 41) whose fertility cycle is complete, the mean number of total children born per woman is 5.58, while the mean number of surviving children is 2.24. Population growth appears to have been as slow historically as it is now. According to tax records in Kathmandu, there were 61 houses in Tarangpur in 1846, 63 in 1868, and 74 in 1908. For my purposes, there are 83 "houses"—that is, separate cooking hearths—even though they may be within the same physical structure. But for Panchayat purposes—that is, if voluntary labor is needed, or contributions are being raised—there are 77 houses.

At some more remote time, the population may well have been higher than it is now. The existence of terraces which have been abandoned for so long that no one can remember when they were cultivated, or by whom, suggests some precipitous drop in population to present levels. The total population of the 13 villages and scattered homesteads of Tichurong was 2,370 in 1969.

7. Using a list of 100 basic words (Swadesh 1955), I found that Kaike shared 49% cognates with the Tibetan dialect spoken in Tichurong, 49% with the very

Tarangpur Population Structure

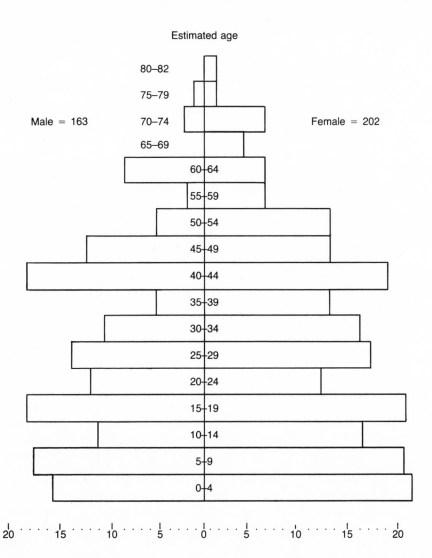

Estimated age

Male = 163   Female = 202

closely related Tibetan dialect spoken in what Snellgrove calls "Inner Dolpo," 35% with Kham, and 23% with Magar. The degree of proximity of each language to the other is as follows:

Words available		Percent cognates among five Tibeto-Burman languages			
		Kaike	*Kham*	*Magar*	*Dolpo Tibetan*
100	Tichurong Tibetan	49	32	18	77
98	Dolpo Tibetan	49	29	17	
99	Magar	23	25		
78	Kham	35			
100	Kaike				

For a fuller treatment of Kaike lexical material, see Fisher (1973). The probable historical development is shown in the following chart, adapted from Glover's (1970) adaptation of Shafer's classification (1955).

8. As will become apparent, Buddhism and Hinduism are historical accretions. The Magars and other Tibeto-Burman groups were apparently neither Buddhist nor Hindu originally. As an earlier observer noted, "there is a Mon-pa [a term which refers to cis-Himalayan tribal groups generally] group called Mā-kra [Magar?] and a Kla-klo group called Kha-si [Khas?] in that country, who are neither Buddhists nor non-Buddhists (i.e., Hindus). They are just like the Kha-khra Klo-pa (Blāma Btsan-po implies that they are devoid of any religious teachings whatsoever)" (Wylie 1970).

9. That is, it is as Hindu as a single, isolated, low-caste can be; their mostly shamanistic religion centers on the worship of such deities as Masta (cf. Gaborieau 1969).

10. See note 29 below.

11. This account of Prasad's trek to Jumla via Tichurong describes "Tarabhot," a term Prasad and other Nepalese sometimes use to refer to the Tibetan (Nepali, "Bhotia") atmosphere of what are sometimes collectively and loosely referred to as the Tara villages (Tarangpur, Tarakot, Tupa, and Gomba). But the Taralis insist on "Tarakot" to refer to both the village and the region. Prasad's passages describing Tichurong are brief and, as far as they go, reasonably accurate. But there is a tendency to describe the passes into Tichurong from the south in exaggerated and melodramatic terms. Thus Purna Prasad reports that ten or twenty lives are lost on the two 15,000-foot passes every year. This is journalistic fantasy. These twin passes serve as Himalayan double doors, and since the normal itinerary requires spending a night between them, there is always the danger of being caught in the middle by a blizzard, making it impossible to advance or retreat out of the trap. But although Tichurong villagers often talk (to anthropologists as well as journalists) about how difficult and dangerous the passes are (severe snow blindness is frequent) and how many people have been

Classification of
Sino-Tibetan Languages

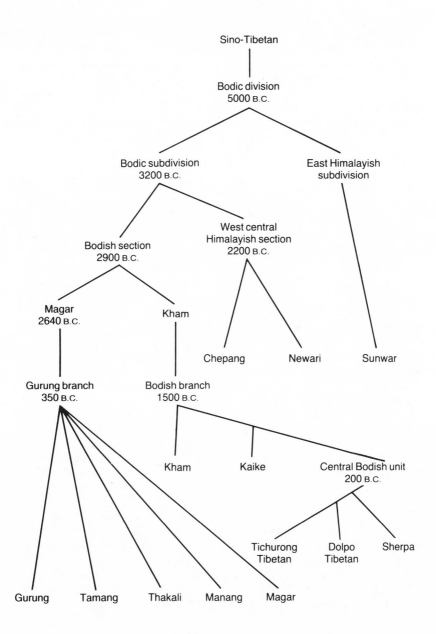

killed on them, I could find very few specific instances of such deaths occurring within living memory. It is a rare year in which anybody is killed.

The author also states that the passes can be crossed only between mid-May and mid-August, and Cluett (1966) reports that they are open only in July and August. In fact, they are always open from May to September, and generally for far longer periods. In the dead of winter they can never be crossed and in the middle of summer they always can be, but in between these two extremes there are a few months when they cannot be crossed after a storm but can be traversed after several sunny days during which the snow has melted sufficiently. Thus during my residence (when winter arrived atypically late), occasional crossings were made as late as the latter part of December.

12. For a more recent Nepalese traveler's account, see Sakya's *Dolpo* (1978), which devotes eight pages to Tichurong.

13. The English Tibetologist David Snellgrove devotes half a chapter to Tichurong in *Himalayan Pilgrimage*. Although this publication records for the first time the Tibetan name for this region, the rest of the information is so inaccurate that it would be pointless to recite the encyclopedia of errors it contains. To cite just one example of the level of factual and analytical penetration achieved, he describes the Magars of one of the villages as "so far tibetanized as to speak Tibetan, wear Tibetan clothes and practice Tibetan religion. . . . Yet so strangely perverse is human nature, that they choose to consider themselves of higher caste than the real Tibetans to the north, with whom intermarriage would be rather scandalous. Their staple food is buckwheat, barley and potatoes" (1961:36).

The empirical facts are rather different. The inhabitants of the village to which he refers do not speak Tibetan except, of course, as an ancillary language, just as they also speak Nepali. Their own language is Kaike. Even the small plate reproduced shows clearly a Tibetan man wearing Tibetan clothes behind the Magar villagers wearing Magar clothes. The two styles are unmistakably distinct. Snellgrove apparently paused briefly in the village, spoke to a few Tibetans who had spent the winter there and had not yet returned to their homes in the north (and to a few Magars who replied in the language in which they had been addressed) and concluded that he was in what was for practical purposes just another Tibetan village, thus completely misunderstanding the unique linguistic and cultural setting. And any account which attempts to explain marriage rules in terms of the perversity of human nature was obviously not written with an anthropological audience in mind. Finally, their staple food, in addition to buck-wheat, is a kind of millet almost as distinctive as their language. Barley, on the other hand, is used primarily for brewing beer; potatoes are eaten as a side dish by all, and seasonally as a staple by the few poverty-stricken people whose millet and buckwheat stores will not quite stretch from one harvest to the next. To say that these people practice Tibetan religion is at best a quarter-truth, since their religious life is a rich complex of several historically and conceptually different religious traditions. The book as a whole is conceived and executed as a chronologically fashioned travelogue in the style of the nineteenth century, although—with its lists of divinities with classical Tibetan and Sanskrit names scattered here and there in the text—it is a high-level one.

14. In a trilingual setting, nouns can be tricky: for example, Ba is not the local name for Tichurong but the Tibetan name for Tarangpur, and Kaike refers to the language, not the speakers of the language.

15. Three such publications are an untitled pamphlet published by the Ministry of Home and Panchayat (1966); a pamphlet published by the "Back to the Village National Campaign" called *Dhaulagiriko Parichaya (A Preface to Dhaulagiri)*, by Shrestha (ca. 1967); and the particularly useful and detailed *Himāchhadit Dolpā Jillāko ek Jhalak (A Glimpse of Snow-Covered Dolpā District)*, by Thakali (1968).

16. It is not clear whether Tucci's question mark reflects uncertainty over location or spelling; the site seems to have been unknown to Tucci, although on his trek to Jumla in 1954 he crossed the Byas River (unnamed on maps) and walked within a few feet of the supposed site of this raja.

17. One raja stayed between the villages of Lawan and Bantara at or near a place called Dāhrā Pāni; he was called the Dahral Raja. Another raja stayed, apparently, in Tarakot; presumably, he was the great nephew of Suratha Sah, who appears in Tucci's chronicles. A third stayed, as already mentioned, by the Byas River. There may have been others as well.

18. Compare Montgomerie's map (1875). Snellgrove's map (1961:296) shows some of the other Tichurong villages, but incorrectly transposes the names for Tupa and Tarangpur; Snellgrove's Nepali versions of these names are also misspelled.

19. This local estimate accords well with the Gorkha conquest of the area in 1786.

20. During this same period, the total number of rupees paid in taxes from Tarangpur village decreased from Rs. 239 to Rs. 231, but this mainly reflects changed value after conversion of the old rupee (equivalent to 16 gandis) to the new (equivalent to 100 paisa). The difference in value is expressed by a ratio of 16:22.

21. Some versions of the myth report three goddesses.

22. Another version relates that he cut his finger so that it would sting when he ate rice in the evening and thus remind him.

23. According to another variant he was to catch the angel by spitting on her, another way of destroying her powers through a confrontation with impurity.

24. One folk etymology for the language name *Kaike*, suggested by the late evangelical lama, Shang Rinpoche, is "god's language," where *kai* is a mutation of *lha* (Tibetan and Kaike, "deity"), and *ke* retains its meaning in Tibetan of "language."

25 The term *Gharti* is used elsewhere in Nepal to refer to descendants of slaves, but I found no evidence of any such connotation in Tichurong.

26. The Palpali Budhas intermarry and are therefore classified as a marriage class rather than as a clan (see chap. 7).

27. Other clan names (in addition to those mentioned so far) cropped up in

census records of the other Tichurong villages. These names include: Bhanari, Thapa, Budatoki, Baiji, Bista, Lama, Bora, Rana, Rawal, Gurung, and Sherchand (the latter an obvious immigrant from Thakkola). "Thapas" and "Boras" emigrated from Khasan three generations ago as *gharjuwāin* (a son-in-law who lives in his wife's house, when she has no brother to inherit in the usual way). Tarangpur informants said that "Rana" is used, especially in other parts of Nepal, as the equivalent of "Jhankri." The fact that the "Gurungs" were actually Tibetan refugees suggests that a process of "clanization" is occurring in which Tichurong people without a clan appropriate some name—almost any will do— by which they can be identified. Historically, tax records show that Rokaya, Budha, and Gharti households have always predominated in Tarangpur. The following table lists the "clan" names in Tarangpur from past years:

	Number of houses				
Clan name	1846	1854	1868	1908	1969
Budha	30	30	33	32	43[a]
Rokaya	10	15	14	15	21
Gharti	5	6	5	7	2
Tudup	1	1	0	1	
Raul	1	1	0	0	
Bhadari	6	4	9	5	
Radi	2	1	0	1	
Batāro	1	0	0	0	
Khatri	1	1	0	0	
Wathālo	0	1	0	0	
Kalatro	0	0	0	3	
Unknown	4	1	2	1	
Jhankri	0	0	0	0	7
Thakuri	0	0	0	0	7
Damai					1
Thakkali					1

[a]Includes 11 "Lama" families.

28. That there are exceptions is demonstrated by the existence, on the Tara River in Baglung District, of Tara village, founded five or six generations ago by two families from "Tarabhot" (see n. 11 above). Their Magar descendants today speak only Nepali.

29. The table on the following page shows the number of houses and the population of each of the thirteen Tichurong villages, with the percentages of its marriage partners who came from each village, or from outside Tichurong.

Percent of marriage partners from

No. of houses	Pop.		Tarangpur	Tarakot	Tupa	Gomba	Khani	Kola	Tachen	Lawan	Pale	Bhantara	Chilpara	Byas	Riwa	Outside[d]
83	365	Tarangpur	41	6	18	20	9	—	—	—	—	2.5	—	—	—	3.5
21	119	Tarakot	43	21	4	21	—	—	—	4	—	—	—	—	—	7
52	274	Tupa	26	3	50	7	3	—	—	—	—	1	—	—	—	—
63	294	Gomba[a]	27	3	6	46	4	9	1	1	1	—	—	—	—	1
31	167	Khani	20	5	2	23	20	7	—	5	9	—	—	2	5	2
33	163	Kola	5	7	—	14	7	47	9	2	—	2	—	—	2	4
14	63	Tachen	—	5	—	21	—	32	32	—	—	—	—	—	—	10
26	142	Lawan[b]	5	—	12	2	14	5	—	31	12	17	—	2	—	—
52	249	Pale	—	—	—	—	1	—	—	—	85	—	—	10	—	4
43	215	Bhantara	6	—	6	3	1	1	4	—	7	25	25	3	6	13
20	105	Chilpara	—	—	3	—	—	—	—	13	—	32	48	—	—	3
25	118	Byas	—	—	—	—	—	—	—	—	56	—	—	44	—	—
18	76	Riwa[c]	—	—	—	—	7	7	—	—	3	26	—	—	45	19

[a] Includes the hamlet of Rikh. [b] Includes the hamlet of Dara. [c] Riwa is composed entirely of Kamis. [d] Mostly Tibetan refugees or Kami families.

30. Nepali, as a lingua franca understood throughout most of Nepal, is certainly a unifying factor, especially in view of India's seemingly intractable search for an acceptable national language; about one half of the population in Nepal speak Nepali as their mother tongue; the rest speak a bewildering variety of Indo-European, Tibeto-Burman and, to a negligible extent, Dravidian languages.

3. Himalayan Farmers

1. For a quantitatively ambitious assessment of a neighboring group, see Macfarlane's study of the Gurungs (1976).
2. Tichurong's interstitial jurisdictional position is perhaps responsible for the vague and unsystematic nature of land classification and evaluation. Lal Singh Budha, a former Mukhiya for Tarakot, wrote to His Majesty's Government in 1907: "This is the region lying between the boundaries of Jumla and Bhot. Unlike in other regions, *asmani* [estimated] tax has been imposed on this region. It has not yet been distinguished here which land is *khet* [level field] and which land is *pākho* [sloping field]. Therefore separate tax rates have not been fixed for khet and pakho here. Taxes are assessed here mainly by guesswork" (document 9).
3. The geographer Dobremez describes the north-facing forests of Tichurong as follows (in Jest 1971):

At 2,200 meters, subtropical pines (Pinus roxburghii)
Between 2,200 and 2,750 meters, cedar (Cedrus deodara) and cypress (Cupressus torulosa)
Between 2,750 and 3,300 meters, pine (Pinus excelsa) and spruce (Picea smithiana)
Between 3,300 and 3,800 meters, fir (Abies spectabilis), birch (Betula utilis) and rhododendron (Rhododendrom campanulatum)
Above 3,800 meters, alpine grasses and bushes, particularly high-altitude varieties of rhododendron

4. Here and elsewhere in the text, I often use words like "average" and "typical" in the casual, nontechnical sense of "ordinary" or "usual." What these terms mean in a more precise, quantitative way can be grasped by referring, for example, to figs. 3, 4, and 6.
5. The earliest recorded land taxes for Tarangpur were paid in 1837, although no one in Tarangpur knows how or when the land settlement for these taxes was made. See chap. 6 for a discussion of land taxes; see also n. 2 above.
6. See Caplan (1970) for an alternative method of measuring land.
7. The myth states that "in the beginning" there was a three-year famine; during the first year people ate a root called *gānshing;* the second year they ate a vegetable, *pimilyacha;* and the third year they ate a plant similar to buckwheat called *chau(w)palā.* After some time there was another famine. Meanwhile, people heard that one of their ancestors who was in a foreign land had died. A

learned man said that if a bone of the ancestor were brought back, there would never be famines again. Some people went looking for the ancestor's grave, which they found after three years, but only after much searching could they find a bone as big as a needle, and when they did find it a cloud appeared in the sky. Near Dhorpatan they made a throne of stone for the bone, but it refused to stay there. They tried again and again to make a throne for the stone at various places, including sites on or near the Jangla passes but in vain. Finally they made a throne near the village, and there the bone stayed. Since then, they have had only bumper crops. One of the phrases used by the priest of the local mountain-god cult is "please let us never have famine."

8. Since grain is usually measured by volume in Nepal, I give volume equivalents in English; different grains have different weights.

9. Professor von Fürer-Haimendorf (1964) has similarly ascribed great importance to the introduction of the potato among the Sherpas.

10. Such use of marijuana produces no intoxication; the intoxicating effect that can be acquired by smoking marijuana is well known to Tarangpurians, but they say they never smoke it, probably because it is a custom they associate with low castes. They have no corresponding aversion to the use of alcohol, however.

11. Cooking oil is sometimes produced from walnuts; other sources of cooking oil include mustard, ghee, and several wild fruits.

12. A mana is officially 545 cc—nearly the same as a pint (568 cc). Since in Tarangpur the "homemade," hollowed-out wooden vessels used to measure a mana are rarely exact, we may conveniently ignore the very small difference between an official pint and an official mana and consider them the same.

13. All conversions from Nepali rupees to U.S. dollars are based on the official exchange rate during 1968–1970: $1.00 = Rs. 10.1.

14. The low-caste tailor family is considered outside the scope of this rule, since their entire livelihood is based on employment by others, and because, despite their 40 years in the village, they regard themselves, and are so regarded by others, as "temporary."

15. Pant (1935) reports a similar division of labor in the Kumaon hills, but it is unknown whether the ideological basis is the same.

16. See Jest (1975:115) for a line drawing of the plow.

17. Agricultural change is not utterly absent, though—witness the introduction of corn and potatoes in recent years. Productivity of these crops is too high to be ignored, and their contribution to the surplus does not go unnoticed by anyone, including men.

4. Transactions: The Salt Circuit

1. A few villagers own yak, but unlike Bhotias, they do not use them for transport.

2. Females also have these relationships, but they tend to be contracted locally, rather than over long distance.

3. These relationships are similar to the "guest-friend" relationship between Navaho and Zuni (see Broom et al. 1954).

4. See chap. 2 n. 3.

5. Sinha (1959) has pointed out that contact with low castes is also a characteristic of Indian tribals.

6. Impression management (Goffman 1959) has been analyzed in another Himalayan context (Berreman 1962) and is implicitly involved in Turnbull's (1962) work.

5. Transactions: The Commodities Circuit

1. More accurately, the amount of fat believed to be on it; Nepalese like fat, and the greater the fat content, the more expensive the animal.

2. The Tibetan boots (*lam*) worn by Tarangpur women are of the cloth type and made in Dolpo; the boots brought from Kalimpong are made of leather and are worn only by men.

6. Control and Use of Wealth: The Traditional Context

1. See chap. 3 nn. 2 and 5. In addition to the land tax and the trading taxes mentioned in chap. 5, there is a new annual tax on houses: half a rupee ($0.05) for a house divided into 3–5 rooms; Rs. 1 for 6–7 rooms; Rs. 3 for 8–9 rooms, and Rs. 4 on any house larger than 9 rooms. Most Tarangpur houses are subdivided into fewer than 5 rooms.

7. Transactions: The Village Context

1. This "Magarization" of a high caste, unlike the "tribalization" to which Srinivas (1967:19) refers, is permanent.

2. See chap. 2, "History: Mythical."

3. See Fisher (1978) for a more detailed discussion of hierarchy in Tarangpur and its relation to the work of Dumont (1970).

4. Nepali, *mukh mildaina*.

5. See the discussion in chap. 2, "History: Mythical."

6. For recent—and fundamental—changes in the social structure and marriage-class system, see chap. 8.

7. The facts of total wealth are private matters, hence the crude estimates that constitute the data of figure 6. By contrast, the question of salary is uninhibitedly public—perhaps because earning a regular salary is such a relatively new phenomenon in Nepal. One of the most frequent questions put to me by people I had never seen before—by travelers resting under the same shade tree on the trail, for example—was, "how much do you make?" Even though I had

only a research stipend and did not, strictly speaking, "earn a salary," I was, by Tarangpur standards, a wealthy man. Our economic impact on the area can be measured by the total expenditures of our own year in the field: Rs. 13,109, or $1,297.92.

8. This title probably originally designated some kind of tax-collecting responsibility; Srivastava reports that tax collectors who assess various tolls on Bhotias trading in Tibet "are known as Thal-Muchis in Tibet and as Thaloos in North-Western Nepal" (1958:9).

9. For a detailed account of the political changes of the 1950s and 1960s, see *The Politics of Nepal* (Rose and Fisher 1970).

10. The Tarangpur school was started in the early 1960s and has been operated sporadically since then, since it has been difficult to find and keep a qualified, reliable teacher. Classes go as high as fifth grade, although very few students get that far. Daily attendance averages about 15.

8. Summary and Conclusions: Ethnicity and Interaction

1. Their main question was whether the astronauts had found a goddess on the moon. They were not particularly curious about the moon itself, and earlier cosmological queries produced little response. Tarangpurians had not thought much about the heavenly bodies. One informant said, when pressed, that because of the distances involved, the stars and moon must be bigger than they appear, a star being the size of a sheep and the moon the size of a yak.

2. See Leach (1964).

Bibliography

Aitken, Robert. "Ploughs (Ards) of West Nepal." *Man* 63, 218(November 1963):169–172.

Barth, Fredrik. *Models of Social Organization*. Occasional Paper No. 2. London: Royal Anthropological Institute, 1966.

———. "On the Study of Social Change." *American Anthropologist* 69(1967): 661–669.

———, ed. *Ethnic Groups and Boundaries: The Social Organization of Culture Difference*. Boston: Little, Brown and Company, 1969.

Berreman, Gerald D. *Behind Many Masks*. Ithaca, N.Y.: The Society for Applied Anthropology, 1962.

———. *Hindus of the Himalayas: Ethnography and Change*. Berkeley and Los Angeles: University of California Press, 1963.

Bista, Dor Bahadur. "The Process of Nepalization." In *Anthropological and Linguistic Studies of the Gandaki Area in Nepal*, Monumenta Serindica No. 10, 1–20 Tokyo: Institute for the Study of Languages and Culture of Asia and Africa, 1962.

Broom, Leonard, Bernard J. Siegel, Evon Z. Vogt, and James B. Watson. "Acculturation: An Exploratory Formation." *American Anthropologist* 56(1954): 973–1000.

Caplan, A. Patricia. *Priests and Cobblers: A Study of Social Change in a Hindu Village in Western Nepal*. San Francisco: Chandler Publishing Company, 1972.

Caplan, Lionel. *Land and Social Change in East Nepal*. Berkeley, Los Angeles, and London: University of California Press, 1970.

Cluett, C. *Report on a Field Trip to Dunai, Dolpo District*. U.S. Agency for International Development (mimeographed), March 1966.

Dalton, George. "A Note of Clarification on Economic Surplus." *American Anthropologist* 62, 3(June 1960):483–490.

———. "Economic Surplus Once Again." *American Anthropologist* 65, 2(April 1963):389–393.

Document 1. Lāl Mohar to the Subbā of Jumla, 1851 B.S. (A.D. 1794).*

Document 2. Lāl Mohar to the Dheba of Mustang, 1851 B.S. (A.D. 1794).

Document 3, Lāl Mohar to Amāli (village headman) of Tārākot to assist in search for minerals, 1862–1863 B.S. (A.D. 1805–1806).

---

*All entries labeled "document" are manuscripts from Lāgat Phant, Mal Pot Bibhāg (Calculation Division, Land Tax Department, Finance Ministry), Kathmandu Nepal.

Document 4, List of heads of households of Tarangpur and their land taxes, 1894 B.S. (A.D. 1837).

Document 5, Lāl Mohar ordering taxes levied on salt, wool, cloth, goats, and blankets in Tārākot area, 1895 B.S. (A.D. 1838).

Document 6, Lāl Mohar adjudicating a dispute over salt trading jurisdictions, 1879 B.S. (A.D. 1822).

Document 7, Lāl Mohar ordering changes in taxes and salaries, 1903 B.S. (A.D. 1846).

Document 8, Lāl Mohar specifying certain tax concessions, 1921 B.S. (A.D. 1864).

Document 9, Correspondence between His Majesty's Government and Tārākot Mukhiyā concerning land taxes, 1964 B.S. (A.D. 1907).

Dumont, Louis. *Homo hierarchicus.* Chicago: University of Chicago Press, 1970.

Evans-Pritchard, E. E. *The Nuer.* London: Oxford University Press, 1940.

Field, A. R. "Himalayan Salt: A Political Barometer." *Modern Review,* 105, 6(June 1959):460–463.

Firth, Raymond. "Social Organization and Social Change." *Journal of the Royal Anthropological Institute* 84(1954):1–28.

———. "Themes in Economic Anthropology: A General Comment." In *Themes in Economic Anthropology,* ed. Raymond Firth, ASA monograph 6. London: Tavistock Publications, 1967.

Fisher, James F. "Tara—Ek Anubhaw." *Swatantra Bishwa* 8, 3(November 1970):23–25.

———. "Nouns of the Kaike Language." In *Clause, Sentence, and Discourse Patterns in Selected Languages of Nepal,* Publication No. 40 (Part IV, Word Lists), 46–299. Kathmandu, Nepal: Summer Institute of Linguistics, Publications in Linguistics and Related Fields, 1973.

———. "Three Nepalese 'Jokes.'" *Journal of South Asian Literature* (special issue on folk literature) Vol. XI, Nos. 1 & 2 (Winter 1975a).

———. "Tarali Magarharu (Kaike Speaking People of Dolpo)." In Nepali. In *Mechidekhi Mahākālisamma (Coronation Gazetteer)* 3:582–586. Kathmandu, Nepal: His Majesty's Government, Department of Information, 1975b.

———. "Homo hierarchicus Nepalensis: A Cultural Subspecies." In *Himalayan Anthropology: The Indo-Tibetan Interface,* ed. James F. Fisher, 43–52. The Hague: Mouton Publishing Company, 1978.

von Fürer-Haimendorf, Christoph. *The Sherpas of Nepal.* Berkeley and Los Angeles: University of California Press, 1964.

———. *Himalayan Traders.* New York: St. Martin's Press, 1975.

Gaborieau, M. "Note preliminaire sur le dieu Masta." *Objets et Mondes 9,* 1(1969):19–50.

Geertz, Clifford. "Thick Description: Toward an Interpretative Theory of Culture." In *The Interpretation of Cultures,* 3–30. New York: Basic Books, 1973.

Glover, Warren W. "Cognate Counts via the Swadesh List in Some Tibeto-Burman Languages of Nepal." In *Tibeto-Burman Linguistics,* Vol. III, ed. F. K. Lehman. Champaign-Urbana: University of Illinois, Department of Linguistics, 1970.

Goffman, Irving. *The Presentation of Self in Everyday Life.* Garden City, N.Y.: Doubleday, 1959.

Hamilton, Francis. *An Account of the Kingdom of Nepal, and of the Territories Annexed to This Dominion by the House of Gorkha.* Edinburgh: A. Constable, 1819.

Harris, Marvin. "The Economy Has No Surplus?" *American Anthropologist* 61, 2(1959):185–199.

Hitchcock, John T. "A Nepalese Hill Village and Indian Employment." *Asian Survey* 1, 9(1961):15–20.

———. "Sub-Tribes in the Magar Community in Nepal." *Asian Survey* 5, 4(April 1965):207–215.

———. *The Magars of Banyan Hill.* New York: Holt, Rinehart and Winston, 1966.

———. "An Additional Perspective on the Nepali Caste System." In *Himalayan Anthropology: The Indo-Tibetan Interface,* ed. James F. Fisher, 111–120. The Hague: Mouton Publishing Company, 1978.

———. *The King's Ward.* Manuscript in preparation, no date.

Jest, Corneille. "Traditions et croyances religieuses des habitants de la Valee de Tichurong (Nord-Ouest du Nepal)." *L'Ethnographie,* 65(1971):66–86.

———. *Dolpo Communautés de Langue Tibetaine du Nepal.* Paris: Centre National de la Recherche Scientifique, 1975.

Kapferer, Bruce. "Introduction: Transactional Models Reconsidered." In *Transaction and Meaning,* ed. Bruce Kapferer. Philadelphia: Institute for the Study of Human Issues, 1976.

Kirkpatrick, William. *An Account of the Kingdom of Nepaul, Being the Substance of Observations Made during a Mission to that Country in the Year 1793.* London: W. Miller, 1811.

Kosambi, D. D. *Ancient India.* New York: Pantheon Books, 1965.

Leach, E. R. *Political Systems of Highland Burma.* Boston: Beacon Press, 1964.

McDougal, Charles. *Village and Household Economy in Far Western Nepal.* Kirtipur, Nepal: Tribhuvan University, 1968.

Macfarlane, Alan. *Resources and Population, A Study of the Gurungs of Nepal.* Cambridge: Cambridge University Press, 1976.

Malinowski, Bronislaw. *Argonauts of the Western Pacific.* London: Routledge and Kegan Paul, 1922.

Mandelbaum, David G. *Society in India,* Vol. I. Berkeley, Los Angeles, and London: University of California Press, 1970.

Marriott, McKim, ed. *Village India.* Washington, D.C.: American Anthropological Association, Memoir 83, 1955.

———. *Caste Ranking and Community Structure in Five Regions of India and Pakistan.* Poona, India: Reprinted from the Bulletin of the Deccan College Research Institute, 1965.

———. "Hindu Transactions: Diversity without Dualism." In *Transaction and Meaning,* ed. Bruce Kapferer. Philadelphia: Institute for the Study of Human Issues, 1976.

Mauss, Marcel. *The Gift.* New York: W. W. Norton and Co., 1967.

Ministry of Economic Planning. *Physical Input-Output Characteristics of Cereal Grain Production in Selected Agricultural Areas in Nepal, Crop Year 1965–66.* Ministry of Economic Planning, His Majesty's Government, and Economics and Commerce Departments, Tribhuvan University, Kirtipur, Nepal 1966.

Ministry of Home and Panchayat, Planning Section, Publicity Subdivision. Untitled pamphlet giving general information about Dolpā District (no author listed). Kathmandu, Nepal, 2023 B.S. (A.D. 1966).

Montgomerie, Thomas George. "Extracts from an Explorer's Narrative of His Journey from Pitogarh in Kumaon via Jumla to Tadum and Back Along the Kali Gandak to British Territory." Communication by T. G. Montgomerie, *Journal of the Royal Geographic Society of London,* 45(1875):350–363.

Murdock, George Peter. *Social Structure.* New York: Macmillan, 1949.

Nitzberg, Frances Lou. "Land, Labor and Status: The Social Implications of Ecologic Adaptation in a Region of the Western Himalayas of India." Unpublished Ph.D. dissertation, Harvard University, Cambridge, Mass., 1970.

Okada, Ferdinand E. "Ritual Brotherhood: A Cohesive Factor in Nepalese Society." *Southwestern Journal of Anthropology* 13, 3(1957):212–222.

Oldfield, Henry Ambrose. *Sketches from Nipal . . . to which Is Added an Essay on Nipalese Buddhism and Illustrations . . . from the Author's Own Drawings.* London: Allen, 1880.

Orans, Martin. *The Santal: A Tribe in Search of a Great Tradition.* Detroit, Mich.: Wayne State University Press, 1965.

———. "Surplus." *Human Organization* 25, 1(1966):24–32.

Pant, S. D. *The Social Economy of the Himalayas.* London: George Allen and Unwin, 1935.

Pearson, Harry W. "The Economy Has No Surplus: Critique of a Theory of Development." In *Trade and Market in the Early Empires,* eds. K. Polanyi, C. M. Arensberg, and H. W. Pearson. Glencoe, Ill.: The Free Press, 1957.

Prasad, Purna. *Mero Jumla Yātrā.* Kathmandu: Munal Prakasan, Ltd. Baisakh, 2020 B.S. (April 1963).

Radcliffe-Brown, A. R. "On Social Structure." In *Structure and Function in Primitive Society,* by A. R. Radcliffe-Brown, 188–204. London: Cohen and West, 1952.

Redfield, Robert. *The Primitive World and Its Transformations.* Ithaca, N.Y.: Cornell University Press, 1953.

Regmi, Dilli Raman. *Modern Nepal. Rise and Growth in the Eighteenth Century.* Calcutta: Mukhopadhyay, 1961.

Regmi, Mahesh C. *Landownership in Nepal.* Berkeley, Los Angeles, and London: University of California Press, 1976.

Regmi Research Project. *Hāmra Anchalharuko Parichayātmak Vivaran (Introductory Details about Our Zones),* Part 2. Translated into English. Kathmandu, Nepal: The Ministry, Jeth, 2025 B.S. (June 1968), 215–290 (mimeographed).

Rose, Leo E., and Margaret W. Fisher. *The Politics of Nepal.* Ithaca, N.Y.: Cornell University Press, 1970.

Sahlins, Marshall D. "On the Sociology of Primitive Exchange." In *The Relevance of Models for Social Anthropology,* ed. M. Banton, ASA monograph 1. London: Tavistock Publications, 1965.

Sahlins, Marshall D., and Elman R. Service. *Culture and Evolution.* Ann Arbor, Mich.: University of Michigan Press, 1960.

Sakya, Karna. *Dolpo: The World Behind the Himalayas.* Kathmandu, Nepal: Jore Ganesh Press, 1978.

Shafer, Robert. "Classification of the Sino-Tibetan Languages." *Word* 11(1955): 94–111.

Shrestha, Govinda Man. *Dhaulagiriko Parichaya (A Preface to Dhaulagiri).* Kathmandu, Nepal: Back to the Village National Campaign, no date (1967?).

Sinha, Surajit. "Tribal Culture of Peninsular India as a Dimension of the Little Tradition: A Preliminary Statement." In *Traditional India: Structure and Change,* ed. Milton Singer. Philadelphia: American Folklore Society, 1959.

Snellgrove, David Liwellyn. *Himalayan Pilgrimage.* Oxford: B. Cassirer, 1961.

———. *Four Lamas of Dolpo. Vol. 1: Introduction and Translation.* Oxford: B. Cassirer, 1967.

Srinivas, M. N. *Social Change in Modern India.* Berkeley and Los Angeles: University of California Press, 1967.

Srivastava, Ram P. "The Bhotia Nomads and Their Indo-Tibetan Trade." *Journal of the University of Saugar* 7, 1, Section A(1958):1–22.

Swadesh, Morris. "Towards Greater Accuracy in Lexicostatistic Dating." *International Journal of American Linguistics* 21(1955):121–137.

Thakali, Shanta Ram. *Himāchhadit Dolpā Jillako ek Jhalak (A Glimpse of Snow-Covered Dolpā District).* Kathmandu, Nepal: His Majesty's Government (mimeographed), 2025 B.S. (A.D. 1968).

Tucci, Giuseppe. *Preliminary Report on Two Scientific Expeditions in Nepal.* Rome: Istituto Italiano per il Medio ed Estremo Oriente, 1956.

———. *Nepal: The Discovery of the Malla.* Translated from the Italian by Lovett Edwards. New York: E. P. Dutton, 1962.

Turnbull, Colin M. *The Forest People.* New York: Simon and Schuster, 1962.

Turner, Ralph L. *A Comparative and Etymological Dictionary of the Nepali Language.* London: Routledge and Kegan Paul, 1931.

Vansittart, Eden. *Gurkhas.* Compiled under the Order of the Government of India, revised by Major B. V. Nicolay. Calcutta: Superintendent of Government Printing, 1915.

Whitehead, Alfred N. *Modes of Thought.* Glencoe, Ill.: The Free Press, 1968.

Wolf, Eric R. *Peasants.* Englewood Cliffs, N.J.: Prentice-Hall, 1966.

Wright, Daniel. *History of Nepal.* Translated from Parbatiya by Munshi Shew Shunker Singh and Pandit Sri Gunanand, with an introductory sketch of the country and people by the editor, Daniel Wright. Cambridge: Cambridge University Press, 1877.

Wylie, Turrell. *A Tibetan Religious Geography of Nepal.* Seria Orientale Roma XLII. Rome: Istituto Italiano per il Medio ed Estremo Oriente, 1970.

Index

Agriculture, 46–86; altitude affects, 56; climate affects, 55–56; decision-making in, 76–77; fertilizer in, 54, 55, 56–57; men's role in, 81, 82, 124; technology in, 82–83, 84; tools in, 69–70 (*see also* Plow); women's role in, 76–77, 78, 81, 117. *See also* Crops; Grain
Altitude, 20, 50, 56
Amaranth, 57
Animal, sacrificed, 24, 97, 101, 151–152. *See also* Livestock

Badri Sah, 30
Baglung, 34
Balirāj, 29, 31
Barbung River, 18, 20
Barley, 55, 124, 125, 210–211 n. 13; for brewing, 57, 63; traded, 88
Barphun, 24
Barth, Fredrik, 96, 184, 185; on anthropological units, 1–2; on transactions, 3–4, 44–45, 46
Beans, 57–58, 89
Beer, 57, 63
Behavior, 184; passing, 95, 130
Bhakti Thapa, 30
Bhantara, 25
Bheri River, 18, 19, 20, 26, 117, 141
Bhot/Bhotias, 19, 42; as grain-deficient, 84–85, 86; Hindus on, 94; livestock trade by, 62, 125; as polluting, 92, 95; religion of, 92; as salt source, 62, 88, 184; as term of abuse, 94; trade with, 90, 117, 124, 125; weaving by, 107; as winter labor, 84–85, 92, 93, 160; as wool source, 106, 125

Birth ceremonies, 66, 95, 144–145, 190
Bista, Dor Bahadur, 190
Blacksmith caste (Kāmis), 10, 70, 93, 180–182; grain paid to, 181–182; own land, 181
Bon, 19, 206 n. 5
Boundaries: ethnic, 2; land, 53, 141
Buckwheat, 55, 56, 124, 210–211 n. 13; exchange rates for, 63; in rituals, 57, 149–150; surplus of, 184; sweet, 57, 150; traded, 62, 88, 89
Buddhism: influence of, 19, 28, 32, 33, 34, 35, 42, 92, 96, 186, 189, 190; of life-cycle rituals, 23; Mahayana (*see* Lama); Tibetan, 19, 28, 32, 33, 34, 44, 91, 92, 190
Budha, Takla Tsering, 13
Budha clan, 38, 40–41, 157, 160; Palpali, 40–41, 160–161
Bullock, 70, 82, 178
Butwal, 77, 116

Calcutta, 117, 185
Calendar: Hindu, 23, 145–146, 154; Nepalese, 145, 154; Tibetan, 23–24, 154
Capital, working, 69–70
Caplan, A. Patricia, 86
Carpenter caste, 10, 70. *See also* Blacksmith caste
Cash, 64, 101, 115, 125, 186; as gift, 146; trade for, 104
Caste, 3, 92; Hindu, 93, 94, 161, 163. *See also* Blacksmith caste; Carpenter caste; Tailors
Chickens, 144, 151–152
Choice, 5, 6, 7; canalized, 185; in

Designer: U.C. Press Staff
Compositor: Prestige Typography
Printer: Malloy Lithographing, Inc.
Binder: John H. Dekker & Sons